Immigration

Immigration

STUART ANDERSON

Greenwood Guides to Business and Economics
Wesley B. Truitt, Series Editor

AN IMPRINT OF ABC-CLIO, LLC
Santa Barbara, California • Denver, Colorado • Oxford, England

Library of Congress Cataloging-in-Publication Data

Anderson, Stuart.
Immigration / Stuart Anderson.
p. cm. — (Greenwood guides to business and economics)
Includes bibliographical references and index.
ISBN 978-0-313-38028-0 (hard copy : alk. paper) — ISBN 978-0-313-38029-7 (e-book)
1. United States—Emigration and immigration. 2. United States—Emigration and immigration—Economic aspects. 3. Immigrants—United States. I. Title.
JV6456.A53 2010
304.8'73—dc22 2010007888

ISBN: 978-0-313-38028-0
EISBN: 978-0-313-38029-7

14 13 12 11 2 3 4 5

This book is also available on the World Wide Web as an eBook.
Visit www.abc-clio.com for details.

Greenwood
An Imprint of ABC-CLIO, LLC

ABC-CLIO, LLC
130 Cremona Drive, P.O. Box 1911
Santa Barbara, California 93116-1911

This book is printed on acid-free paper ∞

Manufactured in the United States of America

Copyright Acknowledgments

Portions of the text used by permission of the American Immigration Council (formerly American Immigration Law Foundation), the National Foundation for American Policy, the National Venture Capital Association, NAFSA: Association of International Educators, and the Merage Foundation.

Portions of chapter 1 in this volume were written by Stuart Anderson for the *Changing Face of North America: Immigration Since 1965*, published by Mason Crest Publishers (Broomall, PA: 2004), a series of books for students on which the author was the senior consulting editor. The author appreciates the permission from Mason Crest to utilize that material in this book.

Contents

Series Foreword

Scanning the pages of the newspaper on any given day, you'll find headlines like the following.

"OPEC points to supply chains as cause of price hikes"

"Business groups warn of danger of takeover proposals"

"U.S. durable goods orders jump 3.3%"

"Dollar hits two-year high versus yen"

"Credibility of WTO at stake in trade talks"

"U.S. GDP growth slows while Fed fears inflation growth"

If this seems like gibberish to you, then you are in good company. To most people, the language of economics is mysterious, intimidating, impenetrable. But with economic forces profoundly influencing our daily lives, being familiar with the ideas and principles of business and economics is vital to our welfare. From fluctuating interest rates to rising gasoline prices to corporate misconduct to the vicissitudes of the stock market to the rippling effects of protests and strikes overseas or natural disasters closer to home, "the economy" is not an abstraction. As Robert Duvall, president and CEO of the National Council on Economic Education, has forcefully argued: "Young people in our country need to know that economic education is not an option. Economic literacy is a vital skill, just as vital as reading literacy."[1]

Understanding economics is a skill that will help you interpret current events playing out on a global scale or in your checkbook, ultimately helping you make wiser choices about how you manage your financial resources—today and tomorrow.

It is the goal of this series, Greenwood Guides to Business and Economics, to promote economic literacy and improve economic decision making. All books in the series are written for the general reader; high school and college student; or the business manager, entrepreneur, or graduate student in business and economics looking for a handy refresher. They have been written by experts in their respective fields for nonexpert readers. The approach throughout is at a "basic" level to maximize understanding and to demystify how our business-driven economy really works.

Each book in the series is an essential guide to the topic of that volume, providing an introduction to its respective subject area. The series as a whole constitutes a library of information, up-to-date data, definitions of terms, and resources, covering all aspects of economic activity. Volumes feature such elements as timelines, glossaries, and examples and illustrations that bring the concepts to life and present them in historical and cultural context.

The selection of the titles and their authors has been the work of an Editorial Advisory Board whose members are the following: Alan Carsrud, Ryerson University; Alan Reynolds, Cato Institute; Wesley Truitt, Pepperdine University; Walter E. Williams, George Mason University; and Charles Wolf Jr., RAND Corporation.

As series editor, I served as chairman of the Editorial Advisory Board and want to express my appreciation to each of these distinguished individuals for their dedicated service in helping bring this important series to reality.

The volumes in the series are as follows:

The Corporation by Wesley B. Truitt, School of Public Policy, Pepperdine University

Demography, Education, and the Workforce by Robert I. Lerman, American University and Urban Institute, and Stephanie Riegg Cellini, George Washington University

Energy by Joseph M. Dukert, Center for Strategic and International Studies

Entrepreneurship by Alan L. Carsrud, Ryerson University, and Malin Brännback, Åbo Akademi University

Globalization by Donald J. Boudreaux, George Mason University

Immigration by Stuart Anderson, National Foundation for American Policy

Income and Wealth by Alan Reynolds, Cato Institute

Money by Mark Dobeck and Euel Elliott, University of Texas–Dallas

The National Economy by Bradley A. Hansen, University of Mary Washington

Real Estate by Mark F. Dobeck, Cleveland State University

The Stock Market by Rik W. Hafer, Southern Illinois University–Edwardsville, and Scott E. Hein, Texas Tech University

Special thanks to our original editor at Greenwood, Nick Philipson, for conceiving the idea of the series and for sponsoring it within Greenwood Press, and many thanks to our current senior editor, Brian Romer, for skillfully steering the continuation of the series.

The overriding purpose of each of these books and the series as a whole is, as Walter Williams so aptly put it, to "push back the frontiers of ignorance."

Wesley B. Truitt, Series Editor

NOTE

1. Quoted in Gary H. Stern, "Do We Know Enough about Economics?" *The Region*, Federal Reserve Bank of Minneapolis, December 1998.

Acknowledgments

While authoring a book is a solo activity, you find quickly it is impossible to write a book without help from a lot of people. My wife, Maria, and children, John and Julia, typed in most of the words that appear on these pages, since I preferred writing long sections of the book by hand. They deserve credit for their effort and an uncanny ability to read my handwriting.

I appreciate Dan Griswold of the Cato Institute for recommending me to the publisher, and Wesley B. Truitt and Jeff Olson of Greenwood for asking me to write the book. Brian Romer, also of Greenwood, came late to the project and provided key assistance, as did Randy Baldini.

Several people provided valuable insights and perspectives that are incorporated in the book, especially Jason Riley, Crystal Williams, Greg Siskind, Philip G. Schrag, Mark J. Perry, Lynn Shotwell, and Rebecca Peters. Interviews for the book were conducted via e-mail and telephone. For sharing their views and knowledge over the years on the practical impact of immigration policy on American business, education, politics, and other sectors, I would like to thank Marlene Johnson, Robert Gelfond, Jenifer Verdery, Paula Collins, Aman Kapoor, Warren Leiden, Daryl Buffenstein, T. J. Rodgers, Paul Gigot, Vivek Wadhwa, Marshall Kaplan, Robert Hoffman, Angelo Amador, Jeanne Butterfield, Alice Tornquist, Ben Hamson, Tom Klingenstein, the late Julian Simon, Frank Sharry, Bob Borens, Stephen Moore, Lee Otis, and Cesar Conda.

For help with some specific factual issues that arose when writing the book, I appreciate the help of Heather Stewart, Tanya Broder, Jonathan Blazer, Michael Fix, Jeffrey Passel, Michael Hoefer, and Ron Haskins.

I owe particular gratitude to those who gave me the opportunity to work for them on immigration policy—Senators Spencer Abraham and Sam Brownback, and former INS Commissioner Jim Ziglar. These men taught me the importance of standing on principle and displaying grace under fire. Ed Crane and David Boaz of the Cato Institute gave me the chance to become the institute's first fulltime policy analyst devoted to working on immigration, and many of the ideas that appear in the book grew out of my early work at Cato.

Charlie Oppenheim and Mark Regets provided assistance in interpreting government data utilized in certain places in the book. Geri Mannion of the Carnegie Corporation of New York and Lew Lehrman of the Lehrman Institute helped support research that appears in this book.

One

History of Immigration to the United States

Competing storylines dominate America's centuries-long tale of immigration. Immigrants engage in heroic struggles to build a better future and learn a new language in a strange land, while natives complain that these new immigrants take jobs and harm the nation's culture. Foreign-born sojourners come to America inspired by opportunity, while two generations later the offspring of those immigrants warn about how different the new immigrants are compared to those of the past.

The history revolves around a country whose policies for two centuries were so open that one could write its few restrictions on immigration on the back of an envelope. However, years later, policies emerged in the form of an immigration code so complex it may rival the law enforced by the Internal Revenue Service.

Did the same government that once helped recruit immigrants to the country's shores later impose harsh restrictions based on the presumed skull sizes of ethnic groups? Could a legislative body that once let states enact more immigration rules than the federal government later so micromanage immigration policy it hired eugenicists to consult in the selection of immigrants?

Oscar Handlin once noted that the history of immigration to America is, in fact, the history of America.[1] And he was right—there is no way to tell the story of immigration without retelling parts of American history.

The dictionary definition of *immigrate* is "to come into a new country . . . in order to settle there."[2] By this meaning, those who came to America and stayed in the years before and after the nation's founding were immigrants. In fact, it was the relative success of the first immigrants that encouraged the rest to come, resulting in lands populated by those of English, Dutch, and German descent.

"Immigration had so long been a familiar aspect of American development that it was not until the end of the 19th century that any question was raised to the propriety of its continuance," wrote Handlin. "The whole history of peopling of the continent had been one of immigration. The 17th century movement of population had brought the first settlements to the Atlantic seacoast."[3]

Two aspects of immigration to the United States have rarely changed. First, immigrants have come to America for a variety of reasons, primarily for economic opportunity and the chance to live in a free society. "The motives for immigration . . . have been very similar from first to last; they have been always a mixture of yearnings—for riches, for land, for change, for tranquility, for freedom, and for something not definable in words," wrote Maldwyn Allen Jones in her book *American Immigration.*[4]

Second, opposition to immigration has always existed in America, with the degree of practical obstacles to those immigrating influenced by the country's economic circumstances and Americans' perceptions of international events. A political cartoon once showed two American Indians on a shore watching the Pilgrims arrive at Plymouth Rock. One Indian knowingly says to the other: "Illegal immigrants." Although the first settlers to America at Jamestown and Plymouth were immigrants, they were not breaking any immigration laws, since none existed. In fact, it would be a long time before those coming to America would face any serious impediments or legal restrictions.

EARLY HISTORY

In 1607, the first immigrant settlers to America arrived in Jamestown. To say these first settlers experienced hardship would understate the case. "The hard winter of the Starving Time [1608] reduced a population of about 500 to barely sixty. . . . Everything from the horses . . . to rats, snakes, mice and roots dug from the forest were consumed, and emaciated survivors took to eating the dead."[5]

In 1610, the surviving settlers decided to abandon Jamestown, but were soon met at sea by ships with supplies and new settlers and chose to return to the colony. The settlement became important as an example of self-government. While King James and later his son, Charles I, retained the authority to enact laws and govern the colony, the settlers had the right, they believed, to decide purely local matters and established an assembly of burgesses.

The English Crown formally approved the assembly as a representative body many years later. "The colonists had kept it alive through fifteen years of neglect by king and council. Now the colonists would enjoy the fruits of self-government and pass to their American posterity from Ottawa to Buenos Aires the grand idea of a representative legislature," writes historian David Robinson. "A year before the Pilgrims landed at Plymouth, the people of Virginia had begun to work out the basic equation of checks and balances that today apportions political power between the legislative, the executive, and the judicial. . . . It is one of history's little jokes that an achievement that changed the world took place on a piece of land that has fewer inhabitants now than it did after the first colonists settled there."[6]

The first immigrants at Plymouth Rock endured many hardships but also became an important model of self-government in America. Unlike the Jamestown settlement, which was organized by the Virginia Company, the Pilgrims sailed to America as a group of like-minded religious individuals and families seeking freedom to worship without interference from governmental authority. "The First Thanksgiving marked the conclusion of a remarkable year. Eleven months earlier the Pilgrims had arrived at the tip of Cape Cod, fearful and uninformed," writes Nathaniel Philbrick, author of *Mayflower*. "They had spent the next month alienating and angering every Native American they happened to come across. By all rights, none of the Pilgrims should have emerged from the first winter alive. . . . That it worked out differently was a testament not only to the Pilgrims' grit, resolve, and faith, but to their ability to take advantage of an extraordinary opportunity."[7] (The opportunity was a diplomatic rapprochement with Native Americans, a give-and-take approach that more or less kept the peace for the Pilgrims for half a century and provided a chance to prosper in the new land.)

The immigrants quickly learned a lesson about food production and private property that three centuries later Joseph Stalin and Mao Zedong failed to grasp, resulting in the unfortunate deaths of millions in twentieth-century China and the Soviet Union. The lesson was simple—people work harder when they own property and can enjoy the fruits of their labor for themselves and their families.

Nathaniel Philbrick explained: "The fall of 1623 marked the end of Plymouth's debilitating food shortages. For the last two planting seasons, the Pilgrims had grown crops communally—the approach first used at Jamestown and other English settlements. But as the disastrous harvest of the previous fall had shown, something drastic needed to be done to increase the yield. In April, Bradford had decided that each household should be assigned its own plot to cultivate, with the understanding that each family kept whatever it grew. The change in attitude was stunning. Families were now willing to work much harder than they had ever worked before. . . . The Pilgrims had stumbled on the power of capitalism. Although the fortunes of the colony still teetered precariously in the years ahead, the inhabitants never again starved."[8]

Historian Bernard Bailyn estimates total migration to Colonial America between the founding of the Jamestown colony and 1760 of "at least 700,000," including slaves forced to America against their will.[9] The scale of immigration from 1630 to 1775 was large given the population sizes of America and the sending countries. Even in the 1630s and 1640s, concerns about religious persecution sent another 21,000 Puritan immigrants to New England.[10] Between 1630 and 1660, an estimated 210,000 British immigrants came to America. Approximately 75,000 German immigrants arrived between 1727 and 1760, while about 100,000 to 150,000 Scotch-Irish came to the colonies from 1717 to 1760.

The pace of immigration increased after 1760. Bailyn calculates approximately 221,500 arrivals between 1760 and 1775, an average of about 15,000 a year compared to about 5,000 annually in earlier decades. About 3 percent of Scotland (40,000 people) and 2.3 percent of Ireland (55,000) came to the colonies from 1760 to 1775.[11] In comparison, Bailyn points out that French immigration to its colonies in the Western Hemisphere, Canada, and the Caribbean averaged less than 600 people a year in the late 1600s.

A prescient writer in the *London Chronicle* in 1773 understood the significance of the large flow of migrants from Britain: "America will, in less than half a century, form a state much more numerous and powerful than their mother-country. . . . What then will they be in fifty years time when their numbers will be more than trebled by natural propagation only, without the addition of thousands who fly every year to that happy country, where they can live with freedom and get their bread with ease."[12]

In certain periods during the Colonial era, a significant portion of immigrants were indentured servants or "redemptioners," meaning a ship captain, a merchant or a middleman, paid for their passage to America in exchange for a set term of service (typically four years).[13] Bailyn found that between 1773 and 1776, approximately 48 percent of the 9,364 English and Scottish immigrants that appeared in a public register were indentured servants.[14] People immigrating as families were much less likely to be indentured. "[A] large part of British migration to America was the movement of a labor force, working people seeking some kind of economic security and a more promising way of life," writes Bernard Bailyn.[15]

THE REVOLUTIONARY PERIOD: THE INFLUENCE OF ONE IMMIGRANT

The new immigrants brought with them the desire to work and also to be free from the political and social strictures of their native lands. Thomas Paine, one of America's earliest immigrants, was perhaps its most influential. Within only 14 months of arriving in America, he wrote and published

Common Sense (1776), a pamphlet that helped galvanize public opinion in the colonies in favor of independence from England. In *The Crisis*, Paine wrote, "When the country, into which I had just set my foot, was set on fire about my ears, it was time to stir. It was time for every man to stir. Those who had been long settled had something to defend, those who had just come had something to pursue; and the call and the concern was equal and universal."[16]

One should not view American independence as inevitable, since divisions existed not only between those who remained loyal to the Crown and those dissatisfied with English rule, but even among those who held grievances against the king. It is estimated that no more than one-third of the members of the Second Continental Congress favored declaring independence between late 1775 and early 1776.[17]

"The publication of Paine's *Common Sense* could not have been better timed," writes Cornell University historian Isaac Kramnick. "The delegates who read it on the January day it appeared in Philadelphia were, like most Americans at the time, confused and ambivalent. Tied by kinship, culture, commerce and decades of loyalty to England, they found themselves suddenly at war with His Majesty's troops. But Paine, the Englishman, had no doubt about the right course. Boldly he announced that America's purpose in these battles was to achieve complete independence, to break all ties with corrupt and tyrannical Britain."[18]

An estimated 500,000 copies of *Common Sense* were distributed in 1776, a total equal to 20 percent of the population of the American colonies at that time. Paine used plain language to argue for independence on moral and practical grounds, noting the numerous civil and European wars the British Crown had become entangled in and skewering the notion that men should be ruled by kings who inherited their power without receiving the consent of the governed. During the Revolutionary War, Paine rallied colonists during difficult times by producing *The Crisis*, a series of essays that George Washington read to his troops. Still, although he remained active in public life for many years, it was his work in 1776 that proved most important to his adopted country. "No single event seems to have had the catalytic effect of Paine's *Common Sense*," notes Kramnick.[19]

IMMIGRATION AFTER THE AMERICAN REVOLUTION

After the victory over the British and the establishment of a new Constitution and Bill of Rights, the federal government did not act in formulating a federal immigration policy. In fact, the absence of strong federal interference in state policies overall left immigration, like other issues, largely up to the states. The lack of uniformity among the states in establishing the terms for becoming a U.S. citizen led Congress to pass the Act of March 26, 1790, which set a national standard of two years of residence before an individual could be naturalized. Congress raised the residency requirement for citizenship to five years in 1795.[20]

In 1798, Congress passed the Alien Enemy Act, which granted the president the authority to order the deportation of any non-U.S. citizen judged "dangerous to the peace and safety of the United States" or suspected of engaging in "treasonable or secret machinations against the government."[21] E. P. Hutchinson notes that although the law lasted only two years, "the act is of some note in the history of American immigration legislation for its direct antialien character and for its initiation of two lasting elements of policy: deportation and manifesting."[22] (Manifesting is imposing a responsibility on ships or other potential carriers in an immigration context.)

In his inaugural address (1801), Thomas Jefferson spoke out against lengthy terms for naturalization and anti-immigrant attitudes more generally, citing America's unique history: "And shall we refuse to the unhappy fugitives from distress that hospitality which the savages of the wilderness extended to our fathers arriving in the land? Shall oppressed humanity find no asylum in this globe?"[23]

The U.S. government began maintaining annual immigration statistics in 1820, a year that saw only 8,385 new immigrants, representing a small fraction of the U.S. population of 9.6 million.[24] However, by 1830, the number of new immigrants had nearly tripled to 23,322, and rose to 79,340 in 1837.

By 1847, the annual number of new immigrants reached 234,968 and as high as 427,833 by 1854. The U.S. Civil War lowered immigration levels, though the United States still admitted 193,418 immigrants in 1864 and over 318,000 in 1866, a year after the war ended.

Examining the data between 1820 and 1900 tells the story of immigration to America in the nineteenth century. The Irish and Germans dominated much of the immigration flow during this period. Between 1820 and 1829, approximately 51,000 Irish men, women, and children immigrated to the United States. However, more than 656,000 Irish immigrated between 1840 and 1849, about 45 percent of all the immigrants in that decade. Irish immigration increased to 1,029,486 for the years 1850 to 1859, representing approximately 37 percent of immigration to the United States during the decade. Although Irish immigration did not reach that level in subsequent decades, it averaged approximately 450,000 a decade until 1910.

German immigration witnessed a similar rise over the course of the nineteenth century. The number of Germans immigrating to America rose from only 5,753 between 1820 and 1829, to 976,072 between 1850 and 1859.[25]

Even these large numbers did not represent the height of German immigration to the United States. Between 1880 and 1889, more than 1.4 million Germans immigrated to America. The large German ethnic population became a source of tension during World War I, when the loyalty of German-Americans was questioned.

The first German immigrant to serve as a U.S. Senator was Carl Schurz, who also became a Union Army major general during the Civil War. In an 1859 speech, Schurz described how he desired to immigrate to America after growing frustrated as a young man in Germany when he "saw that nation crushed down again, not only by overwhelming armies but by the dead-weight of customs and institutions and notions and prejudices which past centuries had heaped upon them. . . . Then I turned my eyes instinctively across the Atlantic Ocean, and America and Americanism, as I fancied them, appeared to me as the last depositories of the hopes of all true friends of humanity."[26]

While historians have focused primarily on German and Irish immigration in the nineteenth century, immigrants to America came in significant numbers from other nations as well. Immigration from the United Kingdom averaged about 50,000 a year between 1850 and 1879, and increased to 810,900 in the years 1880 to 1889.[27] Immigrants from Canada (and Newfoundland) reached a high of 492,865 between 1880 and 1889. Similar numbers can be seen in that decade for immigrants from what was then known as Austria-Hungary. Then, between 1900 and 1919, more than 3 million people emigrated from Austria-Hungary. Immigrants from Sweden totaled 401,330 from 1880 to 1889 and over 230,000 during the next two decades.

Recruiting immigrants to America became an accepted business practice in the 1800s. "Here the railroads played a key role, as they did throughout the economy," according to historian John Higham. "They needed immigrants not just for construction but to buy the great railroad land grants and to insure future revenues. Following the example set by the Illinois Central in the 1850s, the Burlington, the Northern Pacific, and other lines sent agents to blanket northern Europe with alluring propaganda."[28]

The beginning of the twentieth century saw significant numbers of Italians and Russians, many Jewish, immigrating to America. Close to 2 million Italian immigrants and 1.5 million Russian immigrants came here between 1900 and 1909, and more than 1 million came from each country in the years 1910–1919.

Throughout the history of immigration, one can see both "push" and "pull" factors working to draw immigrants to the United States. The pull of economic opportunity enticed both Russians and Italians seeking to escape poverty. In the case of Jews, freedom from anti-Semitism in Russia was a factor.

THE MARCH TOWARD RESTRICTION

The surest way to change the law in America is not by lobbying Congress but by convincing enough of the public the law must be changed. That generally is best done not by elected officials themselves but by outside actors who genuinely believe, rightly or wrongly, in the moral and political rectitude of their cause. The most hostility against any immigrant group in the history of the country was focused against the Chinese, many of whom came to work on the railroads or elsewhere in industry in the mid- to late 1800s. "No variety of anti-European sentiment has ever approached the violent extremes to which anti-Chinese agitation went in the 1870s and 1880s," wrote Higham. "Lynchings, boycotts, and mass expulsions still harassed the Chinese after the federal government yielded to the clamor for their exclusion in 1882."[29]

In her book *Driven Out,* Jean Pfaelzer describes how Chinese immigrants did not remain passive in the face of discrimination. They filed lawsuits for lost property, testified against vigilantes, won the right to send their children to public schools, defended themselves with firearms, and protested against a government order to make Chinese immigrants prove their legal status by the use of identity cards.[30]

Members of Congress introduced a series of bills in the 1870s to restrict Chinese immigration. President Chester A. Arthur vetoed such legislation against the Chinese on treaty and foreign policy grounds. Yet Arthur declined to veto a modified version of the legislation that became the Chinese Exclusion Act of 1882. The new law prevented Chinese immigrants from becoming citizens, provided for the deportation of Chinese "found unlawfully within the United States," and suspended Chinese immigration to America for 10 years.[31]

As significant as the human toll the legislation exacted was the precedent it set for the targeted exclusion of "undesirable" immigrants through legislative means. Other legislation in 1882 gave the Treasury Department more power over arriving ships, and court rulings against state immigration laws set the stage for the greater assumption of federal power over immigration policy.[32] For those seeking to restrict immigration, convincing a majority of Congress became the goal.

Economic concerns, nationalism brought about by World War I, and a tilt toward a smaller percentage of new immigrants with English as their native language contributed to moving public sentiment toward restricting immigration. "By the time of the Great War, unrestricted immigration already appeared a lost cause," writes historian Paul Johnson. "In 1915 an itinerant Georgian minister, William Simmons, founded the Ku Klux Klan as an organization to control minority groups which it identified with moral and political nonconformity. Its aims were powerfully assisted by the publication, the following year, of Madison Grant's presentation, in an American context, of European 'master-race' theory, *The Passing of the Great Race*."[33]

From the turn of the century until application by the Nazis helped to discredit the theories, the pseudoscience of eugenics carried great sway in Western intellectual and policy circles. Eugenics is the belief in improving the qualities of the human race by preventing the reproduction of people deemed to have genetic defects or undesirable characteristics and/or encouraging increased reproduction by those with supposed desirable inheritable characteristics. In 1927, members of the U.S. Supreme Court became convinced enough of the merits of eugenics that they ruled 8 to 1 in *Buck v. Bell* to uphold a New Jersey law that led to the forced sterilization of Carrie Buck, a poor woman who had become pregnant. In a now infamous passage from the majority opinion, Justice Oliver Wendell Holmes argued that sterilizing Buck against her will was not a punishment and that the woman should have viewed it as an obligation to society: "It is better for the world, if instead of waiting to execute degenerate offspring for crime, or to let them starve for their imbecility, society can prevent those who are manifestly unfit from continuing their kind. The principle that sustains compulsory vaccination is broad enough to cover the fallopian tubes. Three generations of imbeciles are enough."[34]

This belief in eugenics became decisive in the effort to reduce immigration. While some supporters of immigration restrictions may argue that the national origins quota laws of 1921 and 1924 were a necessary "pause" in immigration flows, in fact, supporters based the case for such restriction on science that today would be labeled ridiculous.

In *The Passing of the Great Race*, Madison Grant laid out his theory about races and skull sizes. Grant wrote, "In dealing with the European populations the best method of determining race has been found to lie in a comparison of proportions of the skull."[35] Grant sought to dispute arguments that immigrants could develop improved skull sizes through time spent in the United States: "Recent attempts have been made in the interest of inferior races among our immigrants to show that the shape of the skull does change, not merely in a century, but in a single generation. In 1910, the report of the anthropological expert of the Congressional Immigration Commission gravely declared that a round skull Jew on his way across the Atlantic might and did have a round skull child; but a few years later, in response to the subtle elixir of American institutions as exemplified in an East Side tenement, might and did have a child whose skull was appreciably longer; and that a long skull South Italian, breeding freely, would have precisely the same experience in the reverse direction."[36]

In formulating restrictive immigration legislation, the House Judiciary Committee relied on expertise offered by a eugenics consultant, Harry Laughlin, who had drafted the "model eugenics law" that served as the basis for forced sterilization in Virginia.[37]

In February 1921, President Woodrow Wilson vetoed—via a "pocket veto"—a bill to establish strict new immigration quotas. In the new session of Congress that began in March 1921, chief restrictionist legislators Senator William P. Dillingham and Rep. Albert Johnson introduced new versions of their bills, which moved quickly through Congress.

The 1921 bill aimed to restrict the immigration of Jews, Italians, and other Southern and Eastern European immigrants not of "Nordic" descent. To keep Italians, Russians, and others out of the country, the legislation established an annual quota of admitting no more than 3 percent of foreign-born from a country based on the number of that nationality in the 1910 census. This would reduce entry from nationalities represented in more recent waves of immigrants. The bill maintained a bar on immigration from Asian countries and exempted residents of the Western Hemisphere. Interestingly, the bill encouraged a preference "so far as possible" to relatives of U.S. citizens, including spouses, parents, and siblings and provided an exemption from the quota for children of U.S. citizens under 18 years old.[38]

The bill received overwhelming Congressional support, with an early version of the 1921 legislation receiving a vote in the U.S. Senate of 78 to 1.[39] After the 1921 bill became law, legislators opposed to immigration wasted little time in pursuing even more restrictive measures, since the 1921 bill had a "sunset" provision. They succeeded with the passage of the Immigration Act of 1924. To further diminish the number of supposed inferior immigrants, the law set a quota from a particular country of no more than 2 percent of the 1890 population of that country of origin—a date selected because it preceded the large waves of immigrants from Italy and Russia in particular.[40] To appreciate how drastically these quotas and other immigration regulations affected immigration levels, note that from 1910 to 1919, 1.1 million Russian immigrants came to America, compared to 2,463 from 1930 to 1939, a decline of more than 99 percent.[41]

The 1921 and 1924 bills affected the lives of millions of people and its effects lasted generations. The 1921 and 1924 acts also influenced the plight of those who sought refuge from Nazi policies of the 1930s and 1940s and enshrined in U.S. law for decades a racial and ethnic basis for denying entry to people based on bizarre and false distinctions among nationalities.

Advocates of the bills played up anti-Jewish sentiment in gaining legislative support. Representative Johnson used a document quoting U.S. consuls abroad as saying barring legislative action the United States would face an onslaught of Jews who were "abnormally twisted," "inassimilable," "filthy, un-American, and often dangerous in their habits." Historian John Higham notes, "The House Committee on Immigration appended these comments to its own report in favor of the suspension bill and used them to suggest that the present immigration was largely Jewish. This strategy made a strong impression. It left a conviction in various quarters that the chief purpose of the immigration law of 1921 was to keep out the Jews."[42]

At a Congressional hearing held on Ellis Island in 1997, Sen. Spencer Abraham (R-MI), then chair of the Senate Immigration Subcommittee, summarized the historical record of these bills that profoundly shaped the destinies of so many people: "Some argue for another timeout to immigration, yet when we look back at the theories and sentiments that drove Congress to close the door to immigrants, we should realize that those were sad chapters in America's past, not guideposts to its future."[43]

PRE- AND POST-WORLD WAR II

During World War I, the federal government required all travelers to the United States to obtain a visa at a U.S. consulate or diplomatic post abroad. By making that requirement permanent in 1924, Congress had established the framework of temporary (non-immigrant) visas for study, work, or travel, and immigrant visas (for permanent residence) that we have today.[44]

Under the Hoover Administration, consular officers were instructed to be more vigilant in preventing the admission of anyone who did not have a job waiting in the United States or self-sustaining personal wealth. Author Laura Fermi explains: "In response to the new cry for restriction at the beginning of the [Great Depression] . . . the consuls were to interpret very strictly the clause prohibiting admission of aliens 'likely to become public charges; and to deny the visa to an applicant who in their opinion might become a public charge at any time.'"[45]

In the early 1900s, over one million immigrants a year came to the United States. In 1930—the first year of the national origin quotas—approximately 241,700 immigrants were admitted. But under the State Department's strict interpretations, only 23,068 immigrants came in during 1933, the smallest total since 1831.[46]

AFTER WORLD WAR II

The Displaced Persons Act of 1948, the nation's first refugee law, allowed many refugees from World War II to settle in America. The law put into place policy changes that had already seen immigration rise from 38,119 in

1945 to 108,721 in 1946 (and later to 249,187 in 1950). One-third of those admitted between 1948 and 1951 were Poles, with ethnic Germans second.[47] (See Chapter 6 for a broader discussion of the history of U.S. policies toward refugees.)

The 1952 Immigration and Nationality Act is best known for its restrictions against those who supported communism or anarchy. However, the bill's other provisions were quite restrictive and were passed over the veto of President Harry S. Truman. The 1952 Act retained the national origin quota system for the Eastern Hemisphere. The Western Hemisphere continued to operate without a quota and relied on other qualitative factors to limit immigration. Moreover, during that time, the Mexican Bracero program, from 1942 to 1964, allowed millions of Mexican agricultural workers to work temporarily in the United States.

The 1952 Act set aside half of each national quota to be divided among three preference categories for relatives of U.S. citizens and permanent residents. The other half went to aliens with high education or exceptional abilities. These quotas applied only to those from the Eastern Hemisphere.

AN END TO THE NATIONAL ORIGIN QUOTAS

The Immigration and Nationality Act of 1965 became a landmark in immigration legislation by specifically striking the racially based "national origin" quotas. It removed the barriers to Asian immigration, which later led to opportunities to immigrate for many Filipinos, Chinese, Koreans, and others. The Western Hemisphere was designated a ceiling of 120,000 immigrants but without a preference system or per-country limits. Modifications made in 1978 ultimately combined the Western and Eastern Hemispheres into one preference system and one ceiling of 290,000.

The 1965 Act built on the existing system—without the national origins quotas—and gave somewhat more priority to family relationships. Yet it did not completely overturn the existing system but rather carried forward essentially intact the family immigration categories from the 1959 amendments to the Immigration and Nationality Act. Even though the text of the law prior to 1965 indicated that half of the immigration slots were reserved for skilled employment immigration, in practice, Immigration and Naturalization Service (INS) statistics show that 86 percent of the immigrant visas issued between 1952 and 1965 went for family immigration.[48]

A number of significant pieces of legislation since 1980 have shaped the current U.S. immigration system. First, the Refugee Act of 1980 removed refugees from the annual world limit and established that the U.S. president would set the number of refugees allowed to be admitted each year after consultations with Congress.

Second, the 1986 Immigration Reform and Control Act (IRCA) introduced sanctions against employers who "knowingly" hired undocumented immigrants (those here illegally). It also provided amnesty for many undocumented immigrants.

Third, the 1990 Act increased legal immigration by 40 percent. In particular, the act increased the number of employment-based immigrants significantly, up to 140,000, while also boosting family immigration.

Fourth, the 1996 Illegal Immigration Reform and Immigrant Responsibility Act (IIRAIRA) significantly tightened rules that permitted undocumented immigrants to convert to legal status and made other changes that tightened immigration law in areas such as political asylum and deportation.

Fifth, in response to the September 11, 2001, terrorist attacks, the USA Patriot Act and the Enhanced Border Security and Visa Entry Reform Act tightened rules on the granting of visas to individuals from certain countries and enhanced the federal government's monitoring and detention authority over foreign nationals in the United States.

In a dramatic reorganization of the federal government, the Homeland Security Act of 2002 abolished the Immigration and Naturalization Service and transferred its immigration service and enforcement functions from the Department of Justice into a new Department of Homeland Security. The Customs Service, the Coast Guard, and parts of other agencies were also transferred into the new department.

Today, the Department of Homeland Security, with regards to immigration, is organized as follows: U.S. Customs and Border Protection (CBP) contains customs and immigration inspectors, who check the documents of travelers to the United States at air, sea, and land ports of entry; and Border Patrol agents, the uniformed agents who seek to prevent unlawful entry along the southern and northern borders. U.S. Immigration and Customs Enforcement (ICE) employs investigators, who attempt to find undocumented immigrants inside the United States; and Detention and Removal officers, who detain and seek to deport such individuals. The new U.S. Citizenship and Immigration Services (USCIS) is where people go, or correspond with, to become a citizen or obtain permission to work, adjust their status, or extend their stay in America.

Those involved in the September 2001 attacks were not immigrants—people who become permanent residents with a right to stay in the United States—but holders of temporary visas, primarily visitor or tourist visas. Following the September 2001 attacks, the Department of Justice adopted several measures that did not require new legislation to be passed by Congress. Some of these measures created controversy and raised concerns about civil liberties. For example, Federal Bureau of Investigation (FBI) and INS agents detained for months over 1,000 foreign nationals of Middle Eastern descent and refused to release the names of the individuals. The Department of Justice also began requiring foreign nationals from primarily Muslim nations to be fingerprinted and questioned by immigration officers upon entry or to report to the immigration service if they had been living in the United States.

RECENT LEGISLATIVE BATTLES: 1996 AND THE WAR OVER LEGAL IMMIGRATION

A review of recent legislative battles provides context for future debates over immigration in Congress. The Republican takeover of Congress in the 1994 midterm election portended great changes in the politics of immigration. Being in the majority in the House or Senate allows the chair of a committee or subcommittee to seize control of an issue and lead it through the legislative process. In 1995, two motivated individuals who opposed immigration—Rep. Lamar Smith (R-TX) and Sen. Alan Simpson (R-WY)—became the chairs of the House and Senate subcommittees on immigration. Both moved quickly to hold hearings and develop legislative proposals.

Three developments aided Smith and Simpson in their efforts. First, concerns about illegal immigration were reaching a crescendo, manifesting itself in the California referendum Proposition 187 winning 59 percent to 41 percent. Although the referendum was later ruled unconstitutional and did not go into effect after Gov. Gray Davis ended the appeals process, it would have barred illegal immigrants from receiving public education and social services. Changes in immigration enforcement funneled more illegal immigrants into routes that entered California and Arizona. Moreover, public images of obvious enforcement gaps, such as Mexican border crossers running en masse across highways in San Diego, California, fueled public resentment.

Second, lingering economic concerns made immigration restriction more appealing. While by 1995 national unemployment rates had fallen from 7.5 percent in 1992 to 5.6 percent, public perceptions lag economic data. The 1992 presidential election had been fought over economic issues.

Third, a commission chaired by the late Rep. Barbara Jordan (D-TX), which had been established by law in 1990, was well placed to provide cover for immigration opponents. Pro-immigration critics of its reports noted the commission staff seemed to work hand in glove with the staffs of Smith and Simpson when producing the commission's recommendations.

Smith and Simpson largely adopted the Jordan Commission's recommendation to slash legal immigration by prohibiting American citizens from sponsoring for immigration their adult children and siblings, while also reducing and restricting high-skill immigrants and even refugees. In essence, Representative Smith and Senator Simpson hoped to capitalize on public sentiment against illegal immigration by cutting legal immigration.

To many opponents of immigration, it makes little difference whether immigrants are legal or illegal because, in their view, these foreigners may still "take" a job from an American, harm the culture, or add to the country's population. Most of the larger organizations against immigration are focused on population control—seeking to limit or reduce the population of the United States, to which immigration contributes. In that light, to opponents, the impact of a legal immigrant is much the same as someone who entered illegally.

However, most Members of Congress and the general public make distinctions between legal and illegal immigration. For example, after the October 2003 California recall election of Gov. Gray Davis, in which driver's licenses for illegal immigrants was a debated issue, voters surveyed displayed positive attitudes toward legal immigrants. A total of 69 percent of voters surveyed said legal immigration has had a "very positive" or "somewhat positive" impact on California, with only 19 percent saying the impact was "somewhat negative" or "very negative." In contrast, only 24 percent of voters surveyed said the impact of illegal immigration on California has been "very positive" or "somewhat positive," compared to 64 percent who said the impact has been "somewhat negative" or "very negative."[49]

The success or failure of legislation often hinges on the actions and strategies of those outside Congress. In 1995 and 1996, a pro-immigration advocate named Rick Swartz organized meetings of representatives of various groups that supported immigration. Most of the people in these meetings could be described as left of center, including those in groups such as the National Council of La Raza.

One day, Stephen Moore, then an economist at the libertarian think tank the Cato Institute, listened to people at the meeting express alarm that it would be impossible to stop an immigration bill from becoming law given all the concerns and media attention surrounding illegal immigration. Moore, who had attended few meetings, interrupted and said, "Why don't you split the bill?" Realizing more explanation was needed, he said that since members of Congress seemed determined to look tough on illegal immigration, then the only way to save legal immigration was to "split" off the measures on legal immigrants—in other words, make sure provisions on legal immigration are not in the same bill as the more popular measures cracking down on illegal immigrants. This proved to be the most important insight of the debate. Although immigration advocates at the local level accused groups in Washington, DC, of "selling out" illegal immigrants, in fact, there was no way politically to save the relatively liberal provisions in the U.S. immigration law that allowed illegal immigrants to forestall or prevent deportation. The only question was whether to attempt something politically achievable—saving legal immigration—as opposed to concentrating on a quixotic effort on illegal immigration that would give opponents of immigration a complete legislative victory.

While those outside Congress adopted the "split the bill" strategy, none of that would have mattered if the most junior man in the U.S. Senate, newly elected Sen. Spencer Abraham (R-MI), had not declared on his own to oppose cuts in legal immigration. Motivated by the immigrant heritage of his four grandparents, all born in Lebanon, Abraham possessed an optimistic conservative worldview in sync with former President Ronald Reagan. Abraham decided he would take on fellow Republican Alan Simpson and his effort to restrict the admission of family, business, and humanitarian immigrants.

As a courtesy, Abraham met with Simpson to tell the Wyoming senator he planned to oppose his bill when it came before the Senate Judiciary Committee. Simpson believed he had little to fear from Abraham. He was wrong.[50]

Simpson's bill united in opposition a strong coalition of businesses, ethnic organizations, and religious groups. His bill would have limited refugee admissions to 50,000 a year, severely restricted the ability of anyone to apply for asylum in the United States, reduced legal immigration by 40 percent or more, and eliminated the ability of U.S. citizens to sponsor children 21 years or older, siblings, and in practice, parents. Immigrant visas for skilled foreign nationals would have been slashed by more than one-third, a new $10,000 tax would have been levied on each skilled immigrant, and recruiting international students off U.S. college campuses to work in the United States essentially would have been prohibited by requiring two years of work experience abroad for a skilled temporary visa.[51]

Senator Abraham's opposition brought other Republicans along, particularly fellow freshman senator Mike DeWine (R-OH), the father of eight children, who argued against Simpson's family restrictions by asking: Why, for immigration purposes, would hypothetically DeWine's 19-year-old daughter be a member of his family but under the bill his 22-year-old son would be considered some type of outcast? DeWine also opposed the bill's provisions on businesses and especially the proposed refugee and asylum restrictions. Another benefit of young Republican Senators like Abraham and DeWine opposing the bill was that they prevented Senator Simpson from cutting a deal with key Democrats, who would have been embarrassed if Republicans had proved to be better allies of civil rights and ethnic organizations than Democratic lawmakers. With the possibility foreclosed of salvaging a deal with Sen. Ted Kennedy (D-MA), who aligned himself with Senator Abraham, Simpson was mostly on his own.

In the key procedural vote in the Senate Judiciary Committee to "split" off all legal immigration provisions from the bill, Senator Simpson lost

12 to 6. He tried to reattach his legal immigration restrictions on the Senate floor but lost by an even larger margin, 80 to 20.

Meanwhile, a few weeks later, in March 1996, Rep. Lamar Smith moved his bill to the House floor. If his legal immigration reductions made it through the House, it would still be possible to combine them with the Senate's illegal immigration only bill when the two bills would be reconciled in a legislative conference. For that reason, the effort to "split the bill" continued on the House floor in the form of amendments. Similar to in the Senate, it was Reagan-oriented freshmen Republicans who led the effort, in this case Rep. Sam Brownback (R-KS) and Rep. Dick Chrysler (R-MI). California Democrat Rep. Howard Berman joined them in the bipartisan effort.

The Chrysler-Berman-Brownback amendment was straightforward—eliminate the measures on legal immigration reductions from the bill, while leaving the new provisions to crack down on illegal immigration intact. The education effort inside and outside of Congress as to how negative the bill would be toward family and other elements of legal immigration if enacted proved effective.[52] The Chrysler-Berman-Brownback amendment prevailed by a vote of 238 to 183. The new restrictions on legal immigration proposed by Lamar Smith and Alan Simpson had been defeated.

The effort by Senator Abraham in the Senate and similar efforts by his allies in the House have allowed hundreds of thousands more legal immigrants to join close relatives, fill skilled positions, or gain refuge in the United States since 1996. "The restrictionists wanted to impose a regime that was as close as America could ever get to Europe's zero-immigration policies and that goal was within their grasp. . . . It was an astonishing victory," said Frank Sharry, then executive director of the National Immigration Forum.[53]

2006 AND 2007

The Congressional debates in 2006 and 2007 differed significantly from 1996. A central issue in 2006 and 2007 became the best approach to dealing with approximately 11 million illegal immigrants living in the United States.

The story of 2006 and 2007 really began with the turn of history in September 2001. President George W. Bush left the statehouse in Texas and moved to the White House determined to forge closer ties with Mexico. A key part of those closer ties involved reaching an immigration agreement with Mexico that would aid Vicente Fox, the country's new president. The goal was to establish new temporary visas to ease the pressure to immigrate illegally and address the situation of Mexicans (and potentially others) in the country illegally. In early September 2001, talks with Mexico and internal Bush Administration discussions had proceeded far enough that legislation was likely to be introduced with the Administration's imprint to liberalize U.S. immigration laws. The terrorist attacks of September 11, 2001, changed that.

The September 11, 2001, attacks focused the nation's attention on national security, including gaps in our immigration system. Moreover, the temporary downturn in the economy increased anxieties about unemployment. Concerns about porous borders and immigrants "taking" jobs proved too much to overcome, and the U.S.-Mexico immigration talks were pushed to the backburner and later ended.

In 2004 and 2005, President Bush reiterated his support for immigration reform. However, he made the same tactical mistake that continues to be made on this issue—emphasizing the goal of legalizing the status of millions of illegal immigrants above all other issues, rather than viewing legalization as part of a broader compromise on the issue of immigration.

In 2006, President Bush continued to urge Congress to legalize those here illegally but also put more emphasis on border security and a temporary visa program. The White House worked with Sen. Ted Kennedy and Sen. John McCain (R-AZ) on legislation that encompassed those three aspects of immigration policy. However, as the bill moved forward in the legislative process, the provisions on temporary visas were whittled back by amendments. It became unclear whether the numbers would be too low and the process too cumbersome for the temporary visas to be effective in reducing illegal immigration. In the end, the bill passed the U.S. Senate, but few found the legislation ideal.

In the House of Representatives, a completely different effort had been underway. Led by Judiciary Committee Chair Rep. Jim Sensenbrenner (R-WI), House Republicans opposed any effort at legalizing those in the country and instead filled their bill with many restrictive measures on illegal immigration. While the Senate bill contained a variety of pro-immigration measures on family and high skill immigration, the House legislation contained no provisions on legal immigration.

Outside efforts influenced the Congressional debate in ways both intended and unintended. April 2006 saw for the first time truly large immigrant rights protests that were national in scope. NBC News described the rallies: "Angered by the direction Congress appeared to be taking, hundreds of thousands of Latino immigration-rights protestors took to the streets of major metropolitan areas, arguing that illegal immigrants should not be treated as criminals. On April 10 [2006] they marched in 102 different U.S. cities. It was mostly an ad-hoc effort, organized by church and labor groups and publicized by Spanish-language radio personalities. Conservative critics were offended by the fact many of the demonstrators carried huge Mexican flags."[54]

Even at the time it should have been evident such protests were more likely to repel, rather than attract, Americans to their cause. In addition to the poor optics of some individuals carrying Mexican flags, the core message of the march organizers was off the mark. The issue was not the "rights" of illegal immigrants, since clearly under the law they did not have the right to be here. After all, a key part of the Senate's legislation was designed to give illegal immigrants a legal basis for remaining in the United States without fear of deportation. Civil rights marches in the 1960s emphasized rights, but those marchers could argue they already possessed the rights under the Bill of Rights. Marchers in the 1960s just needed the government at different levels to protect their constitutional right to vote and not be persecuted because of the color of their skin. The distinction is important.

Americans are far more open to an "opportunity" argument than a rights-based argument on immigration. Advocates for illegal immigrants both in 1996 and today should argue illegal immigrants want an opportunity to live the American Dream, just like that enjoyed by American citizens and their families. The immigrants want the opportunity to work and live in freedom and to raise their children as Americans. Like other immigrants in the past, they have pride in their former land but will be Americans by choice, or at least would be if granted the grace and opportunity by the elected representatives of the American people. As illegal immigrants, they should state it was wrong to break the law but they felt it was a necessary transgression to help their families escape poverty and provide a better future for their children. And they should realize it is necessary to make amends for these transgressions and be willing to do so in order to become a full participating member of American society. Opportunity, not "rights," appeals to Americans' pride in our country's history as a nation of immigrants, as well as our citizens' compassion and willingness to give people a second chance.

In the end, Republican House leaders, buoyed by faxes and phone calls opposing the legislation, and spurred on by talk radio hosts, refused to meet with the Senate to reconcile differences between the two bills. This effectively killed immigration efforts in 2006.

In 2007, the effort at immigration reform resembled the attitude of Colonel Nicholson, played by Alec Guinness in the film *Bridge on the River Kwai*. In the movie, captured POW Colonel Nicholson decides, with single-minded determination, that he will build the Japanese the best bridge they ever saw as a way to demonstrate British superiority and improve morale among his men. He forgets the reason British soldiers are fighting is to win the war and defeat the Japanese, not to build bridges to show up a Japanese commandant. As a consequence, Nicholson ends up building the Japanese military a bridge of enormous strategic importance. The bridge is so important that a small British-led commando squad is organized to blow it up.

Col. Nicholson belatedly uncovers the plot and tries to stop the commandos and save the bridge. In a way, in both 2006 and even more so in 2007, Administration and some other advocates for immigration reform became a little like Colonel Nicholson—so eager to achieve the goal of passing a bill, any bill, they lost sight of the bigger picture.

In 2007, the bigger picture involved the Senate almost eviscerating the legal immigration system, in essence preventing Americans from allowing close relatives to immigrate legally as part of a political deal to grant legal status to several million illegal immigrants. In exchange for support for legalization, Sen. Jon Kyl (R-AZ) and some Senate Republican allies asked for the elimination of most family immigration categories and even employment-based preference categories. In their place would be a legislatively mandated point system to select legal immigrants.

The point system in the Senate bill was so poorly conceived it should have embarrassed its supporters. The point system aimed to give preference to those with higher education degrees, English language ability, work experience in the United States, and jobs in fields of high projected growth, which included jobs in fast food restaurants. A National Foundation for American Policy analysis concluded a Nobel Prize–winning physicist who worked abroad could receive more points and have a better chance of gaining admission under the point system if he was offered a job preparing hamburgers at McDonald's than teaching at MIT. The designers of the point system did not seem to understand how the immigration law's per-country limit would produce absurd results under the proposed point system. For example, if 100,000 people from India scored 80 points or higher but 1,000 individuals from Luxembourg scored 40 points or less, in practice all 1,000 individuals from Luxembourg would receive green cards, while perhaps 80,000 or 90,000 people from India with higher scores would not be allowed to immigrate to America.[55] U.S. citizens would have been unable to sponsor most close family members and U.S. employers prevented from sponsoring specific employees, instead being forced to leave it up to the vagaries of the point system to determine whether a valued worker could gain permanent residence. Employers understood the best determinant of an individual's ability to integrate and have value in the U.S. economy was not "paper" qualifications for achieving points in a government "test" but whether an employer was willing to hire the individual to be part of his or her company.

In the end, the immigration reform effort in 2007 fell of its own weight in the Senate and never proceeded in the House. The opposition to the Senate bill centered on how to address the situation of those in the country illegally. There simply was not enough political support in the Senate to make major changes to immigration law. In 2008 and 2009, no serious effort was mounted, owing to the failures in 2006 and 2007 and, in 2009 in particular, the poor economy.

CONCLUSION

The history of immigration is filled with surprises. Looking back, it is surprising immigration with virtually no restrictions lasted in the country from 1607 to 1921. Reading about the virulent anti-Semitism and bizarre eugenics theories that dominated U.S. immigration policy before and even, for a time, after World War II, should also surprise the modern reader. The ability to change policy back to a pro-immigration direction in 1965 and 1990 shows Americans, at heart, are proud of our history as a nation of immigrants. Yet concerns about illegal immigration that resulted in more restrictive legislation in 1996 and the blocking of legalization for illegal immigrants in 2006 and 2007 demonstrate American compassion is finite.

NOTES

1. Oscar Handlin, *The Uprooted: The Epic Story of the Migrations That Made the American People*, 2nd ed. (New York: Little, Brown, 1979), 3. "Once I thought to write a history of the immigrants in America. Then I discovered that the immigrants *were* American history," wrote Handlin.
2. *Webster's New World Dictionary*, Third College Edition (New York: Simon & Schuster, 1988), 702.
3. Oscar Handlin, ed., *Immigration as a Factor in American History* (Englewood Cliffs, NJ: Prentice-Hall, 1959), 1.
4. Maldwyn Allen Jones, *American Immigration*, 2nd ed. (Chicago: University of Chicago Press, 1992), 4.
5. Ivor Noel Home, "We Are Starved," in *1607: Jamestown and the New World* (New York: Rowman & Littlefield, 2007), 73–74.
6. Ibid., David Robinson, "Accepte our poore indevour," 159–160.
7. Nathaniel Philbrick, *Mayflower* (New York: Penguin Group, 2006), 119.
8. Ibid., 165.
9. Bernard Bailyn, *Voyagers to the West* (New York: Vintage Books, 1986), 25.
10. Philbrick, 173.
11. Bailyn, 26.
12. Ibid., 42.
13. Ibid., 166.
14. Ibid., 166–167.
15. Ibid., 243.
16. Thomas Paine, *Common Sense* (Middlesex, UK: Penguin Books, 1986), 25.
17. Ibid., 8.
18. Ibid., 8.
19. Ibid., 9.

20. E. P. Hutchinson, *Legislative History of American Immigration Policy, 1798–1965* (Philadelphia: University of Pennsylvania Press, 1981), 11.

21. Ibid., 15.

22. Ibid., 15.

23. Ibid., 17.

24. All figures in this section are derived from Tables 1 and 2 of the *2008 Yearbook of Immigration Statistics*, Office of Immigration Statistics, Department of Homeland Security, 2009.

25. Between those decades saw 124,726 Germans immigrating in the 1830s and 385,434 in the 1840s.

26. Michelle Houle, ed., *Immigration, Great Speeches in History* (New York: Greenhaven Press, 2004), 35.

27. According to the *2008 Yearbook of Immigration Statistics*, "Since 1925, data for United Kingdom refer to England, Scotland, Wales and Northern Ireland."

28. John Higham, *Strangers in the Land, Patterns of American Nativism 1860–1925* (New York: Atheneum, 1973), 16.

29. Ibid., 25.

30. Jean Pfaelzer, *Driven Out* (New York: Random House, 2007).

31. Hutchinson, 80–84.

32. Hutchinson, 83–84.

33. Paul Johnson, *Modern Times* (New York: HarperCollins, 2001), 203.

34. Elof Axel Carlson, *The Unfit: A History of a Bad Idea* (Cold Spring Harbor, NY: Cold Spring Harbor Laboratory Press, 2001), 254–255.

35. Madison Grant, *The Passing of the Great Race*, 4th ed. (New York: Charles Scribner's Sons, 1922), 19.

36. Ibid., 17.

37. Elof Axel Carlson, 250, 255–256.

38. Hutchinson, 179–180.

39. Ibid., 179–180.

40. Ibid., 194.

41. Table 2, *2008 Yearbook of Immigration Statistics.*

42. Higham, 309–310.

43. "Should America Remain a Nation of Immigrants," hearing before the Subcommittee on Immigration, Committee on the Judiciary, U.S. Senate, August 11, 1997, 3.

44. Interview with C. D. Scully, former Department of State Consular Affairs Officer.

45. Laura Fermi, *Illustrious Immigrants* (Chicago: University of Chicago Press, 1968), 26.

46. Examination of annual immigration statistics in Table 1 of the *2008 Yearbook of Immigration Statistics.*

47. Parts of this summary of U.S. immigration history were written by Stuart Anderson for the *Changing Face of North America: Immigration since 1965*, published by Mason Crest Publishers (Broomall, PA, 2004), a series of books for

students on which the author was senior consulting editor. The author appreciates the permission from Mason Crest to utilize that material in this book.

48. Data supplied by the Immigration and Naturalization Service.

49. Luntz poll of California voters, October 7, 2003. The poll was commissioned by the Federation for American Immigration Reform.

50. John Heilemann, "Do You Know the Way to Ban Jose?" *Wired Magazine*, August 1996.

51. Ibid.

52. Ibid. I played a role in these public education efforts by consulting with Congressional staff and writing reports and articles.

53. Ibid.

54. George Lewis, "NBC: '06 Saw Battle over Immigration," NBC News, December 20, 2006.

55. Stuart Anderson, *The Point System's Impact on Foreign Nurses and Other Potential Immigrants* (Arlington, VA: National Foundation for American Policy, 2007).

SUGGESTED READINGS

Handlin, Oscar. *The Uprooted: The Epic Story of the Migrations That Made the American People*, 2nd ed. New York: Little, Brown, 1979.

Higham, John. *Strangers in the Land: Patterns of American Nativism, 1860–1925.* New York: Atheneum, 1973.

Hutchinson, E. P. *Legislative History of American Immigration Policy, 1798–1965.* Philadelphia: University of Pennsylvania Press, 1981.

Jones, Maldwyn Allen. *American Immigration*, 2nd ed. Chicago: University of Chicago Press, 1992.

2008 Yearbook of Immigration Statistics. Washington, DC: Office of Immigration Statistics, Department of Homeland Security, 2009.

Two

The Contributions of Immigrants

Immigration, like many issues, can become dominated by statistics. In reality, the issue is really about people and their lives. Like any individual, the greatest impact an immigrant will exert is on family, friends, and coworkers. However, there are immigrants, taken as a group or individuals, who also make substantial contributions to America in fields as diverse as national defense, sports, science, business, and the arts. The children of immigrants also can contribute in ways rarely reported in the daily newspapers.

IMMIGRANT ENTREPRENEURS

Immigrants are more likely than natives to start businesses, according to the Kauffman Foundation. "For immigrants, 530 out of 100,000 people start a business each month, compared to 280 out of 100,000 native-born people," notes the foundation.[1] Other studies have found a similar propensity of immigrants to start companies.

Many of America's leading high-technology companies have utilized venture capital funding and grown successful enough to be traded on a U.S. stock exchange. A study by Stuart Anderson and Michaela Platzer conducted for the National Venture Capital Association found "Over the past 15 years, immigrants have started 25 percent of U.S. public companies that were venture-backed, a high percentage of the most innovative companies in America. . . . The largest U.S. venture-backed public companies started by immigrants include Intel, Solectron, Sanmina-SCI, Sun Microsystems, eBay, Yahoo!, and Google."[2]

Researchers from Duke University and University of California–Berkeley, interviewed executives at U.S. technology and engineering companies and reached conclusions similar to those of the National Venture Capital Association study: "Of the 2,054 companies we interviewed, 25.3 percent reported that at least one of their key founders was an immigrant. Extrapolating from this sample, we estimate that all companies founded by immigrants from 1995 to 2005 produced $52 billion in sales and employed 450,000 workers in 2005," according to Vivek Wadhwa, AnnaLee Saxenian, Ben Rissing, and Gary Gereffi.[3]

Some critics of immigration have argued immigrants are no more likely than natives to start businesses, though the data suggest otherwise. Yet even if immigrants were no more likely to be entrepreneurs, it would still be good for the United States. After all, starting a business or receiving a patent does not preclude someone else from engaging in these economically positive activities.

Economist Mark J. Perry points out that small business creation is essential to economic growth and job creation, so the more small businesses the better, regardless of who starts the business. "The characteristics of entrepreneurs is irrelevant for economic growth and jobs, and it doesn't matter if more people from Virginia start businesses than people in Maryland or California, or if more people with blue eyes start businesses compared to people with brown eyes," says Perry. "Those are all just artificial distinctions, like the artificial distinction between Americans and immigrants." He notes, "Small businesses that directly create new jobs, also create or support other jobs indirectly from the spending and consumption, investment and savings from the new workers who spend their earnings."[4]

A 2008 study by the Small Business Administration found, "Immigrants are nearly 30 percent more likely to start a business than are nonimmigrants, and they represent 16.7 percent of all new business owners in the United States." The report concluded: "Immigrant business owners make significant contributions to business income, generating $67 billion of the $577 billion in U.S. business income, as estimated from 2000 U.S. Census data. They generate nearly one-quarter of all business income in California—nearly $20 billion—and nearly one-fifth of business income in New York, Florida, and New Jersey."[5]

It is instructive to go beyond the numbers and look at some individual immigrants who have made interesting and unique contributions as entrepreneurs. Their stories remind us there are many ways to find success in America.

NANCY CHANG, TAIWANESE-BORN CO-FOUNDER OF TANOX

"If you really believe in something, the best approach is to invest yourself in that idea," said Dr. Nancy Chang, co-founder of Tanox, a biotechnology company based in Houston, Texas that was purchased by Genentech.[6]

Not many people take undergraduate classes from one professor who is a future Nobel Prize winner (Yuan T. Lee) and another who would go on to become the nation's prime minister. Nancy says her good fortune to learn from these teachers gave her the courage to leave Taiwan and study at Brown University in 1974, barely able to speak English. On the plane ride to America, she read James Watson's book on the discovery of the double helix, which led her to change her academic focus to biology, even though she had never taken a course on the subject.

Nancy Chang became one of the first international students to attend Harvard Medical School and, she was told, the medical school's first major entrepreneur. After Harvard, Dr. Chang was hired at Hoffman-La Roche on a work visa and later became director of the molecular biology group for Centocor. She also has taught at the Baylor College of Medicine and holds seven patents.

In 1986, Dr. Chang co-founded Tanox and served as CEO from 1990 to 2006. Starting Tanox was "part passion and dream and went against the textbook" by developing an asthma drug that focused on the allergy-related basis of asthma. At the time, this ran counter to the central belief about how asthma operated. The perseverance paid off when in June 2003, the Food and Drug Administration (FDA) approved Xolair, the first biotech product cleared for treating those with asthma related to allergies. Xolair was developed under an agreement among Tanox, Inc., Genentech, Inc., and Novartis Pharma AG.

When Tanox went public in April 2000 on the NASDAQ, it raised $244 million, which at the time was the largest biotech initial public offering (IPO). Dr. Chang said she is passionate about AIDS, since as a young researcher she worked in one of the first laboratories to confront the disease. Tanox developed TNX-355, an antibody for the treatment of HIV/AIDS. Genentech licensed TNX-355, known as Ibalizumab, to TaiMed Biologics.[7]

"I came to the United States frightened and scared. But I found if you do well and if you have a dream you will find people in America willing to help and give you an opportunity," said Dr. Chang. "Life is very rich. I just love this country."[8]

SAID HILAL, LEBANESE-BORN FOUNDER OF APPLIED MEDICAL RESOURCES

Said Hilal came to America from Lebanon as a teenager to study at California State, Long Beach, where he received a BS and MS in mechanical engineering, and later an MBA from the University of Southern California. With school ending and the situation in Lebanon worsening, Hilal chose to stay in America. Most importantly, while in college he married a native Californian. "I was deeply in love with both my new wife and my new country."

He started out working for a company developing scuba diving and commercial diving equipment. But Hilal notes the business took a downturn, particularly after the release of the blockbuster film *Jaws*. "People were afraid to go in the water."

Hilal considers himself a "reluctant" entrepreneur. He decided to start a new company only after Baxter bought Edwards Laboratory, a place where he had risen quickly through the ranks. With his mentors gone or leaving, and the culture changing, Hilal decided it was time to move on.

In 1988, he secured venture capital from Institutional Venture Partners (and later the private equity firm 3i and Security Pacific/Bank of America) to start Applied Vascular and Applied Urology, the predecessors to Applied Medical Resources. Hilal believes he gained funding more for the concept of his new company than from the more traditional approach of having developed a specific technology that needed financial backing. The new company's model was to listen closely to the customer and produce medical devices that married improved clinical outcomes with better value. Within three years, the company had turned a profit.

The privately held Applied Medical Resources, based in Rancho Santa Margarita, California, must contend with being a relatively small company in a field dominated by large players. In 2002, *Inc.* magazine named the company one of the top 50 innovative companies in America with revenues below $100 million. Applied Medical Resources has over 700 pending or issued patents spanning 25 technologies and over 800 products for cardiac and vascular surgery, general surgery, urology, colorectal surgery, and OB/GYN surgery. The company employs over 1,500 people and continues to manufacture all of its devices in Orange County, California.

"Lebanon was a wonderful country for a curious kid, and its educational system prepared me well for my college years. Unfortunately, the whole region is still tied to past and present conflicts," said Hilal. "We're very blessed in the United States to be a people focused on the future."[9]

PATRICK LO, CHINESE-BORN FOUNDER OF NETGEAR

"Sometimes one must take chances to secure a better life for your family." That is a lesson Patrick Lo said he learned when his parents decided to escape China and Mao Zedong's Cultural Revolution in the 1960s. Separating to increase their odds of success, Lo left China with an aunt and went to Macao. However, his parents were captured and sent to a re-education camp until Mao died in 1975.

Living with his grandparents in Hong Kong, Lo managed to win a full scholarship, reserved for students from developing nations, to attend Brown University. To secure the $400 needed for the plane ticket to America, he held a fundraiser, which he describes as his first experience in raising capital. After paying for the cab ride, he had only $170 to his name upon arriving in America.

Lo received a BS in electrical engineering from Brown University, but later returned to Hong Kong to seek employment. Hewlett-Packard hired him in its Asia office and eventually transferred him to Silicon Valley. He later started working for Bay Networks, which allowed him to establish Netgear as an "independent company-within-a-company, with separate budgets and personnel." Netgear's focus was computer networking for homes and small- and medium-sized businesses. When Nortel purchased Bay Networks, it expressed little interest in Netgear. Lo raised sufficient funds to purchase Netgear.

By 2003, the company had shown a sufficient enough track record of profitability that Lo could take the company public. Today, the company, based in Santa Clara, California, employs over 500 people. One of Netgear's home-networking devices, which can be plugged into any wall socket, has been favorably reviewed in the *Wall Street Journal* and other publications.

"If I stayed in Hong Kong I would have ended up fixing radios," said Patrick Lo. "It was America's culture that encouraged me to be ambitious."[10]

ZVI OR-BACH, ISRAELI-BORN FOUNDER OF eASIC

Israeli-born Zvi Or-Bach came to America in 1981 on an H-1 visa, the precursor to the H-1B visa. After working at Honeywell for two years, he returned to Israel. His brief work experience in the United States convinced him that some day he could return and find niches in the U.S. marketplace. And that was what Zvi did.

In 1990, he started Chip Express, an 80-person company with a patented laser technology useful in producing prototypes of chips within 24 hours. Like many other immigrant entrepreneurs, Or-Bach went on to start another company, eASIC, based in Santa Clara, California. The privately held company, founded in 1999, uses a combination of chips and software to enable end customers, such as providers of consumer electronics, to introduce custom products into the marketplace quickly and cheaply.

Or-Bach, who holds over 30 patents, primarily in the field of semi-custom chip architectures, helped eASIC survive its start-up phase by spreading its workforce among the United States, Malaysia, and Romania. The core of the company resides in the United States, but his experience and contacts from Chip Express helped establish eASIC's multinational design and production capabilities.

Or-Bach is concerned that current immigration policies are harming his adopted country. "It's painful to see. Because of immigration restrictions, such as on H-1B visas, we're losing many great minds," said Zvi. "Having worked in the United States for the last 20 years, it's clear that immigration is vital to the growth of the U.S. and being competitive internationally. There's no question immigration is America's secret weapon."[11]

ASA KALAVADE, INDIAN-BORN CO-FOUNDER OF TATARA SYSTEMS

Twenty years ago, it would have been considered improbable for a young woman in India to found her own technology business. "Even when I just started studying engineering, people came to my parents to talk them out of it, never mind starting my own company," said Asa Kalavade.

She came to America as an international student and received an MA and PhD in electrical engineering and computer science from the University of California–Berkeley. While most people think of wireless networks and streaming as new technologies, Kalavade has worked on these technologies for a decade and a half. Early in her career at Bell Labs, she invented patent-pending technologies for wireless multimedia streaming, network interfaces, and real-time multiprocessor digital signal processing (DSP) systems. She holds multiple patents.

After serving as vice president of technology at Savos, Kalavade founded Tatara Systems along with an immigrant from China, Hong Jiang. Based in Acton, Massachusetts, the privately held Tatara Systems, which provides technology for mobile services for companies like Vodafone, employs 60 people. Kalavade's two siblings are both in the United States working as electrical engineers. Her Indian-born husband has started his second company, Tizor Systems. "We're serial entrepreneurs," said Kalavade.[12]

NOBEL PRIZES AND ACHIEVEMENTS IN SCIENCE

In 2009, the world received further confirmation of the benefits of America's melting pot when immigrants in the United States were awarded Nobel Prizes in medicine, physics, and chemistry. Four of the seven Americans to win Nobel Prizes in the science categories in 2009 were immigrants.

University of California–San Francisco professor Elizabeth Blackburn, born in Australia, shared the 2009 Nobel Prize for Medicine with fellow immigrant Jack Szostak (Harvard Medical School), born in London, and American-born Carol Greider (Johns Hopkins University School of Medicine). Greider was Elizabeth Blackburn's student in 1985 when they "published a paper announcing the discovery of the enzyme telomerase."[13] Dr. Blackburn and Dr. Szostak also were able to establish that "repeated DNA sequences make up the tips of each chromosome."[14] Since the enzyme serves an important function in the health of cells, the discovery has helped launch research into cancer, cardiovascular disease, and other age-related illnesses.[15]

Willard S. Boyle, an immigrant from Canada, and George E. Smith shared the 2009 Nobel Prize for Physics with Charles K. Kao, who immigrated to the U.K. from Shanghai. Boyle and Smith worked together at Bell Labs and invented semiconductor technology (a charge-coupled device) now used in digital cameras.[16]

Venkatraman Ramakrishnan, a naturalized U.S. citizen born in India, shared the 2009 Nobel Prize in Chemistry with American-born Thomas Steitz and Ada Yonath of Israel. Their work using x-ray crystallography has provided "fundamental information about the workings of the cellular machinery at the atomic level and is already being exploited by pharmaceutical companies working to make new, more effective antibiotics."[17]

Immigrants to America have a long history of achievement in Nobel Prizes and other forms of international recognition in the sciences. "It is fairly clear that Americans with recent foreign roots are overrepresented in any classification of Americans who have brought honor and recognition to the United States," concluded the National Research Council, a part of the national Academy of Sciences, in its 1997 report *The New Americans.*[18] As of 1997, the National Research Council found immigrants made up between one-quarter to one-third of the U.S. Nobel Prize winners: 26 percent in chemistry, 32 percent in physics, 31 percent in physiology medicine, 31 percent in economics, and 27 percent in literature.[19]

Some who oppose immigration more generally—or high-skill immigration specifically—argue they have no problem with America admitting Nobel Prize winners, just not others of lesser distinction. They argue we should only allow in skilled foreign nationals who can gain the equivalent of an "Einstein Visa" by showing established genius. Of course, at some point in his life, a younger Albert Einstein would not have qualified for an "Einstein visa."

The problem is that even America's recent Nobel Prize winners were often just promising students when they first began the process of immigrating to the United States. For example, Elizabeth Blackburn first came to America in 1975, more than three decades before earning the Nobel Prize in Medicine and 10 years before she published her seminal paper that led to the prize. More generally, there are valuable contributions that can be made to the economy and society that would never be recognized by a Nobel Prize Committee.

Dr. William Ganz developed a "revolutionary catheter to measure blood flow and heart functions" with co-inventor Dr. Jeremy Swan, an immigrant from Ireland. Ganz, a Jew in Czechoslovakia during the Nazi invasion, managed to survive World War II and came to Los Angeles in 1966, no longer wishing to live under a communist regime. The Swan-Ganz device produced "a phenomenal impact on the understanding of cardiovascular disease," according to Dr. Jeffery W. Moses, director of the Center for Interventional Vascular Therapy at Columbia University Medical Center. In the 1980s, Ganz worked with Dr. P. K. Shah, an immigrant from India and currently director of cardiology at Cedars-Sinai Heart Institute, in developing clot-dissolving therapies now considered standard for helping victims of heart attacks.[20]

RESEARCH ON THE CONTRIBUTIONS OF THE FOREIGN BORN

Paula Stephan (Georgia State University) and Sharon G. Levin (University of Missouri-St. Louis) performed extensive research on the contributions of the foreign born in six areas of scientific achievement. Those areas included election to the National Academy of Sciences/National Academy of Engineering, the launching of biotechnology companies, and authors of scientific publications. After examining a study group of more than 4,500 scientists and engineers, Stephan and Levin wrote, "Individuals making exceptional contributions to science and engineering in the U.S. are disproportionately drawn from the foreign born. We conclude that immigrants have been a source of strength and vitality for U.S. science and, on balance, the U.S. appears to have benefitted from the educational investments made by other countries."[21]

Among the findings in the Stephan-Levin research:

- 19.2 percent of the engineers elected to the National Academy of Engineering are foreign born, compared to the 13.9 percent of the engineers who were foreign-born in 1980.
- Members of the National Academy of Sciences are "disproportionately foreign-born"; 23.8 percent of the scientists and engineers elected to the National Academy of Sciences (NAS) are foreign-born, compared to 18.3 percent non-natives in the U.S. workforce.[22]
- "We find the foreign-born to be disproportionately represented among those making exceptional contributions in the physical sciences . . . more than half of the 'outstanding' authors in the physical sciences are foreign-born compared to just 20.4 percent of physical scientists who are foreign-born in the scientific labor force as of 1980."[23]

The research by Stephan and Levin indicate America may be wise to make it easier for those who receive their schooling abroad to immigrate, particularly at the PhD level. "We also find evidence contributions to U.S. science and engineering are disproportionately drawn from the foreign-educated, both at the undergraduate and at the graduate level," note Stephan and Levin.[24]

THE NEXT GENERATION OF SCIENTISTS

It is striking how a restrictive policy toward immigration could carry implications beyond the immediate future. At the 2004 Intel Science Talent Search, the nation's premier science competition for America's top high school students, I conducted interviews to determine the immigration background of the 40 finalists. The results were instructive. An astonishing two-thirds of the Intel Science Talent Search finalists were the children of immigrants. In other words, if America had adopted a more restrictive immigration policy, most of the coming generation's top scientists would not be here in the United States today, since we never would have allowed in their parents.[25]

After examining the immigration backgrounds of the Intel Science Talent Search finalists, the most significant finding relates to the high proportion of student finalists whose parents came to the United States as professionals on H-1B temporary visas. The finding indicates the United States gains more than was previously realized by the entry of skilled professionals. Nearly half—18 of 40—of the finalists at the Intel Science Talent Search in 2004 had parents who entered the country on H-1B visas (known as H-1 prior to 1990). In contrast, only 16 of the 40 finalists had parents born in the United States. (The other six students had parents who immigrated in the family, refugee, or diversity category.) To put this in perspective: More than 85 percent of the U.S. population is native born, while well less than 1 percent of the population consists of current or former H-1B visa holders. Yet parents who entered the country on an H-1/H-1B visa were more likely to have a child be a finalist at the Intel Science Talent Search competition than a parent born in America.

Students from immigrant families seem acutely aware of the opportunity to excel that their parents gave them by immigrating to the United States. Qilei Hang, who lives in Cumberland, Maryland, was born in China. She came here as an eight-year-old when her father pursued a PhD in engineering and later obtained an H-1B visa. "If I were in China, I'd be preparing for the big exam, the one that decides whether you go into blue collar work or get to go to college. In China, it's a one-shot deal," she said. Her work on using mathematical modeling to increase the efficiency of mineral reclamation is used today and has been recognized by the Society for Mining, Metallurgy, and Exploration.

Russian-born Boris Alexeev, whose father arrived on an H-1B visa to teach at the University of Utah, garnered a second-place finish for mathematical work, the applications of which range from deciphering the genome and DNA to optical character recognition. Boris also was one of the top scorers in the 2004 U.S. Math Olympiad.

The mother of Romanian-born Andrei Munteanu came to the United States after winning the sometimes-criticized Diversity Visa Lottery (see Chapter 3). Inspired by the movies *Armageddon* and *Sudden Impact*, Andrei performed research that could contribute to saving us all—literally. He invented a new algorithm to predict collisions between Earth and asteroids. Similarly, Lisa Doreen Glukhovsky, whose parents came to the United States as refugees from Russia, developed a "method of measuring near-Earth asteroids [that] could one day help mitigate the danger of asteroid collisions with Earth." In an extraordinary feat for an amateur astronomer, she used high-resolution asteroid images at both a European and a U.S. observatory to develop a new approach to measuring the distances of asteroids. Like many of the Intel Science Talent Search finalists, Lisa is fluent in multiple languages (English, French, Russian, and Hebrew) and plays classical music (piano and violin).

Both Daniel Chimin Choi and Duy Minh Ha are in the United States because of family-sponsored immigration. Choi, whose South Korean-born parents were sponsored by a sibling, plans to pursue a PhD in biomedical engineering. He constructed a fuel cell "that derives electricity from bacterial respiration," which improved generation by 750 percent compared with similar fuel cells. Duy Minh Ha was born in Vietnam and came to the United States after relatives sponsored his family. Ha wants to dedicate his life to studying neurodegenerative disorders. His research on the impact of long-term estrogen replacement therapy on white and gray brain matter may provide clues for lowering the risk of Alzheimer's disease.

The immigration background of the parents of the 2004 U.S. Math Olympiad top scorers is similar to that of the Intel Science Talent Search finalists. More of the Math Olympiad top scorers have parents who received H-1B visas (10) than parents born in the United States (7). Twenty percent (4) of the parents entered first as international students. Two of the 20 top scorers for the 2004 U.S. Math Olympiad—Tony Zhang, born in China, and Jongmin Baek, born in South Korea—came to the United States when their U.S.-based relatives sponsored their parents for immigration. Oleg Golberg arrived with his family as a refugee from Russia. Interviews with the parents and students reveal a strong family culture of encouragement at an early age. In a number of cases, one finds a parent's professional experience in mathematics, and, in several instances, a student's interest in music. Math and music are similar, according to Jae Bae, who was born in South Korea and lives today in Hackensack, New Jersey. Bae used to play the piano and believes that a good head for math and music go together.

The presence of many immigrant children in the U.S. Math Olympiad is so notable it is even a source of humor among native-born U.S. parents. "My son is the Jewish Caucasian representative," joked Elizabeth Batson, the mother of Joshua Batson who was an honorable mention top scorer in the 2004 U.S. Math Olympiad. She credits immigrant parents for much of their children's success. "There's a different attitude and different priorities about how kids spend their time."

"Most Asian American children don't see themselves growing up to be NBA players, captains of industry, or politicians. . . . But many believe that if they do well in mathematics and science, they can succeed. They can become scientists, engineers, computer programmers, physicians," writes *Count Down* author Steve Olson. "All new immigrants to the United States must work hard to succeed, and they expect their children to work hard, too."[26]

Olson argues that immigrant success in the U.S. Math Olympiad is not coincidental. In addition to the drive of the individuals and their families, he points out that because the students or their parents are recent immigrants, "they speak more than one language and have experience with multiple cultures, which, as [Dean Keith] Simonton demonstrated, can be a source of creativity." Olson adds, "From an early age they absorb the lesson that they must work hard to do well in the United States and that, if they master mathematics and science, they are more likely to succeed. Given the precarious position of immigrant families in U.S. society, the intensity of their drive to succeed is hardly surprising.[27]

Nearly half the members of the U.S. Physics Team in 2004 were the children of immigrants—11 of 24, or 46 percent. In addition, 9 of 24 (or 38 percent) were born outside the United States, primarily from China.

BASEBALL

Yankees fans who watched their team win the 2009 World Series should be pleased at U.S. immigration policies that allow foreign-born athletes to play in America. Japanese-born Hideki Matsui was the 2009 World Series Most Valuable Player (MVP) after he knocked in six runs in the final game, hit in the go-ahead run in Game 2 and batted an amazing .643 for the series. Dominican-born pitcher Mariano Rivera gave up no runs in 5.1 innings as the Yankees closer, a role he has filled successfully in earlier Yankees championship seasons going back more than a decade.

The impact of foreign-born baseball players on the World Series should not have surprised those who have followed recent international trends in sports. A National Foundation for American Policy analysis completed near the end of the 2006 season found 23 percent, or 175, of the 750 players on active major league rosters were born outside the United States.[28] Foreign-born players accounted for 31 percent of the players selected for the 2006 All Star Game, higher than their proportion of 23 percent on major league active rosters. Seven of the 16 starting position players at the 2006 All Star Game—44 percent—were foreign-born: David Ortiz, Vladimir Guerrero, and Ichiro Suzuki started for the American League, and Jason Bay, Edgar Renteria, Albert Pujols, and Alfonso Soriano started for the National League.

The percentage of foreign-born players in the major leagues has more than doubled from 10 percent since 1990. Even though only a fixed number of jobs exist on active major league rosters—unlike the ebb and flow of jobs in the rest of the U.S. economy—one never hears complaints about "immigrants taking away jobs" from Americans in the major leagues.

Increased competition from foreign-born players has not resulted in lower salaries for native ballplayers. Since 1990, average major league player salaries more than quadrupled (in nominal dollars) from $578,930 to $2.87 million in 2006, while the proportion of foreign-born players in the league more than doubled from 10 percent to 23 percent. A sustained or increased quality of play, to which foreign-born players have contributed, may have helped increase revenues, as major league ballpark attendance rose from 54.8 million to 74.9 million between 1990 and 2005.

In 2009, Albert Pujols, born in the Dominican Republic, was unanimously named the National League's MVP, an honor he was won three times. Carlos Pena, also born in the Dominican Republic, tied for the lead in home runs in the American League, while the Seattle Mariners' Felix Hernandez, born in Venezuela, led the league in wins and was near the top in strikeouts and earned run average. Ichiro Suzuki (Japan) and Miguel Cabrera (Venezuela) placed second and fourth in batting average in the American League.

The Dominican Republic, followed by Venezuela, has been the leading source of foreign-born players for the major leagues. There are many high-caliber baseball players in Cuba, but the communist government will not allow its players to leave; Cuba is one of the few nations in the world today to forbid the emigration of its citizens.

Cubans wishing to play baseball in the major leagues have been forced to defect, escaping from Cuba at much personal risk. The Cuban government banned Kendry Morales from playing inside Cuba after it suspected him of a desire to defect. "Determined to get on the field again, Morales says he tried to escape 12 times, usually failing because of rough seas. Thrice he was caught, spending a mandatory 72 hours in jail each time. . . . On June 8, 2004, 12 days short of turning 21, Morales finally made it out on a rowboat that took him and other passengers to a larger boat, which carried them to

Florida," reported *USA Today.*[29] In 2009, Morales led the American League West Division Champion Angels in home runs and runs batted in.

Other U.S. sports have become more international over time. The National Hockey League has always boasted Canadians, but the fall of communism has allowed American fans also to see many great players from the former Soviet Union and Eastern Europe. In 2007, David Beckham, the world's most famous soccer player, signed a contract to play for the Los Angeles Galaxy. In the past 15 years, the National Basketball Association has opened its door to more international players than ever before, including players from Iran (Hamed Haddadi with Memphis) and Israel (Omri Casspi with Sacramento).[30]

CONTRIBUTIONS OF IMMIGRANTS TO NATIONAL DEFENSE

Immigration helped transform the United States into a superpower. American Enterprise Institute scholar Ben Wattenberg has pointed out that population size has remained an important component of power throughout history and up to the present day. America economically can avail itself of more talent, more ideas, more innovations, and a greater national output with a larger base of people to draw upon. That traditionally has translated into greater military power as well.[31]

"To no small degree, U.S. international power and national security today can be traced, both in a specific sense and more broadly, to its approach to immigration. For reasons intrinsic to its political order, migration has on balance dramatically enhanced U.S. security. Immigration has made it possible for the United States to transform itself from a small political experiment into a superpower," writes Harvard University demographer Nicholas Eberstadt.[32]

Research by the U.S. Census Bureau's Campbell Gibson shows that the U.S. population would be one-half its present size if there had been no immigration to the country since 1790. As of 1996, instead of a population of 265 million, the United States would have had only 127 million people if immigration had ceased after the founding of the Republic.[33] In 1940, on the eve of World War II, rather than 132 million people, America would have had only 70 million people and, consequently, a far smaller economy with which to gear up for war. In 1940, Japan had 72 million people, while Germany had a population of 69 million in 1938.[34]

WEAPONS DEVELOPMENT

A scientific infrastructure and people capable of developing products and advanced weaponry have proven to be valuable to a country's economic and military strength. In this regard, immigrant military contributions to U.S. war and peacetime efforts have been vital.

In 1939, the race was on between Germany and the United States to see who would be the first to develop a bomb that could provide enormous, perhaps even decisive, influence over world affairs. Unfortunately, the U.S. military was barely aware such a race had started.

Fission had first been discovered in Germany, and that greatly disturbed the foreign-born scientists who had immigrated to America to flee persecution. They feared that Hitler's military establishment would be the first to develop a weapon of mass destruction. Italian-born physicist Enrico Fermi, a winner of the Nobel Prize, contacted the U.S. Navy about these concerns but could not convince officials of the gravity of the situation. Hungarian-born scientist Leo Szilard, Fermi and other scientists knew they needed to leapfrog the bureaucracy.

The scientists contacted the German-born Albert Einstein, believing he was among the few men of sufficient stature able to gain the attention of President Franklin Roosevelt. Einstein, Szilard, and Russian-born Alexander Sachs drafted a letter to the president. When Sachs managed to meet with Roosevelt, he showed him Einstein's letter and convinced him of the need to act.

> "Alex, what you are after is to see that the Nazis don't blow us up," the president said.
>
> Sachs replied, "Precisely."
>
> Roosevelt called in an aide and told him, "This requires action."[35]

That planted the seeds of the Manhattan Project to develop the atomic bomb.

Before practical work on the atomic bomb was even conceived of, substantial theoretical work by the European refugees who arrived between 1930 and 1937 laid the groundwork. The most significant work was done by Eugene Wigner (who came from Hungary), George Gamow (Russia), Felix Bloch (Switzerland), Hans Bethe (Germany), Edward Teller (Hungary), and Victor Weisskopf (Austria). This theoretical underpinning paved the way for Niels Bohr, born in Denmark, and Enrico Fermi to make their breakthrough.

Edward Teller and George Gamow had set up a series of meetings among astronomers and theoretical physicists who shared the goal of exploring the key energy issues of the period. It was at that Washington conference in 1939 that Bohr and Fermi first publicly addressed the idea that neutrons were emitted when uranium fission takes place. This opened the way to "chain reaction" and the development of the atomic and hydrogen bombs.

Leading up to and during the Manhattan Project, considerable collaboration between American and foreign-born scientists took place. "At every point where European and American scientists came together, there was the same high degree of acceptance. As the atomic project grew and many more Americans and Europeans joined in, cooperation became even more prominent," writes Laura Fermi, author of *Illustrious Immigrants*, which chronicles the European immigrants of the 1930s and 1940s.[36]

While there is still debate about the issue, many historians believe the decision to drop the atomic bomb on Japan shortened the war and saved thousands of American lives that would have been lost in a land invasion of Japan. The United States benefitted both during World War II and during the cold war in being the nation to develop nuclear weapons first. But the immigrants who arrived as refugees from Europe produced a legacy that outlasted the Manhattan project.

In 1954, the Atomic Energy Act established a distinguished award to recognize scientific achievements in the field of atomic energy. The first winner was the Italian-born Enrico Fermi. In all, five of the first eight winners of what became known as the Enrico Fermi Award (so named after his death) were immigrants. In addition, four of the nuclear scientists who came to the United States from Europe in the 1930s later received a Nobel Prize for physics: Felix Bloch, born in Switzerland, won it in 1952; Emilio Segre (Italy) won in 1959; and Maria Mayer (Poland) and Eugene Wigner (Hungary) won the award in 1963.

The development of the atomic bomb at a secret site in Los Alamos, New Mexico, is one of the great scientific and military accomplishments of the modern era. Many scientists played important roles but among the key figures were George Kistiakowsky, a Russian émigré who designed the bomb's plutonium core, and Hungarian-born John von Neumann, who devised a computer language that turned mathematical procedures into a language to instruct the computer. Hans Bethe believed that without John von Neumann, the development of modern computers would at best "have been delayed 10 years or longer."[37]

Why did the immigrant physicists succeed? Clearly these were some of the most highly skilled people on earth, but it was something more. Beyond their skills, Laura Fermi notes the unique characteristics and emotions that the foreign-born scientists brought to the atomic project:

> The determination to defend America at all costs spurred the newcomers no less than the Americans, and the European-born may have come to this determination somewhat earlier than the native-born, driven by stronger personal emotions. The picture of their country under Nazi power in the event of a German victory was something the Americans could imagine only with difficulty. [Not so those who had already seen their countries overrun.][38]

Fermi notes that "it was not only gratitude to the country that had offered them asylum or pride in their new citizenship but also the fear of dictators that drove them to work to the limit of their physical and mental endurance."[39]

SHIPS, SUBS, AND HELICOPTERS

One of the first great military contributions made to America by a foreign-born engineer or scientist was the ironclad ship. Swedish-born John Ericsson followed a pattern similar to many immigrant innovators. Early on, he tried to convince the French of the efficacy of building an armored ship "impregnable to the heaviest shot or shell." The French showed only limited interest. In America, however, the idea caught on. Businessman Cornelius Bushnell took Ericsson's design to Washington and helped convince Abraham Lincoln and a government board to buy his ship.

John Ericsson was awarded a contract to build his ship and had only 100 days to do it. The Swedish-born engineer, of course, was not the only one to conceive of an ironclad ship, but he built and designed one that "was nothing less than the most revolutionary warship of the nineteenth century," notes naval historian Ivan Musicant. "In the basic concept of an armored hull, carrying a revolving gun turret, it set the theory and architecture for the capital ships that dominated naval warfare for the next eighty years."[40]

Another important naval advance came from immigrant inventor John Philip Holland. Born in Ireland, Holland was impressed by the battle between the *Monitor* and the *Merrimack* during the Civil War. Even before he immigrated to America (in 1872) he had begun to design a submarine. While there had been crude submarines dating back to the American Revolution, no one had conceived of anything like John Philip Holland.

Holland's idea was a "true submersible ship, powered by a steam engine on the surface and an electric battery while submerged. He wanted it to be able to attack a surface warship from concealment and survive to repeat the deed."[41] Unable to attract sufficient attention from the U.S. government, Holland relied on an Irish-American military group poised to strike at Britain to attain Irish independence. With a $6,000 grant, Holland built the submarine, but it was never launched and he eventually cut his ties to the group.

It took 20 years but finally John Philip Holland broke through the bureaucracy and convinced the U.S. Navy to purchase one of his submarines. It was commissioned USS *Holland*. The basic design of the submarine that Holland conceived of has changed little these many years later. He came up with the idea of "reserve buoyancy" and "trim tanks," and in 1954 his concept of shaping the hull of the submarine to be like the body of a porpoise was revived and is now standard on submarines.[42] America remains the world's leader in submarine technology, thanks in part to the boost Holland gave the United States early on. The company he helped found, Electric Boat in Groton, Connecticut, is now owned by General Dynamics and remains the world's premier producer of submarines.

Another immigrant who settled in Connecticut also has a legacy that has outlived him—Igor Sikorsky, the Russian-born designer of the modern helicopter. In Russia, Sikorsky had developed aircraft, but the Bolshevik Revolution forced him to flee the country. He landed in France, offered his talents, but set "sail for the U.S. [after] the French did not take up his services."[43]

He arrived in New York on March 30, 1919, a few years before the "national origins" quotas legislation was passed that likely would have barred his entry to the United States. First, he landed an engineering job with the U.S. Army Air Service and spent his free time teaching mathematics to fellow Russian émigrés in New York. By March 1923, Sikorsky had raised sufficient investment capital to build an all-metal, twin-engine passenger airplane. He built the plane off Long Island using Army surplus materials and parts from local junkyards. The S-29A started flying in America by September 1924. The following year, he founded the Sikorsky Manufacturing Corporation, which later became the Sikorsky Aviation Corporation in Stratford, Connecticut.

In the 1930s, Igor Sikorsky returned to his first passion and patented the design for what became the modern helicopter—a single large rotor and small anti-torque tail rotor. By 1940, the helicopter could fly for 15 minutes at a time. In 1942, the U.S. Army Air Corps received the prototype for the American military's first mass-produced helicopter, the Sikorsky S-47. Those associated with Sikorsky Aircraft today emphasize the unique life-saving role that those helicopters have filled. During World War II, the helicopters flew the first Medevac and combat rescue missions.[44]

Igor Sikorsky died in 1972 at the age of 83, but his company is still in business and employs several thousand people. Altogether, more than 30,000 Americans have worked at the company since Igor Sikorsky established it in 1925.

Interviews with government weapons labs and major U.S. defense firms reveal that immigrant scientists and engineers remain key developers of advanced weapons technology for America's national defense. The children of immigrants have also played an important role in U.S. history, both as soldiers, particularly during World War II, and in weapons design. Neil Sheehan describes in his book *A Fiery Peace in a Cold War* the efforts of Air Force Gen. Bernard Schriever, the child of German immigrants, in developing the first intercontinental ballistic missile (ICBM) after World War II. As described by former *Washington Post* reporter Michael Dobbs: "In Sheehan's words, the real contribution of the nuclear weapons designers was to help 'buy the time needed for the Soviet Union to collapse of its own internal contradictions.' In that sense, the ICBM was the first weapon in history that won a war without ever being used."[45]

Another little-known figure in American history is Andrew Higgins, a New Orleans boat builder and the son of Irish immigrants. When historian Stephen E. Ambrose first met Gen. Dwight D. Eisenhower, he was asked by Eisenhower, "I notice you are teaching in New Orleans, did you ever know Andrew Higgins?"

"No, sir," Ambrose replied.

"That's too bad," Eisenhower said, "He is the man who won the war for us."[46]

Andrew Higgins designed and built the landing craft that enabled Allied forces to storm the beaches of Normandy. Eisenhower believed that without those landing craft, the invasion of Normandy would not have been possible.

IMMIGRANTS IN THE U.S. MILITARY TODAY

While a country's population size and its scientists are important to maintaining a strong defense, a nation also needs individuals willing to serve in its armed forces. Logically, countries with smaller populations are more likely to be forced to institute compulsory military service if they are to fill the ranks of their armed forces. Naturalized citizens and lawful permanent residents would be eligible to be drafted in the case of a draft.

In today's all-volunteer military, many immigrants already serve in the U.S. armed forces. A permanent resident (green card holder) may enlist in the American military if he or she meets the requirements for enlistment. Some recent programs have opened up the possibility for foreign nationals other than permanent residents to join the U.S. military.

The age pattern of enlistment provides a natural limit on the proportion of immigrants in the armed forces. Traditionally, the average age new enlisted recruits join the military is before age 21, while approximately 70 percent of legal immigrants enter the country at age 25 or older.[47] "In FY 2004, 87 percent of new active duty recruits were 18 through 24 years of age," according to the Office of the Under Secretary of Defense, Personnel and Readiness.[48]

Still, the data demonstrate that America's all-volunteer military continues to attract immigrants who want to serve in the nation's armed forces, which conforms to the historical experience. "As of June 30, 2009, there were 114,601 foreign-born individuals serving in the armed forces, representing 7.91 percent of the 1.4 million military personnel on active duty," according to Department of Defense data obtained by the Immigration Policy Center. "Roughly 80.97 percent of foreign-born service members were naturalized

U.S. citizens, while 12.66 percent were not U.S. citizens."[49] The Philippines (24 percent) and Mexico (9 percent) are the leading countries of origin for immigrants in the military, followed by Jamaica, South Korea, and the Dominican Republic.[50]

IMMIGRANT MEDAL OF HONOR RECIPIENTS

Of the millions of men who have served in America's armed forces, only a few thousand have received the Medal of Honor. Over 700 of those recipients have been immigrants. "Those who have received the Medal of Honor since it was established in 1861 as the nation's highest decoration are as different as the melting pot population of our country," reads the official guide to Congressional Medal of Honor recipients.[51]

Immigrants comprise more than 20 percent of the total number of Medal of Honor recipients.[52] The criteria for receiving the Medal of Honor are stringent. A recipient must risk his life, his act must be considered beyond the call of duty, and the bravery must be distinguished from other acts, particularly in that no one would justifiably criticize the individual had he acted otherwise. At least two eyewitnesses must have observed the act and provide incontestable evidence that it occurred.

The stories of heroism are as unique as the men who have received the award. These were deeds for which no training could ever prepare a person. In many cases, these were deeds that cost the men who performed them their lives.

Jose Francisco Jimenez, born in Mexico City, Mexico, entered the U.S. Marine Corps in Phoenix, Arizona, and served during the Vietnam War as a lance corporal with Company K (3rd Battalion, 7th Marines, 1st Marine Division). On August 28, 1969, in the Quang Nam Province of Vietnam, Jimenez's unit came upon North Vietnamese soldiers who had concealed themselves in a well-camouflaged position. The North Vietnamese guns, trained on the Americans, started firing. But seizing the initiative, Jimenez, the team leader, plunged forward as his men followed. Jimenez killed several of the enemy and eliminated the anti-aircraft weapon that had been firing on the American planes.

Jimenez moved forward and yelled to his soldiers to keep on going. Slowly, he proceeded to within 10 feet of hostile soldiers who fired automatic weapons at him from a trench. In the face of heavy fire, Jimenez managed to destroy their position.

The remaining enemy soldiers turned their guns on Jimenez, hoping to stop his assault. Still, Jimenez pressed forward and attacked another enemy soldier. This was to be the American lance corporal's final act. He died from the wounds that enemy soldiers inflicted upon him. "Lance Corporal

Jimenez' indomitable courage, aggressive fighting spirit and unfaltering devotion to duty upheld the highest traditions of the Marine Corps and of the U.S. Naval Service," according to the official citation.[53] Jimenez was 23 years old.

Lewis Albanese was born in Venice, Italy, and later immigrated to the United States. During the Vietnam War, he served as a private first class in the U.S. Army. On December 1, 1966, Albanese's platoon advanced through dense terrain, while enemy soldiers fired automatic weapons at them from close range. Despite this, the platoon needed to move forward and establish a blocking position. It was Albanese's job to provide security for his platoon's left flank.

Suddenly, an enemy located in a concealed ditch opened fire on the left flank. Knowing his fellow soldiers were in imminent danger, Albanese fixed his bayonet, plunged into the ditch, and silenced the sniper fire. That enabled the platoon to advance safely toward the main enemy position.

The ditch that Lewis Albanese had entered, however, was not an ordinary ditch but rather an intricate complex of defenses intended to inflict heavy damage on any who attacked the main position. The other members of the platoon could hear heavy firing from the ditch and some of them witnessed what happened next. Albanese moved 100 meters along the trench and killed six snipers, each of whom were armed with automatic weapons. But soon, Albanese was out of ammunition so he proceeded to engage in hand-to-hand combat with North Vietnamese soldiers and killed two of them. But he was mortally wounded in the attack.

"His unparalleled actions saved the lives of many members of his platoon who otherwise would have fallen to the sniper fire from the ditch, and enabled his platoon to successfully advance against an enemy force of overwhelming numerical superiority," read the official citation. "Private First Class Albanese's extraordinary heroism and supreme dedication to his comrades were commensurate with the finest traditions of the military service and remain a tribute to himself, his unit, and the U.S. Army."[54] Lewis Albanese died at the age of 20.

Not all acts of heroism involve directly engaging an enemy in combat. Such was the case with Lieutenant John Koelsch, a London-born immigrant who flew a helicopter as part of a Navy helicopter rescue unit during the Korean War. He had entered the service in Los Angeles, but on the evening of July 3, 1951, he found himself on the Korean peninsula with darkness fast approaching. Word came that the North Koreans had shot down a U.S. marine aviator and that the man was trapped deep in hostile territory amid mountainous terrain. John Koelsch volunteered to rescue him.

Koelsch's aircraft was unarmed and flew without a fighter escort because of the low altitude and the overcast that blocked the sight of everything below the mountain peaks. As he descended beneath the clouds to search in a systematic fashion for the aviator, the enemy fired on him.

After being hit, Koelsch kept going until he found the downed pilot, who had suffered serious burns. While the injured pilot was being hoisted up, a burst of enemy fire struck the helicopter, causing it to crash into the side of the mountain. Koelsch quickly helped his crew and the downed pilot out of the wreckage. He led the men out of the area, barely escaping the enemy troops. For nine days they were on the run, administering medical care to the burned pilot and evading capture by the North Koreans. After days of pursuit, the North Koreans finally captured Koelsch and his men.

John Kelvin Koelsch's trials were not yet over. "His great personal valor and heroic spirit of self-sacrifice throughout sustain and enhance the finest traditions of the U.S. Naval Service," his citation for the Medal of Honor reads. That self-sacrifice, the citation notes, included inspiring other prisoners of war, for during the interrogation he "refused to aid his captors in any manner" and died in the hands of the North Koreans.[55]

During World War II, a number of immigrants and children of immigrants distinguished themselves on the field of battle. This chapter does not include information on Medal of Honor recipients who were the children of immigrants, though judging from the names listed just among World War II recipients such a list might be quite long. First names like Vito and Christos, and surnames like Sarnowski and Cicchetti, pepper the list and would be typical of the offspring of immigrants who arrived during the great wave near the turn of the century.

Macario Garcia, born in Mexico, was 24 years old when he became acting squad leader of Company B (22nd Infantry). Near Grosshau, Germany, Garcia found his company pinned down by the heavy machine gun fire of Nazi troops and by an artillery and mortar barrage. Though wounded and in pain, he refused to be evacuated. Instead, he made a remarkable decision.

Garcia crawled forward, all alone, stopping near one of the enemy's prepared positions. He then lobbed hand grenades into the enemy's emplacement, singlehandedly assaulted the position, and destroyed the gun, killing three German soldiers.

A short time later, he returned to his company, when another German machine gun started firing. Back toward the German position he went. Alone, he stormed the enemy and destroyed the gun, killing three more German soldiers and capturing four prisoners. Private Macario Garcia was later promoted to staff sergeant and returned with the prisoners to his company.[56]

Victory in war is not inevitable. It ultimately depends, in large measure, on the quality of those willing to fight and die. Nicholas Minue, who emigrated from Poland, entered the U.S. Army in Carteret, New Jersey. Whether or not he was prepared to die for his country was answered on April 28, 1943. In Tunisia, near Medjez-el-Bab, his company was being hit hard by a nest of enemy machine gun fire from the flank. On his initiative, "voluntarily, alone, and unhesitatingly, with complete disregard of his own welfare," Minue charged the enemy's entrenched position with fixed bayonet. In the face of soldiers firing at him with machine guns and rifles, Nicholas Minue killed 10 of the enemy.

He destroyed that position and moved forward, proceeding to rout enemy riflemen from their dugout positions. But Minue paid for his actions—he was mortally wounded. The Medal of Honor, presented posthumously, included in the citation that his "courage, fearlessness, and aggressiveness . . . in the face of inevitable death was unquestionably the factor that gave his company the offensive spirit" to advance and drive away the enemy forces.[57]

Two final examples, one from World War I, the other from the Vietnam War, illustrate the variety of heroic acts that have been performed by American soldiers, including immigrant soldiers. In France, September 1918, U.S. Army Pvt. Michael Valente found his company facing withering enemy fire. He and another soldier volunteered for the dangerous task of freeing up the company. Amid the intense machine gun fire, Valente and his compatriot rushed forward and into the enemy nest, where they killed two of the enemy, captured five, and silenced the gun.

Valente saw another enemy nest close by that was pouring "deadly fire" on American soldiers. He and his fellow soldier assaulted that position as well, killing the gunner and silencing that gun, too. They then jumped into a trench, killed two German soldiers and captured 16 men. Despite what the citation calls "conspicuous gallantry and intrepidity" and "utter disregard of his own personal danger," Valente was not killed.[58]

Michael Valente, who was born in Cassino, Italy, saved the lives of many American soldiers that day. Three years later, Congress passed the first "temporary" national origins quotas under the theory that Italians and other Southern Europeans were genetically inferior to native-born Americans and, therefore, should be kept out of the country.

ALFRED RASCON

Nicholas Minue from Poland, John Koelsch from England, Lewis Albanese from Italy, and Jose Jimenez from Mexico are just some of the immigrants who fought and died for America. Their stories are impressive, but they have not been alone in their willingness to sacrifice for their adopted homeland.

Alfred Rascon was born in Chihuahua, Mexico, and immigrated to the United States with his parents in the 1950s. He served two tours in Vietnam, one as a medic, and was known as "Doc." When Rascon volunteered for the service, he was not a citizen but still a lawful permanent resident. He was 17 years old but tricked his mother into signing his papers so he could enlist.

On March 16, 1966, bullets flew and grenades exploded, and Rascon's platoon found itself in a maelstrom of North Vietnamese firepower. When an American machine gunner went down and someone called for a medic, Rascon, 20 at the time, ignored his orders to remain under cover and rushed down the trail amid a hail of enemy gunfire and grenades. To better protect the wounded solider, Rascon placed his body between the enemy machine gun fire and the solider. Rascon turned. He was shot in the hip. Although wounded, he managed to drag the soldier off the trail. Rascon soon discovered the man he was dragging was dead.

Specialist 4th Class Larry Gibson crawled forward looking for ammunition. The other machine gunner was already dead and Gibson had no ammunition with which to defend the platoon. Rascon grabbed the dead soldier's ammo and gave it to Gibson. Then, amid relentless enemy fire and grenades, Rascon hobbled back up the trail, snared the dead soldier's machine gun and, most importantly, 400 rounds of additional ammunition.

The pace quickened and more grenades dropped. One ripped open Rascon's face. It did not stop him. He saw another grenade drop five feet from a wounded Neil Haffy. He tackled Haffy and absorbed the grenade blast himself, saving Haffy's life.

Though severely wounded, Rascon crawled back among the other injured soldiers and gave them aid. A few minutes later, Rascon saw Sgt. Ray Compton being hit by gunfire. As Rascon moved toward him, another hand grenade dropped. Instead of seeking cover, Rascon dove on top of the wounded sergeant and again absorbed the blow. This time the explosion smashed through Rascon's helmet and ripped into his scalp. He saved Compton's life.[59]

When the firefight ended, Rascon refused aid for himself until the other wounded were evacuated. So bloodied by the conflict was Rascon that when soldiers placed him on the evacuation helicopter, a chaplain saw his condition and gave him last rites. But Alfred Rascon survived.[60]

The soldiers who witnessed Rascon's actions that day recommended him in writing for a Medal of Honor. Years later, these soldiers were shocked to discover that he had not received one. Finally, in 2000, after an authorization from Congress, President Bill Clinton awarded the Medal of Honor to Alfred Rascon.

Perhaps the best description of Alfred Rascon's actions came 30 years later from fellow platoon member Larry Gibson:

> I was a 19-year-old gunner with a recon section. We were under intense and accurate enemy fire that had pinned down the point squad, making it almost impossible to move without being killed. Unhesitatingly, Doc [as he was called] went forward to aid the wounded and dying. I was one of the wounded.
>
> Doc took the brunt of several enemy grenades, shielding the wounded with his body. . . . In these few words I cannot fully describe the events of that day. The acts of unselfish heroism Doc performed while saving the many wounded, though severely wounded himself, speak for themselves. This country needs genuine heroes. Doc Rascon is one of those.[61]

Rascon was once asked why he acted with such courage on the battlefield even though he was an immigrant and not yet a citizen. Rascon replied, "I was always an American in my heart."[62]

NOTES

1. Robert W. Fairlie, *Kauffman Index of Entrepreneurial Activity, 1996–2008* (Kansas City, MO: Ewing Marion Kauffman Foundation, April 2009), 11–13.
2. Stuart Anderson and Michaela Platzer, *American Made: The Impact of Immigrant Entrepreneurs and Professionals on U.S. Competitiveness* (Arlington, VA: National Venture Capital Association, November 2006), 6.
3. Vivek Wadhwa, AnnaLee Saxenian, Ben Rissing, and Gary Gereffi, "Skilled Immigration and Economic Growth," *Applied Research in Economic Development* 5, no. 1 (2008), 7.
4. Interview with Mark J. Perry.
5. Robert W. Fairlie, *Estimating the Contribution of Immigrant Business Owners to the U.S. Economy,* Small Business Administration, Office of Advocacy, November 2008, Executive Summary.
6. Unless otherwise noted, the profiles of immigrant entrepreneurs in this chapter are based on interviews and information gathered on these individuals that appeared in Anderson and Platzer, *American Made: The Impact of Immigrant Entrepreneurs and Professionals on U.S. Competitiveness.* Information was updated where possible.
7. Mary Ann Azevedo, "Genentech license launches new team at TaiMed Biologics," *Houston Business Journal*, April 2008.
8. Interview with Nancy Chang.
9. Interview with Said Hilal.
10. Interview with Patrick Lo.
11. Interview with Zvi Or-Bach.
12. Interview with Asa Kalavade.
13. Goutam Naik, "U.S. Cell-Aging Researchers Awarded Nobel," *Wall Street Journal*, October 6, 2009, A5.

14. Ibid.

15. Ibid.

16. Kenneth Chang, "Nobel Prize in Physics is Awarded for Advances in the Harnessing of Light," *New York Times*, October 7, 2009, A18.

17. Thomas H. Maugh II, "2 Americans, Israeli Share Nobel Prize in Chemistry," *Los Angeles Times*, October 7, 2009.

18. National Research Council, *The New Americans*, advance copy (Washington, DC: National Academy Press, May 1997), 8–15.

19. Ibid., 8–15.

20. Douglas Martin, "William Ganz, 90, Catheter Inventor," *New York Times*, November 14, 2009, A16.

21. Paula E. Stephan and Sharon G. Levin, "Exceptional contributions to U.S. science by the foreign-born and foreign-educated," *Population Research and Policy Review* 20 (2001): 59.

22. Ibid., 69, 74.

23. Ibid., 70.

24. Ibid., 75. Stephan and Levin do not come to a conclusion in this paper as to whether the presence of the foreign-born adversely affected Americans in these fields. Looking at the PhD level, "the data suggest that U.S. citizens trained in science and engineering have generally been less likely than their immigrant counterparts to hold these jobs and in that sense have been 'displaced' from science and engineering," write Stephan and Levin. "But without additional analysis, we do not know whether displaced U.S. citizens were, on balance, pushed out by the increase in foreign-born or pulled out by higher salaries."

25. For this section, the interviews and additional citations conducted at that time can be found in Stuart Anderson, "The Multiplier Effect," *International Educator*, Summer 2004. Available at: www.nfap.com.

26. Steve Olson, *Count Down* (New York: Houghton Mifflin, 2004), 141, 150.

27. Ibid., 145–146.

28. Stuart Anderson and L. Brian Andrew, *Coming to America* (Arlington, VA: National Foundation for American Policy, 2006), 4.

29. Jorge L. Ortiz, "Five Years after Defecting from Cuba, Morales Has Arrived," *USA Today*, October 7, 2009.

30. Fred Bierman and Benjamin Hoffman, "Growing Pains," *New York Times*, November 29, 2009, Sports, 5.

31. Much of the material in this chapter discussing the contributions of immigrants to national defense and the military appeared in Stuart Anderson, *In Defense of a Nation* (Washington, DC: American Immigration Law Foundation, 1996), and is used with permission.

32. Nicholas Eberstadt, *The Tyranny of Numbers* (Washington, DC: AEI Press, 1995), 263.

33. Campbell Gibson, Population Division, U.S. Census Bureau, "The Contribution of Immigration to the Growth and Ethnic Diversity of the American Population," *Proceedings of the American Philosophical Society* 136, no. 2 (1996), 166. The updated figures for 1996 were done by request.

34. Japanese embassy; German Historical Institute. In 1940, German population data included the annexation of Austria and Czechoslovakia, which increased the population to 79 million.

35. Richard Rhodes, *The Making of the Atomic Bomb* (New York: Simon & Schuster, 1986), 314.

36. Laura Fermi, *Illustrious Immigrants* (Chicago: University of Chicago Press, 1968), 187.

37. Ibid., 290.

38. Ibid., 188.

39. Ibid., 188.

40. Ivan Musicant, *Divided Waters: The Naval History of the Civil War* (New York: HarperCollins, 1995), 159.

41. John A. Barnes, "Irish Immigrant Was Father of the Modern Submarine," *Investor's Business Daily*, March 17, 1995, 1.

42. Ibid.

43. John W. R. Taylor, Michael J. H. Taylor, and David Mondey, *Air Facts and Feats* (New York: Bantam Books, 1978), 166.

44. Information provided by Sikorsky Aircraft.

45. Michael Dobbs, "The Genius General Who Went Ballistic," *Washington Post*, September 27, 2009, B1, B3.

46. Stephen E. Ambrose, *D-Day, June 6, 1944: The Climactic Battle of World War II* (New York: Simon & Schuster), 1994, 45.

47. "The mean age of new active duty recruits was slightly more than 20," according to the Office of the Under Secretary of Defense, Personnel and Readiness, *Population Representation in the Military Services*, 2004, executive summary; Table 9 of the *2008 Yearbook of Immigration Statistics,* Office of Immigration Statistics, Department of Homeland Security, 2009.

48. Office of the Under Secretary of Defense, Personnel and Readiness, *Population Representation in the Military Services*, executive summary.

49. Margaret D. Stock, *Immigrants in the Military 8 Years after 9/11* (Washington, DC: Immigration Policy Center, 2009), 3.

50. Laura Barker and Jeanne Batalova, *The Foreign Born in the Armed Services* (Washington, DC: Migration Policy Institute, 2007), 2–3.

51. *United States of America Congressional Medal of Honor Recipients and Their Official Citations* (Columbia Heights, MN: Highland House II, 1994), xi.

52. See Anderson, *In Defense of a Nation.*

53. *United States of America Congressional Medal of Honor Recipients and Their Official Citations*, 79.

54. Ibid., 18.

55. Ibid., 203.

56. Ibid., 320–321.

57. Ibid., 395.

58. Ibid., 533.

59. Interview with Alfred Rascon.

60. Rex Bowman, "A Medal of Honor Mission," *Washington Times*, July 4, 1996, C8.

61. L. M. G., letter, "Rascon's Acts Worthy of Medal of Honor," *Washington Times*, June 17, 1996, A2.

62. Interview with Alfred Rascon.

SUGGESTED READINGS

Anderson, Stuart. "The Multiplier Effect." *International Educator*, Summer 2004. Available at: www.nfap.com.

Anderson, Stuart, and L. Brian Andrew. *Coming to America.* Arlington, VA: National Foundation for American Policy, 2006. Available at: www.nfap.com.

Anderson, Stuart, and Michaela Platzer. *American Made: The Impact of Immigrant Entrepreneurs and Professionals on U.S. Competitiveness.* Arlington, VA: National Venture Capital Association, 2006. Available at: www.nfap.com.

Fairlie, Robert W. *Kauffman Index of Entrepreneurial Activity, 1996–2008.* Kansas City, MO: Ewing Marion Kauffman Foundation, 2009.

Fermi, Laura. *Illustrious Immigrants.* Chicago: University of Chicago Press, 1968.

National Research Council. *The New Americans.* Washington, DC: National Academy Press, 1997.

Wadhwa, Vivek, AnnaLee Saxenian, Ben Rissing, and Gary Gereffi. "Skilled Immigration and Economic Growth." *Applied Research in Economic Development* 5, no. 1 (2008).

Three

Legal Immigration

The U.S. immigration system affects millions of people every year, whether someone is seeking to work in America, visit, or immigrate to join close family members. Immigration policies also influence the lives of Americans who seek a visa on behalf of a relative or employee, or wish to invite a potential investor to the country. Even people who fall in love are affected by immigration policy if the person they wish to marry is a foreigner.

In 2008, 1,107,126 people immigrated legally to the United States, according to the Department of Homeland Security.[1] Nearly half (44 percent) were classified as the "immediate relatives of U.S. Citizens"—spouses, children (under 21 years old), and parents. A review of the 2008 numbers provides an overview of the legal immigration system (see Figure 3.1).

Employer-sponsored immigrants made up 166,511 of the (legal immigrant) total, which included the dependents (spouses and children) of the sponsored employee. Diversity visas, which are distributed by lottery to applicants from underrepresented countries, went to 41,761 people. The refugee and asylee categories received 90,030 and 76,362 lawful permanent residents respectively. The numbers for asylees reflect a backlog that built up over several years when only 10,000 asylees annually were permitted to become permanent residents.[2] Refugees typically become permanent residents and are counted in the immigration totals a year after arrival, meaning the 2008 numbers reflect mostly people who came to America a year earlier.

Others who became lawful permanent residents in 2008 utilized a mix of past laws and less-publicized statutes. The Haitian Refugee Immigration Fairness Act, passed about a decade earlier, allowed for the admission of 1,580 individuals. Another 29 people became permanent residents under the Nicaraguan Adjustment and Central American Relief Act (NACARA). Approximately 11,000 people in 2008 received "cancellation of removal,"

FIGURE 3.1
"What Part of Legal Immigration Don't You Understand?"

Source: Reason Magazine, October 2008, pp. 32–33. Used by permission from the Reason Foundation.

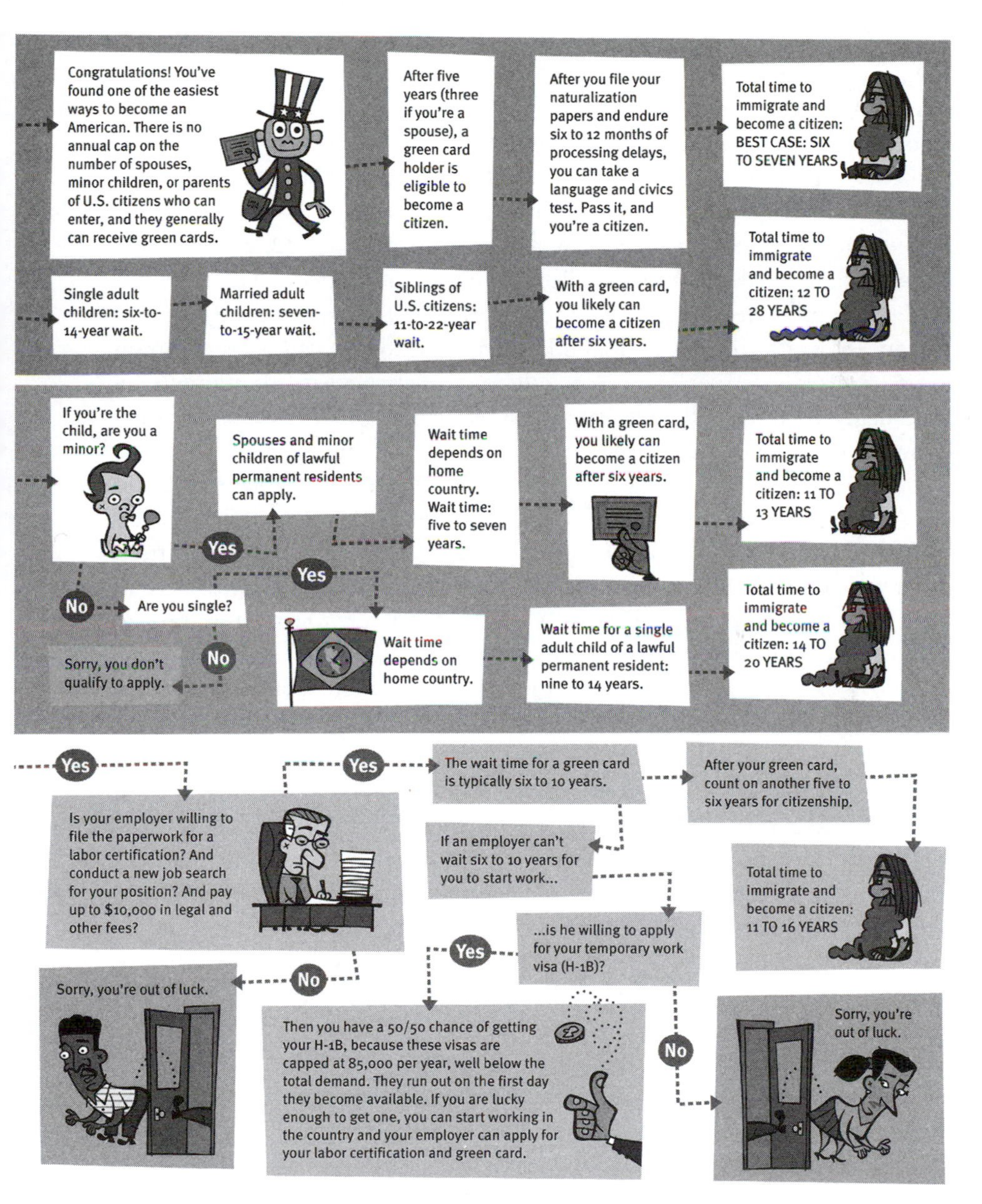

(Flynn is director of government affairs and Dalmia is a senior policy analyst at Reason Foundation. This chart was developed by Reason Foundation in collaboration with the National Foundation for American Policy.)

which means they qualified before an immigration judge to become lawful permanent residents by meeting standards that allowed them to stay in the country and thereby avoid deportation.[3]

Finally, in the family-sponsored preference categories, 26,173 "unmarried sons and daughters (21 or older) of U.S. citizens" immigrated; 103,456 "spouses, children and unmarried sons and daughters of lawful permanent residents"; 29,273 "married sons and daughters of U.S. citizens"; and 68,859 "brothers and sisters of U.S. citizens."

The law on legal immigration has changed little since 1990, which means fluctuations in the annual totals reflect primarily the ability of U.S. Citizenship and Immigration Services (and previously the Immigration and Naturalization Service) to process and adjudicate applications. While it is common to use terms like "arrived" and "came here" to describe legal immigrants, in fact, many of those who receive lawful permanent residence (commonly known as obtaining a green card) were already in the United States.

In 2008, 58 percent of the people receiving lawful permanent residence did so inside the country through "adjustment of status," which is a process by U.S. Citizenship and Immigration Services to change an individual from usually a temporary status (such as a work or student visa) to lawful permanent residence. Other individuals were outside the United States and traveled to a consulate or embassy to complete their application.

Due to their complexity, our immigration laws are compared to the country's tax laws. But a mistake on one's taxes usually results in only a fine or an additional payment to the Internal Revenue Service. In contrast, a mistake or a poor choice on immigration can change one's life forever.

To understand U.S. immigration it is useful to divide it up into the various reasons that people come into contact with the system: visiting, studying, work, investment, marriage, exchange programs, crime, human rights, and sponsoring close family members. By examining each of these areas, we can answer such questions as: Can anyone sponsor a family member or marry a foreigner? What are the wait times for such visas? Can anyone claim persecution and get to stay here? Can anyone with a job offer get a visa, whether for a high- or low-skilled job? Can international students come here and work? How do foreign professional athletes and movie stars work here? And how do foreign visitors convince a U.S. consular officer they deserve a visa to the United States?

THE DIFFERENCE BETWEEN PERMANENT RESIDENCE AND TEMPORARY VISAS AND THE FEDERAL ROLES IN IMMIGRATION

Those who enter or stay in America can do so primarily in one of two ways: (1) obtaining a temporary status, or (2) gaining lawful permanent residence, known as receiving one's "green card." The difference between the two is simple. An individual in temporary status or on a temporary visa (also known as a "nonimmigrant" visa) can stay in the United States for a period of time but is not entitled to remain permanently or become an American citizen. In contrast, once an individual receives a green card or an immigrant visa, that person can remain in the United States for the rest of his or her life (barring certain criminal convictions) and is eligible to become a U.S. citizen.

In general, responsibility for immigration is spread across three cabinet departments. The State Department issues temporary visas abroad in embassies and consulates, while also being responsible for administering many of the applications for permanent residence.

The U.S Department of Labor plays a smaller role in administering and enforcing rules related to work visas, including for workers in fields as diverse as agriculture, hospitality, and high technology.

The Department of Homeland Security (DHS) plays the largest role in immigration policy. Within Homeland Security, U.S. Citizenship and Immigration Services (USCIS) administers immigration applications and naturalization. Immigration and Customs Enforcement (ICE) agents perform the "plainclothes" police duties, such as investigations. Preventing illegal immigration at the borders and between ports of entry is the job of Border Patrol agents. The individuals who screen travelers at air, land, and sea ports of entry into the United States are inspectors. Both inspectors and Border Patrol agents function as part of U.S. Customs and Border Protection (CBP).

VISITING

Not everyone visiting the United States needs a visa. Under the Visa Waiver Program, as of January 2010, nationals of 35 countries can come to America for 90 days or less without a visa. The 35 countries in the Visa Waiver Program are Andorra, Iceland, Norway, Australia, Ireland, Portugal, Austria, Italy, San Marino, Belgium, Japan, Singapore, Brunei, Latvia, Slovakia, Czech Republic, Liechtenstein, Slovenia, Denmark, Lithuania, South Korea, Estonia, Luxembourg, Spain, Finland, Malta, Sweden, France, Monaco, Switzerland, Germany, the Netherlands, United Kingdom, Hungary, and New Zealand.[4]

A national of these countries wishing to stay in the United States longer than 90 days, or to work or study, must obtain a visa. The Visa Waiver Program benefits Americans in at least two ways. First, under reciprocity agreements, visa-free travel for nationals of Visa Waiver countries means U.S. tourists can travel to France or the other 34 countries in the program without a visa. Second, easing the process for travel boosts tourism in the

United States, creating jobs and increasing economic activity. However, some have criticized the Visa Waiver Program, arguing the absence of an interview before a consular officer removes an extra layer of scrutiny, although those on Visa Waiver are still screened by an inspector at a port of entry.

Nationals of countries not in the Visa Waiver Program generally would need an in-person interview at a U.S. embassy or consulate to enter the United States for travel. The primary purpose of the interview is not to "catch terrorists," although individuals can be denied a visa if they are considered a security threat. The key reason an individual might be denied a visitor or other temporary visa is he or she fails to convince a consular officer the individual will not return home after visiting the United States.[5]

Under Section 214(b) of the Immigration and Nationality Act, "Every alien shall be presumed to be an immigrant until he establishes to the satisfaction of the consular officer, at the time of application for admission, that he is entitled to a nonimmigrant status. . . ."[6] According to the State Department: "The most frequent basis for such a refusal concerns the requirement that the prospective visitor or student possess a residence abroad he/she has no intention of abandoning. Applicants prove the existence of such residence by demonstrating that they have ties abroad that would compel them to leave the U.S. at the end of the temporary stay. The law places this burden of proof on the applicant. . . . Strong ties differ from country to country, city to city, individual to individual. Some examples of ties can be a job, a house, a family, a bank account. 'Ties' are the various aspects of your life that bind you to your country of residence: your possessions, employment, social and family relationships."[7]

The waiting times to schedule interviews can be long (at times weeks or months in some countries) and the process can deter people from filing. But most people seeking to travel to the United States for business or pleasure or as an investor or to attend a conference can gain a visa in a timely matter. Canadians are not required to have a visa to enter the United States for periods of generally six months or less, as long as the purpose of the visit is not to work or study. Mexicans can obtain border-crossing cards that allow them to go back and forth from Mexico to the United States.

There are two types of visitor visas: B-1 (temporary visitor for business) and B-2 (temporary visitor for pleasure). In general, neither visa entitles an individual to work in the United States. Describing the length of time for a B-1 visa (for business travel), attorneys Victoria Duong and Lincoln Stone write, "A B-1 visitor may be admitted for no more than one year. The actual period of admission granted by the inspecting officer should be a 'period of time which is fair and reasonable for completion of the purpose of the trip.' Too often this is just 30 days."[8] Generally the length of stay for B-2 visas is six months, though it is possible to apply for and receive an extension from U.S. Citizenship and Immigration Services.

The number of people coming to the United States on these visas is large and can be affected by U.S. policies, which is why the travel industry lobbies on immigration issues. Of the 6.6 million visas issued by the State Department in FY 2008, more than half, in excess of 4 million, were B-1 or B-2 visas.[9]

GETTING MARRIED

If you are a U.S citizen, you can marry a foreigner, and that person can live with you on a permanent basis in the United States. A spouse of a U.S. citizen is considered an "immediate relative" for immigration purposes, which means there is no annual quota to limit the number each year. That does not mean there is no wait.

U.S. Citizenship and Immigration Services has developed a set of procedures to guard against fraudulent marriages. For that reason, the green card issued to the spouse of a U.S. citizen or lawful permanent resident is conditional for two years. At the time of the initial application, USCIS will normally conduct interviews with the married couple to determine if the marriage is bona fide and was not done solely for immigration purposes. "In order to convert to unrestricted permanent resident status, the petitioner and beneficiary must submit a Joint Petition to Remove Conditional Residence . . . together with supporting documents such as tax returns, apartment leases, insurance and financial records, children's birth certificates, etc., to show that the marriage was bona fide when contracted," according to Susan Fortino-Brown.[10]

Immigration attorney Greg Siskind offers advice for Americans intending to marry a foreign national:

> The biggest issue in a case like this is usually the potential separation of the couple while the visa process is underway. There are visas for fiancés (K-1) and visas for spouses of U.S. citizens, and each usually take a number of months to process. The foreign spouse is not permitted to come to the U.S. to wait merely because this application has been filed. So the U.S. citizen must either wait outside the United States for six months to a year (the typical wait) or wait in the U.S. while the spouse is abroad. Some choose to try and come in on a visitor visa and then apply for a green card in the U.S. The problem here is that many USCIS officers would consider entering on a visitor visa with the intention of marrying and applying for a green card to be evidence of fraudulent intent. The visitor visa is generally supposed to be used for tourists and business trips.
>
> Another issue is where to hold the wedding. Planning a U.S. wedding is risky because you cannot predict precisely when a fiancé visa will be granted. So the couple should have some flexibility in case the visa is delayed. A couple also should have a plan and stick to it. For example, if they start out applying for a fiancé visa and plan on marrying in the U.S. and then several months later decide

to marry abroad, the whole application process will need to start again and this can lead to an even longer wait.[11]

MAKING AN INVESTMENT

U.S. immigration law allows foreign nationals to stay and work here if they make investments in America. There are essentially two ways of doing this. First, one can obtain an E visa, which is a temporary visa that enables someone to work at the business in which he or she is investing. A second approach is to receive an immigrant investor visa for, in general, making an investment in the United States, usually $500,000 or more following specific guidelines established by U.S. Citizenship and Immigration Services. "I usually first try and figure out what a client's goals are and then determine whether we can devise an immigration strategy that is consistent with those aspirations," said attorney Greg Siskind. "If, for example, the client tells me that she is really only interested in coming to the U.S. for a few months a year and will keep her primary residence abroad, that would probably lead me to recommend a nonimmigrant, temporary visa strategy over a green card. Or perhaps the client has significant funds to invest but does not want to be involved on a daily basis in the management of a business. Then, investing in a regional center [established for immigrant investor visas] might make sense. Tax planning can factor into the equation since different immigration strategies can have different tax implications."[12]

EXCHANGE PROGRAMS

Many individuals come to the United States on temporary exchange programs, generally utilizing a J-1 visa. This is used for summer youth work programs and is particularly popular among Eastern Europeans, whom many Americans will encounter in jobs at resorts and amusement parks during the summer.

The J-1 is also used for physicians. While there is a requirement that J-1 visa holders return to their native country after two years, many physicians seek waivers to remain and work in the United States.

The most well-known use of the J-1 visa is for au pairs. Every year, Americans apply on behalf of au pairs through agencies. Au pairs help care for the children of American families but also take classes while in the United States. Under U.S. immigration law, it is generally impossible to hire an experienced foreign national as a caregiver, such as a woman from Honduras who has raised children of her own. As a result, many Americans use au pairs as caregivers, even though they are young women often without experience in watching children.

A Q-1 visa can be used for "participants in an international cultural exchange program approved by the Attorney General for the purpose of providing practical training, employment, and to share the history, culture, and traditions of the alien's home country."[13] People from Northern Ireland can use the Q-2 visa to work for a time in the United States.

CRIME-RELATED VISAS

If an individual is a victim of a "severe form of trafficking in persons," then that individual may be eligible to receive a T visa. A victim of certain crimes who helps with the prosecution of a case may receive a U visa. An "informant on a criminal organization" is eligible for an S-5 visa, while an "informant on a terrorist organization" can receive an S-6 visa. These last two are sometimes referred to as "snitch" visas.

HUMAN RIGHTS

If an individual can prove persecution, then he or she can receive status as a refugee (when outside the country) or as an asylee (if already in the United States; U.S refugee and asylum policy is addressed in detail in Chapter 6). One can also receive Temporary Protected Status (TPS) if the Secretary of Homeland Security designates nationals of a country for that status on humanitarian grounds. As USCIS explains: "In 1990 . . . Congress established a procedure by which the Attorney General [now the Secretary of Homeland Security] may provide TPS to aliens in the United States who are temporarily unable to safely return to their home country because of ongoing armed conflict, an environmental disaster, or other extraordinary and temporary conditions. . . . During the period for which a country has been designated for TPS, TPS beneficiaries may remain in the United States and may obtain work authorization. However, TPS does not lead to permanent resident status."[14] Countries whose nationals have been designated temporary protected status in recent years include Honduras, Haiti, Nicaragua, and El Salvador.

DIPLOMATIC AND INTERNATIONAL ORGANIZATIONS

Diplomats and foreign government officials use A visas. A-2 and NATO1-6 are visa classifications utilized by foreign military personnel. G-1–G-5 are used for employees of a designated international organization, while NATO visas are used by employees of the North Atlantic Treaty Organization.

DIVERSITY VISAS

The "fifth wheel" of U.S. immigration policy and a target of critics is the Diversity visa. This visa category offers lawful permanent residence to (approximately) 50,000 persons a year from countries less represented in the legal immigration system. In practice, this provides an opportunity for people to immigrate to America from nations that have not traditionally sent large numbers of immigrants to the United States. For example, the top countries receiving Diversity visas in recent years include Egypt, Ethiopia, Ukraine, and Nigeria. To apply for a Diversity visa, one must possess the equivalent of a high school education or higher, "within the past five years, two years of work experience in an occupation requiring at least two years' training or experience," and be a national of an eligible country. Then, the individual must enter a "lottery," managed by the U.S. Department of State. In recent years, more than 6 million people sent in applications for the 50,000 available slots.[15] The State Department has added procedures in recent years in an attempt to prevent fraud.

WORKING IN THE UNITED STATES

While there are many ways for foreign nationals to work in the United States, gaining approval for an immigrant or temporary employment visa is not easy. Generally, both the job and the individual must fit into specific criteria, and employers must provide a substantial amount of documentation to federal agencies. It is common for the process to require an immigration attorney. (Chapters 4 and 5 contain more in-depth discussions of high- and low-skilled employment-based immigration.)

One can divide employer-sponsored immigration into permanent (green card) and temporary visas. In addition, the alphabet soup of temporary work visas can be separated into high-skilled and low-skilled.

EMPLOYMENT-BASED IMMIGRATION CATEGORIES (FOR PERMANENT RESIDENCE)

To remain in the United States on a permanent basis, a skilled professional generally must receive lawful permanent residence. Temporary visas such as H-1B or L-1 entitle an individual to stay only for limited periods of time. Such individuals cannot be certain of staying long-term in the United States or becoming citizens unless they successfully apply for and are granted a green card. Part of the processing usually requires "labor certification," which involves testing the labor market to demonstrate that equally qualified Americans are not available for the position. The following discussion focuses on green cards, not temporary visas.

Under U.S. law, no more than 140,000 employment-based green cards are issued in a fiscal year. Today, it is this low quota, not bureaucratic delays, that leads to multi-year waits for skilled immigrants, although there were earlier years when inadequate processing prevented the full 140,000 quota from being utilized.[16]

Another factor influencing the availability of green cards is the per-country limit on employment-based immigrants. As the Government Accountability Office explains: "There are also annual numerical limitations on the number of visas that can be allocated per country under each of the preference categories. Thus, even if the annual limit for a preference category has not been exceeded, visas may not be available to immigrants from countries with high rates of immigration to the United States, such as China and India, because of the per-country limits."[17]

Under Section 202(a) of the Immigration and Nationality Act, relating to per-country levels for family-sponsored and employment-based immigrants, it states: "[T]he total number of immigrant visas made available to natives of any single foreign state . . . may not exceed 7 percent . . . of the total number of such visas made available under such subsections in that fiscal year."[18] With an annual quota of 140,000, this would generally limit employment-based immigrants from one country to approximately 10,000 a year. However, there is a provision in the law to allow nationals of a country to pierce this ceiling if additional employment-based visas are available. For example, the availability of additional numbers in the first and second preference in some years has allowed individuals from India and China to exceed the per-country limit.[19] However, in general, the per-country limits work to force individuals from large population countries to wait years longer than people from smaller countries.[20]

The five categories for employment-based immigration are:

- First Preference (EB-1 priority workers): aliens with extraordinary ability, outstanding professors and researchers, and certain multinational executives and managers.
- Second Preference (EB-2 workers with advanced degrees or exceptional ability): aliens who are members of the professions holding advanced degrees or their equivalent and aliens who because of their exceptional ability in the sciences, arts, or business will substantially benefit the national economy, cultural, or educational interests or welfare of the United States.
- Third Preference (EB-3 professionals, skilled workers, and other workers): aliens with at least two years of experience as skilled workers, professionals with a baccalaureate degree, and others with less than two years experience, such as an unskilled worker who can perform labor for which qualified workers are not available in the United States.

- Fourth Preference (EB-4 special workers such as those in a religious occupation or vocation).
- Fifth Preference (EB-5 Employment Creation)."[21] This is also known as an immigrant investor visa.[22]

HIGH-SKILL TEMPORARY VISAS FOR EMPLOYMENT IN THE UNITED STATES

H-1B

These visas for primarily professional jobs require the position to be in a "specialty occupation," which is defined as "an occupation that requires (a) theoretical and practical application of a body of knowledge, and (b) attainment of a bachelor's or higher degree in the specific specialty (or its equivalent) as a minimum for entry into the occupation in the United States."[23] A spouse or minor child can accompany the H-1B visa holder, but these dependents are not eligible to work in the United States. A spouse being unable to work can become an important issue for couples, particularly given the long waits for green cards for employer-sponsored immigrants. A green card would enable the spouse to work.

In a practical sense, an H-1B visa can be the only way an international student or outstanding individual identified from abroad can work long-term in the United States, which is why the category has become so important. The restrictions in other temporary visa categories and the long waits for green cards make the H-1B vital for employers wishing to employ skilled foreign nationals inside the United States. The annual H-1B quota is low relative to the size of the U.S. labor force—less than one-tenth of one percent—and this has caused year-long delays or made it impossible for many employers to hire a foreign national recruited to work in America (see Chapter 5). Eliminating or unduly restricting the use of H-1B visas would have the practical impact of generally barring skilled foreign nationals from working in the United States. That would compel U.S. employers to shift more resources outside of America or lose these skilled individuals to foreign competitors.

L

L visas allow U.S. companies to transfer executives, managers, and personnel with specialized knowledge from their overseas operations into the United States to work. To qualify, L-1 beneficiaries must have worked abroad for the employer for at least one continuous year (within a three-year period) prior to a petition being filed. This would prevent, for example, someone hired overseas from being sent to work immediately in the United States. Also, based on USCIS regulations, an executive or manager is limited to seven years, while an individual with specialized knowledge can stay for five years. While several decades ago these visas would not have been so important, today, in a connected global economy, they have become essential to companies as a means of moving—and integrating—personnel around the world. Efforts to impose new conditions on L-1 visa holders could run afoul of U.S. trade commitments on the movement of people under the General Agreement on Trade in Services. Restricting L-1 visas could also inhibit foreign investment, since companies investing in America often need to transfer executives and other personnel into the country.

O

An O visa is for persons of extraordinary ability, someone who can demonstrate national or international acclaim. An O-1 nonimmigrant (temporary visa holder) must demonstrate "extraordinary ability . . . which has been demonstrated by sustained national or international acclaim," according to the law.[24] "Extraordinary ability in the field of science, education, business, or athletics means a level of expertise indicating that the person is one of the small percentage who have arisen to the very top of the field of endeavor," according to USCIS regulations. "This is a very high standard and applies only to those who are well-established in their fields," notes Crystal Williams, executive director, American Immigration Lawyers Association. While some immigration critics say if H-1B visa holders are truly outstanding, then they should be able to qualify for O visas, in reality that is not the case. Williams explains the difference between an O and an H-1B visa: "The H-1B is for the highly skilled professional who has not yet achieved that level of recognition. In other words, the O-1 is for the person who already has invented advanced fuel cell technology. The H-1B is for the person who shows promise to be the inventor of the next generation of fuel cell technology. Both are important to the American economic engine, but they fall under different standards for qualification."[25] Only 9,014 O-1 visas were issued in FY 2008.[26] Many of those who received O-1 visas in 2008 may have been movie stars, professional athletes, or noted chefs, rather than scientists and engineers.

P

P-1 is used for professional athletes and people in entertainment. It has no annual quota. Previously, minor league baseball players used the H-2B category, but due to the numerical ceilings being reached in some years, teams found foreign players could not begin their minor league seasons in the United States. P-1 is for "individual or team athletes, or members of an entertainment group that are internationally recognized; P-2 . . . applies to artists or entertainers who will perform under a reciprocal exchange program; P-3 . . . applies to artists or entertainers who perform under a program that is culturally unique (same as P-1)."[27]

R

R is for religious workers who will come to work on a temporary visa.

TN

These visas are for professional workers from Mexico and Canada who qualify under the North American Free Trade Agreement (NAFTA). This has been a popular visa for nurses in Canada to work across the border in Michigan. The maximum period of admission for a TN is three years, but U.S. Citizenship and Immigration Services can grant extensions of stay.[28] "There is no limit on the number of years a TN visa holder can stay in the United States. However, the TN visa status is not for permanent residence."[29]

I

These visas are used for foreign journalists and foreign media representatives.

LOW-SKILLED TEMPORARY VISAS FOR EMPLOYMENT

H-2B

H-2B visas are used for short-term seasonal jobs not in agriculture. Under the law, both the type of job and the employer's need to fill the position must be temporary. For example, picking crabs for three to six months qualifies as a job eligible for H-2B, but using the visa to employ a waiter in a restaurant would not be permitted, unless perhaps the waiter would work only for the summer or winter, such as at a resort. In addition to the restrictions on the types of jobs, the small annual quota on H-2B visas has plagued the category. The annual quota is 66,000 a year, which is low relative to a U.S. labor force of over 150 million people. While the existence of the visas may have some impact in preventing individuals from coming here to work illegally, the small quota and limits on the types of jobs make the category too restrictive to have a substantial impact on reducing illegal immigration.

New regulations have made the H-2B process more cumbersome and less predictable for employers, according to attorneys.

H-2A

U.S. employers use H-2A temporary visas to hire workers in agriculture and related specialties, such as nurseries and landscaping. There is no annual limit on H-2A visas, but use of H-2A has been limited by the bureaucratic process that accompanies it, including a risk for employers that an application will not be approved in time to harvest a crop. On the other hand, farm worker advocates would like to make the rules even tighter. Growers and farm worker advocates both favor legislation that would streamline certain rules for growers, while providing legal status for the predominately illegal immigrant labor force now working in agriculture. "The program is indeed cumbersome and litigation-prone. Employers must wade through a regulatory maze in order to achieve some sort of basic understanding of what is required of them," testified John R. Hancock, formerly the Department of Labor's chief of the agricultural certification unit responsible for administration of the H-2A program, before a 1997 House Immigration Subcommittee hearing. "The H-2A program is not currently a reliable mechanism to meet labor needs in situations where domestic workers are not available."[30]

From FY 2005 to FY 2008, the use of H-2A visas increased from 31,892 to 64,404. Experts say the difficulty in finding domestic labor and increased border enforcement contributed to the increase. Despite the greater usage, legal workers on H-2A visas remain in the minority when compared to individuals working illegally in agriculture.

COMING TO AMERICA TO STUDY

Few areas receive less policymaking or media attention than U.S. policies toward international students. In a 2005 report, the National Academy of Sciences and its sister organizations concluded, "International students contribute to U.S. society not only academically and economically, but also by fostering the global and cultural knowledge and understanding necessary for effective U.S. leadership, competitiveness, and security."[31] On policy matters, the report warned: "If the United States is to maintain overall leadership in science and engineering, visa and immigration policies should provide clear procedures that do not unnecessarily hinder the flow of international graduate students and postdoctoral scholars."[32]

While international students aim to better their futures by coming to America, these students also benefit the United States. Their spending creates jobs in both the universities and in the surrounding communities in which they study. Their numbers in graduate schools help support programs that otherwise might possess too few students to be financially viable. International students also allow American students to learn about the lives of people in other parts of the world without even leaving a U.S. campus. As a foreign policy matter, returning international students are likely to return with a positive impression of America and its institutions that can be taken back to their home countries. Finally, many international students, particularly at the graduate level, decide to stay after completing their degrees and continue contributing to the United States.[33]

Today, more than 50 percent of the engineers with PhDs working in the United States are foreign born, according to the National Science Foundation. More than one-third of American university engineering faculty with PhDs are foreign born.[34] "At the doctoral level, foreign-born individuals constitute about half the total number of workers in both engineering (51%) and mathematics/computer sciences (48%), up from 41% and 33% a decade earlier," according to the National Science Foundation.[35] Many of these individuals first came to the United States as international students.

In general, the business community has expressed concern publicly about the impact of visa and international student policies on the long-term competitiveness of U.S. firms. At one point, Microsoft Chairman Bill Gates called the policy "a disaster." General Electric Chairman and CEO Jeffrey Immelt said, "This is a case where our policy to close down on access boomerangs. It moves jobs out of the United States and creates less incentive for people to study in the U.S."[36]

In the wake of the September 11, 2001, attacks, tightened admission policies and lengthened processing times made it less likely for an international student to receive a U.S. visa. This was not a case of unintended consequences. A widespread public perception took hold after the attacks on New York and Washington, DC, that it had become too easy to enter the United States from abroad. Members of Congress, in particular, excoriated consular officers, while criticism of Mary Ryan, assistant secretary of state for consular affairs, forced her retirement from the State Department after she lost support from her superiors. Three of the September 11, 2001, hijackers had some connection to international study, though none were full-time international students enrolled in four-year or graduate degree programs. Two had changed their status from visitor to student to enroll in flight schools and another had enrolled in a language program.[37]

In response to measures passed by Congress, the State Department required nearly all visa applicants to be interviewed in person, significantly increasing the workload in consulates around the world. Additional and more intensive security clearances became required for individuals from certain countries and studying in certain fields. New regulations and tighter enforcement made it more difficult to enter on a visitor visa and change to student status inside the country or to travel back and forth from one's home country to the United States. Perhaps most importantly, visas that may have been approved in the past turned into denials, as signals from Washington, DC, influenced the decisions of consular officers. Between 2001 and 2003, the number of visa applications refused for F-1 students increased from 27.3 percent to 35.2 percent.[38]

Since 2004, the issuance of F-1 visas has increased, reflecting both more stable U.S. policies and continued interest in America as a place to pursue higher education. In FY 2004, the number of F-1 visas issued was 218,898, but rose to 273,870 by FY 2006 and to 340,711 by FY 2008.[39] (In 2008, 10,475 M-1 visas were issued for foreign vocational students.)[40]

In 2009, the Institute of International Education released a report showing recent increases in enrollment, particularly among undergraduate students from China. According to the report, international students at U.S. colleges and universities reached an all-time high of 671,616 in the 2008/09 academic year.[41] The study noted, "International students contribute $17.8 billion to the U.S. economy, through their expenditures on tuition and living expenses, according to the U.S. Department of Commerce."[42]

Despite this positive news, certain problems remain, as reflected in a June 2009 public statement expressing concerns about U.S. visa policies signed by the leaders of more than 30 science and higher education organizations, including the Association of American Universities, the National Academy of Sciences, American Physical Society, NAFSA: Association of International Educators, and others. "As representatives of organizations of U.S. higher education, science, and engineering, we have been deeply concerned about the significant increase in delays experienced earlier this year by many international students, scholars, and scientists who have applied for visas to study, conduct research, or attend conferences in this country," according to the statement. "Lengthy and unnecessary delays frustrate and discourage many of the best and brightest international students, scholars, and scientists from studying and working in the United States, or attending academic and scientific conferences here and abroad. This compromises our ability to attract international scientific talent and maintain scientific and economic leadership."[43]

HOW DOES SOMEONE BECOME AN INTERNATIONAL STUDENT?

To better understand the process and issues facing a typical (in this case, hypothetical) international student, we can examine the case of Susan Lin. Susan is completing an undergraduate degree in Beijing and would like to study abroad to obtain a PhD in electrical engineering to conduct research in nanotechnology, but she has heard so many stories about visa problems that she is uncertain whether to apply to U.S. universities.[44]

Susan has heard from friends that countries besides the United States seem very interested these days in attracting students like her. The statistics bear out this perception. The United Kingdom experienced a 25 percent increase in Chinese student enrollment between 2003 and 2004, according to the British Council director of examinations in China. Australian universities saw a similar growth in Chinese student enrollment after 9/11.[45] Overall, the United Kingdom has increased its enrollment of international students by 77 percent since 1999, while Australia has raised its by 183 percent.[46]

Susan is concerned, too, about costs. One reason she decided not to attend a U.S. university as an undergraduate—as opposed to applying now as a graduate student—is it would have been too much of a financial strain on her family, since few scholarships are available for international students at that level.[47] She understands there is more money available from U.S. universities for international students at the graduate school level. According to the Institute of International Education, more than 40 percent of international graduate students list a U.S. university as their primary source of funds, compared to only 10 percent of (foreign) undergraduate students.[48]

After weeks of indecision, Susan applies and eventually is accepted to three American graduate schools and one British university. She decides to attend the University of Texas–Austin because she is impressed with the engineering program and she was offered a financial aid package that will make the school more affordable for her family.

Unlike a U.S. student, when a foreign national is accepted to an American college, that is only half the battle. To enter the United States to enroll at the University of Texas–Austin, Susan must apply for a visa at the U.S. embassy or at one of the American consulates in China. The State Department gives priority for international student interviews, so she receives her appointment time within a few days. Fortunately, she lives in Beijing and can easily access the embassy. But if she lived far away, she might have to fly and stay in a hotel in order to attend the interview.

A U.S. Embassy official in China has said that he tells "every Congressman and Senator I meet that 214(b) really is a problem for students and U.S. institutions."[49] In other words, U.S. consular officers deny visas to individuals—under 214(b) of the Immigration and Nationality Act—who they believe may stay in the United States after completing their education. That is the case even though it may be beneficial for America if such individuals remained to work or teach here.

It is the reality of this policy that Susan Lin must face when she enters the U.S. embassy for her interview. When the interview starts, Susan grows nervous, knowing a wrong answer (or even her demeanor) could cost her an opportunity to study in the United States.[50] In other words, this interview can change her life. The consular officer reviews the financial records, since an international student must demonstrate he or she is capable of funding the education through personal or other means. It appears that between her family's assets (from the bank records) and the financial package offered by the University of Texas–Austin there is enough money to fund Susan's studies.

"What do you plan to do after you receive your degree in electrical engineering?" asks the consular officer.

Susan knows working in the United States is an uncertain proposition. Moreover, she has learned that three years is a long time and it would appear boastful to tell anyone that after graduating she plans to get a job at a top American company. More importantly, she has heard that consular officers frown upon those who they believe plan to stay in the United States after completing their studies.

"I plan to come back to China after studying in America," says Susan.

"Don't you want a job in America?" he asks.

"I don't know if I would be good enough for that. My father is an engineer and I think he can help me get a job in Beijing once I come back with an American degree," says Susan.[51]

After a few more questions, the consular officer thanks Susan. The interview lasted less than five minutes. If the officer believed Susan intended to stay in the United States, he would have denied her on the spot under 214(b) as an "intended" immigrant. Instead, he tells her she will receive notification in about a month. This is because since Susan is a Chinese national and planning to study at the graduate level in a technology field, her visa application will undergo an additional level of screening.[52]

Weeks go by and Susan worries. She wonders if there is still time to tell the school in England she wants to go there instead. She is unsure what to do. Finally, four weeks after her interview, Susan receives word that her visa application has been approved. While not everyone succeeds, Susan overcame a number of hurdles to be able to enroll at a major U.S. university. She is going to America.

FAMILY IMMIGRATION AND THE LONG WAIT TO IMMIGRATE

Some of the most contentious immigration policy battles in recent years have been over a concept as old as our nation—families reuniting in America. In 1996 and 2007, Congressional critics unsuccessfully fought to eliminate key family preferences categories and reduce the level of family immigration. It is likely critics will renew such efforts in the future.

The wait times for sponsoring a close family member are long, in some cases extremely long. In a November 2009 report, the State Department tabulated more than 3.3 million close relatives of U.S. citizens and lawful permanent residents on the immigration waiting list who have registered for processing at a U.S. post overseas (see Table 3.1).[53] That does not include individuals waiting inside the United States, such as in a temporary visa status, who would gain a green card via adjustment of status at a U.S. Citizenship and Immigration Services office. Counting such individuals as well would likely increase the waiting list to over 4 million.[54]

In general, a U.S. citizen can sponsor for permanent residence a spouse, child, parent, or sibling. A lawful permanent resident (green card holder) can sponsor a spouse or child. The wait times and quotas vary for the categories, with the application of per-country limits creating much longer waits in some preference categories for nationals of Mexico and the Philippines.[55]

An "immediate relative" of a U.S. citizen can immigrate to America without being subjected to an annual quota. This is important, since it is the relatively low quotas in the family and employer-sponsored preference

TABLE 3.1
Family-Sponsored Immigrants Waiting for Processing Abroad, November 2009

Family-Sponsored Preference Categories	Individuals Waiting in Immigration Backlog for Processing at an Overseas Post
1st Preference—Unmarried Adult Children of U.S. Citizens	245,516
2nd Preference (2A)—Spouses and Minor Children of Permanent Residents	324,864
2nd Preference (2B) Unmarried Adult Children of Permanent Residents	517,898
3rd Preference—Married Adult Children of U.S. Citizens	553,280
4th Preference—Siblings of U.S. Citizens	1,727,897
TOTAL	**3,369,455**

Source: "Annual Report of Immigrant Visa Applicants in the Family-sponsored and Employment-based Preferences Registered at the National Visa Center as of November 1, 2009," U.S. Department of State, Bureau of Consular Affairs. Note: The formal names of the categories cited above utilize "sons and daughters" and "brothers and sisters" in place of "adult children" and "siblings." A proportion of individuals on the list may be in the United States but have chosen to be processed at an overseas post. There are also several hundred thousand individuals not on this list who will be processed inside the United States via adjustment of status.

categories that lead to waits of often many years for would-be immigrants. While there is no numerical limit in the immediate relative category, processing would still normally take several months.

The three primary immediate relatives included in the category are:

- Spouses of U.S. citizens.
- Unmarried children of a U.S. citizen. The child must be under 21 years old. An adopted child must be younger than 16 years old.[56]
- Parents of U.S. citizens, if the petitioning citizen is at least 21 years old.[57]

FAMILY-SPONSORED PREFERENCE CATEGORIES AND ESTIMATED WAIT TIMES

Under the law, a minimum of 226,000 immigrants are allowed to become permanent residents each year under the family-sponsored preferences.[58] There are also per-country limits on the number of individuals from one country who can obtain a green card in these preference categories each year.[59]

Following are the descriptions of the four family-sponsored preferences as detailed in the monthly visa bulletin:

First—Unmarried Sons and Daughters of Citizens: 23,400 a year.

Second—Spouses and Children, and Unmarried Sons and Daughters of Permanent Residents: 114,200 A. Spouses and Children: 77 percent of the overall second preference limitation, of which 75 percent are exempt from the per-country limit; B. Unmarried Sons and Daughters (21 years of age or older): 23 percent of the overall second preference limitation.

Third—Married Sons and Daughters of Citizens: 23,400.

Fourth—Brothers and Sisters of Adult Citizens: 65,000.[60]

Enormous backlogs and waiting times plague the family immigration preference categories. For example, the wait time for a U.S. citizen petitioning for a brother or sister from the Philippines exceeds 20 years. This is based on the State Department Visa Bulletin, where, as of January 2010, it stated the U.S. government would only process applications filed prior to May 1, 1987, for siblings from the Philippines. In other words, American citizens with brothers or sisters in that country who filed while Ronald Reagan was still president of the United States and before the Berlin Wall fell are still waiting for their relatives to join them. For siblings from countries other than Mexico and the Philippines the wait times are closer to 10 years (see Table 3.2).[61]

The expected waiting times are quite long for other family categories as well. A U.S. citizen petitioning for either a married (3rd preference) or unmarried (1st preference) son or daughter (21 years or older) from Mexico can expect to wait about 17 years.[62] There is a similar wait time for married sons and daughters from the Philippines. The wait is an estimated six years for U.S. citizens with unmarried sons and daughters in other countries.

The spouses and children of lawful permanent residents (green card holders) also experience long waits for legal immigration. In the second preference (2A), the wait time is estimated to be about four years, with longer waits for Mexicans. The wait for unmarried sons and daughters of lawful permanent residents (2B) is about nine years for all countries except Mexico, which has a 16-year wait, and the Philippines, where the wait is approximately 10 years.

THE PROCESS

"Family reunification has long been an important concept in immigration law," notes attorney Susan Fortino-Brown. "However, helping clients immigrate based on a family relationship can be difficult and complex. Detailed attention to definitions, deadlines, and the interplay of numerous provisions is more important now than ever."[63]

Form I-130 is the alien relative petition that is sent to U.S. Citizenship and Immigration Services for approval. Among other things, it must establish that a family relationship exists between the U.S. citizen or lawful permanent resident filing the petition and the alien relative, also known as the beneficiary. If the relative is in the United States, the processing will take place at USCIS, with the relative hoping to obtain approval of an adjustment of status application (I-485). If the relative is abroad, then a U.S. consulate will process that individual's application. There is also a "self-petition" process for widows, widowers, battered spouses, and battered children, whereby they can apply or complete the immigration process without the involvement of a U.S. citizen or lawful permanent resident sponsor.

A sponsor must file an Affidavit of Support that shows the petitioner, or another individual willing to accept liability, can provide financial assistance to the family member. Under the law, the sponsor must show he or she can support the individual at 125 percent of the poverty level based on family size.[64]

KEY ISSUES AND CONTROVERSIES SURROUNDING FAMILY IMMIGRATION

In 2007, as part of a deal to appeal to critics who argued Congress should not reward *illegal* immigrants, the U.S. Senate came close to changing immigration law to prohibit Americans from sponsoring their own children

TABLE 3.2
Estimated Wait Times for Family-Sponsored Immigrants

	China	India	Mexico	Philippines	All Other Countries
Unmarried Adult Children of U.S. Citizens (1st Preference) 23,400 a year	6 year wait	6 year wait	17 year wait	16 year wait	6 year wait
Spouses and Minor Children of Permanent Residents (2nd Preference—A) 87,934 a year*	4 year wait	4 year wait	6 year wait	4 year wait	4 year wait
Unmarried Adult Children of Permanent Residents (2nd Preference—B) 26,266 a year	8 year wait	8 year wait	16 year wait	10 year wait	8 year wait
Married Adult Children of U.S. Citizens (3rd Preference) 23,400 a year	8 year wait	8 year wait	16 year wait	17 year wait	8 year wait
Siblings of U.S. Citizens (4th Preference) 65,000 a year	10 year wait	10 year wait	14 year wait	20 year wait	10 year wait

*The spouses and minor and adult children of Permanent Residents category is 114,200 annually "plus the number (if any) by which the worldwide family preference level exceeds 226,000." 75% of spouses and minor children of lawful permanent residents are exempt from the per-country limit. Wait times are approximate as of January 2010.

Source: U.S. Department of State Visa Bulletin, January 2010; National Foundation for American Policy.

or other close family members for *legal* immigration. Simply put, Sen. Jon Kyl (R-AZ) wanted something in exchange for agreeing to support the legalization of several million illegal immigrants and that "something" was eliminating the family categories that allowed U.S. citizens to petition for their adult children and siblings for immigration.

The policy rationale offered for eliminating family immigration categories in 1996 and 2007 fails to hold up under scrutiny, appearing more contrived than substantive. For example, some have argued that the wait times in some of the family categories are so long that it gives people "false hope." But this argument strikes one as crying "crocodile tears" for those waiting in line. The fact that long waits exist in some categories simply means that Congress has not raised the limits to correspond with the demand. The solution is not to eliminate categories and guarantee Americans in the future could never reunite with certain loved ones. The more rational approach is to raise the quotas, as the Senate did in its immigration bill passed in 2006. If one argues that long waits encourage individuals to jump ahead in line, then destroying all hope of immigrating legally would provide even more incentive for people to come to the United States and stay illegally. It makes little policy sense to decry illegal immigration by arguing people should immigrate legally and at the same time to eliminate the country's most viable options for legal immigration.

THE MYTH OF "CHAIN MIGRATION"

One argument made for eliminating family categories is it would reduce something called "chain migration." However, "chain migration" is a meaningless and contrived term that seeks to put a negative light on a phenomenon that has taken place throughout the history of the country—some family members come to America and succeed, and then sponsor other family members.

The following example illustrates the myth of "chain migration." In 2010, an immigrant who arrived 6 years before and has now become a U.S. citizen decides to sponsor a sibling for immigration. With a 10-year wait (or 14 to 20 years for Mexicans and Filipinos), that means 16 years would pass between the arrival of the first and second immigrant. It would then take the second immigrant 6 years to become a citizen and, if he or she then sponsors an unmarried adult child, it would take an additional 6 to 16 years for that "third" immigrant to arrive (depending on the country). So under this "chain migration," the time between the arrival of the first immigrant and the third immigrant would be between 28 and 48 years, depending on the country of origin. This is not the continuous "onslaught" that critics have sought to conjure up when discussing this issue. Moreover, all of the immigrants in this example would immigrate under the legal quotas established by Congress.

While it is true approximately 65 percent of U.S. legal immigration in 2008 was family-based, more that half of family immigration was actually the spouses and minor children of U.S. citizens, categories no one has proposed eliminating. Of total U.S. legal immigration in 2008, married and unmarried adult children of U.S. citizens accounted for only about 2 percent each; siblings of U.S citizens accounted for only 6 percent.[65] Eliminating these categories would produce only a small drop in overall legal immigration and lead to great personal hardship for tens of thousands of Americans and their loved ones.

ALREADY HIGH LEVELS OF EDUCATION FOR LEGAL IMMIGRANTS

Some have argued that a rationale for establishing a point system in place of family categories is to improve the skill level of immigrants. In reality, the typical legal immigrant already has a *higher* skill level than the typical native, so upon examination the basic rationale falls apart for eliminating family categories.

- The New Immigrant Survey, which examines only legal immigrants, finds: "The median years of schooling for the legal immigrants, 13 years, is a full one year higher than that of the U.S. native-born."[66]
- The Pew Hispanic Center reports: "By 2004, all groups of legal immigrants in the country for less than 10 years are more likely to have a college degree than natives."[67]
- The Pew Hispanic Center also reports that the average family income for a naturalized U.S. citizen in the country more than 10 years in 2003 was more than $10,000 a year higher than a native ($56,500 vs. $45,900).[68]
- Writing in the May 1999 *American Economic Review*, economists Harriet Duleep, then a senior research associate at the Urban Institute, and Mark Regets, a senior analyst at the National Science Foundation, found that the gap in earnings between new immigrants and natives largely disappears after 10 years in the United States, with immigrant wage growth faster than native (6.7 percent vs. 4.4 percent).[69]

Simply put, while the policy of eliminating family categories would cause real pain for families, it would create little or no net benefit with regard to its stated purpose.

A number of past reports focusing on the skill levels of immigrants have used census data that included many illegal immigrants. Two of the studies cited previously differentiate between legal and illegal immigrants and show that a "low education" level among legal immigrants is not a problem. Legal immigrants do congregate at the top and bottom of the education scale, but less so than census data imply. Besides, economists agree that immigrants increase America's labor productivity most when they fill niches at the top and bottom.

ECONOMIC BENEFITS OF FAMILY IMMIGRATION

Family immigration provides important economic benefits, particularly in fostering entrepreneurship, while also promoting the type of family cohesiveness that political office seekers tell voters is vital to the nation's future. "A large majority of immigrant-owned businesses in the United States are individual proprietorships relying heavily on family labor," testified University of South Carolina professor Jimy M. Sanders before the Senate Immigration Subcommittee. "Our experiences in the field suggest that the family is often the main social organization supporting the establishment and operation of a small business." Sanders notes: "The family can provide important resources to members who pursue self-employment. Revision of federal law in the mid-1960s to allow large increases in immigration from non-Western European societies and to give priority to family reunification increased family-based immigration and contributed to a virtual renaissance of small business culture in the United States. By contrast, labor migration that involves single sojourners who leave their families behind and work temporarily in the United States has produced far less self-employment."[70]

Family members immigrating to support other family members in caring for children and helping to run family owned businesses are likely to benefit the United States economically. In New York City during the 1990s, the number of immigrant self-employed increased by 53 percent, while native-born self-employed declined by 7 percent, according to the Center for an Urban Future.[71]

The Kauffman Foundation's Index of Entrepreneurial Activity has found immigrants are more likely than natives to start businesses. In fact, the foundation's research has found the "gap in the entrepreneurial activity rate between immigrants and natives is large." According to an April 2009 report, "For immigrants, 530 out of 100,000 people start a business each month, compared to 280 out of 100,000 native-born people." The study also found, "Overall, immigrants have much higher low- and medium-income-potential entrepreneurship rates than the native-born. But, immigrants also are more likely to start high-income-potential types of businesses."[72]

John Tu, President and CEO of Kingston Technology, based in Fountain Valley, California, immigrated to America from Taiwan after being sponsored by his sister. He built up his computer memory company with fellow Taiwanese immigrant David Sun. When Tu sold the company for

$1 billion, he did something almost unheard in the annals of business: He gave $100 million of the sale's proceeds to his American employees—about $100,000 to $300,000 for each worker. This decision changed the lives of those working at Kingston, allowing many to fund dreams for themselves and their children. Kingston employee Gary McDonald said, "Kingston's success came from a philosophy of treating employees, suppliers, and customers like family, this being based upon the Asian family values of trust, loyalty, and mutual support practiced by John and David."[73]

Jerry Yang, co-founder of Yahoo!, one of America's top Internet companies, came to this country at the age of 10. "Yahoo! would not be an American company today if the United States had not welcomed my family and me almost 30 years ago," said Yang.

In addition to economic benefits, it is important to remember that family immigration has always been the foundation of America's immigration system. It is part of the country's tradition, going back from the Mayflower through Ellis Island and to the present day. The historical records at Ellis Island make clear that most immigration prior to the 1920s was family-based, and such unification never entirely lost its role.

A report of the House Judiciary Committee on the 1959 legislation states, "The recognized principle of avoiding separation of families could be furthered if certain categories of such relatives were reclassified in the various preference portions of the immigration quotas." Joyce Vialet of the Congressional Research Service analyzed the 1965 Immigration Act and concluded, "In response to the demand for admission of family members, Congress enacted a series of amendments to the Immigration and Nationality Act (INA), beginning in 1957, which gave increasing priority to family relationship. The family preference categories included in the 1965 Act evolved directly from this series of amendments. Arguably, the 1965 Act represented an acceptance of the status quo rather than a shift to a new policy of favoring family members."[74]

A POINTLESS POINT SYSTEM

In place of certain family categories, in 2007, President Bush dropped his support for family immigration as part of a deal with some Republican Senators who sought to eliminate certain family immigration categories. In order not to appear hostile toward immigrants, the proposal was couched in the form of instituting a Canadian-style point system. Such a point system would have worked by establishing a "score" and assigning admission "points" for age, education level, and other characteristics for those immigrants who seek entry. Only those who achieved the score could immigrate.

The proposal in the U.S. Senate in 2007 to establish a point system was a Trojan horse designed to reduce family immigration. It was not intended to help employers. Not only did employer groups oppose establishing a point system, but such a system would have prevented companies from sponsoring individual employees.

As noted in Chapter 1, the 2007 Senate legislation displayed a lack of understanding of the overall immigration system. If it became law, the per-country limit retained in the bill would have allowed almost anyone with a college degree born in a small country to gain admission to the United States over people with a master's degree or higher born in large population countries such as China or India. That is because no matter how many "points" individuals from China or India earned, the overall per-country limit for those countries would have limited how many Chinese or Indians could immigrate each year under that system. At the same time, someone from Ghana, Syria, or Bulgaria would need a comparatively low point total to qualify for entry because those countries would never reach the per-country limit. In many ways, the proposal was little more than a glorified "Diversity" visa, an immigration category many of these same members of Congress have criticized.

A point system would transfer power from Congress to federal bureaucrats at the expense of individuals, families, and employers. "A point system has many imperfections," concedes point system advocate George Borjas, an economist at Harvard University. "A few hapless government bureaucrats have to sit down and decide which characteristics will enter the admissions formula, which occupations are the ones that are most beneficial, which age groups are to be favored, how many points to grant each desired characteristic and so on."[75] (One should note a similar problem with removing authority from Congress and empowering bureaucrats in a "commission" to regulate the number of foreign professionals and lesser-skilled workers permitted into the United States each year.)[76]

After noting that the list of occupations, each assigned points, takes up 10 pages in the Canadian system, Borjas writes, "Most of these decisions are bound to be arbitrary and clearly stretch the ability of bureaucrats to determine labor market needs well beyond their limit."[77] But bureaucrats are not well suited at all to handle labor market decisions on behalf of employers. Moreover, no government test can ever measure life's most important intangibles: drive, individual initiative, and a commitment to family.

Borjas concedes that keeping out Mexicans is a likely end product of a point system. "Most likely," he writes, that under a point system, "the predominance of Mexican immigrants and of immigrants from some other developing countries will decline substantially."[78] Whether or not the intended goal of proponents of a point system is to prevent immigration from Mexico and Central America, it is the most likely outcome.

One should note that the Canadian point system is designed with a different purpose in mind. Given its relatively small population, Canada needs to attract immigrants to the country. In the United States, attracting skilled immigration is not a problem. The American problem is straightforward—Congress has failed to increase the quotas for H-1B temporary visas and employment-based green cards.

Research by economists Harriet Orcutt Duleep and Mark Regets questions the alleged economic benefit of eliminating family categories in favor of admitting individuals under a Canadian-style point system. Duleep and Regets found that while family-based immigrants have lower earnings upon entering the United States, they experience higher earnings growth than employment-based immigrants. "This result . . . challenges assumptions about the presumed productivity gains that would be achieved if the United States were to increase employment-based immigrant admissions at the expense of family-based admissions."[79]

The research found immigrants admitted via family categories "catch up" to those admitted for employment purposes within 11 to 18 years, according to the estimates.[80] Duleep and Regets believe the faster earnings growth for family-based immigrants may be associated with "increased investment in human capital" by such immigrants. Overall, the economists believe the research raises many questions about the presumed advantages of a point system to admit immigrants. Duleep and Regets conclude, "From a policy perspective, this finding, in tandem with previous research showing no clear-cut labor market effects of the Canadian admission system, suggests that any efforts to increase skills-based U.S. immigration at the expense of family-based immigration should be preceded by a lot more thought and research."[81]

LOOKING AHEAD

Family immigration quotas are inadequate and result in needless separation and long waits for Americans, lawful permanent residents, and their close family members. Eliminating family categories, as some have proposed in the past, would go against America's heritage and lead to false distinctions about the value of different family members. One way to look at this issue is to put it at the personal level. Most Americans—and members of Congress—would agree they would have a difficult time welcoming the immigration of their 19-year-old son, while barring the door to their 22-year-old daughter.

If Congress wants to increase the number of skilled immigrants in the country, the best way is through the existing set of temporary visas and the employment-based immigration system. A point system or a commission that attempts to "bean count" the correct number of skilled immigrants represents a fatally flawed endeavor. U.S. employers want to hire specific skilled individuals, not skilled people in general. And the best evidence that an individual has desirable skills in the U.S. economy is the answer to a straightforward question: Does an employer want to hire that person?

Companies thrive on certainty. While the current backlogs and delays in green cards create uncertainty, at least employers are able to sponsor specific individuals. Not so with a point system or a commission to regulate skilled labor or a point system where bureaucratic mandates will override the individual labor market decisions of employers and employees.

Denying U.S. citizens the ability to sponsor adult children, parents, or siblings is unnecessary and politically divisive. The bill the Senate passed in 2006 raised quotas for both family and employment-based immigrants, and Congress can do so again. The most effective policy to promote skilled immigration is not to reduce family immigration but to exempt from the current quotas employer-sponsored immigrants with a master's degree or higher, eliminate the per-country limits for employment-based immigration, and allow international students an easier path to remain in the country after completing their studies.

To encourage international student enrollment and maintain a steady flow of talented individuals into fields important to America, while also balancing security concerns, it is necessary to change certain policies and promote new approaches to international education. These changes would involve government, business, and universities.

First, change the requirement that to obtain a visa individuals pursuing master's and doctorates in the United States must demonstrate they will return to their home country. Amending 214(b) as it applies to graduate students, an action recommended by a National Academy of Sciences panel, would increase the ability of U.S. universities to attract outstanding students.[82] It could also be more politically saleable than attempting to eliminate it entirely for all international students.

Catheryn Cotten, formerly director of the international office at Duke University, relates the story of a Chinese student earning a PhD in a scientific field who went home to visit and could not receive another visa because the consular officer accused her of wanting to stay in the United States to work after completing her PhD. This demonstrates the self-defeating nature of U.S. policy. American officials should *hope* a scientist receiving a PhD from Duke University wants to stay in America. After a number of months, the student from China was eventually allowed to reenter the United States, but as Catheryn Cotten says, "Students are scared. They need to go home, they need to travel, but are now often afraid to do so."[83]

Second, the United States should streamline the immigration process for international graduate students in science, engineering, and other fields. It is in America's interest to make it feasible for such individuals to stay and work in the private sector, perform research in our labs, or teach at U.S. universities. "We have heard from faculty who travel abroad that the prospect that people won't be able to work in the United States after completing their studies is a major concern," says Cotten.[84] An opportunity to work in America can be part of the attraction of studying here, often justifying the enormous financial investment international students must endure to attend a U.S. college.

Third, to deal with both policy and processing problems, the U.S. government needs to both increase accountability and improve coordination among the numerous departments with authority over international students. One approach would be to require a single administration official to coordinate policy and act as an "ombudsman" on international student issues. This would lead to a logical setting of priorities to balance security and other interests, and would inject accountability into policies affecting international education. Marlene Johnson, Executive Director and CEO of NAFSA: Association of International Educators, believes such an individual needs to be located in the White House, and that the message from that official should be connected to our overall message to the world about the United States.[85]

Fourth, U.S. universities need to increase their marketing abroad to attract international students to the United States. "Schools should absolutely increase their marketing," says NAFSA's Marlene Johnson. "While we need a marketing plan as a nation for international education, individual universities need to compete abroad to attract students." She notes some schools rely primarily on India and China for their international students, and it would be beneficial to maintain a more "diversified" source of students. She also explains an increasing number of Chinese students are financially "sponsored" by the government, which means they are obligated to return home after completing their undergraduate/graduate studies in the United States. This could have competitive implications for U.S. businesses.[86]

Fifth, universities, businesses, and the U.S. government should work together on a strategic plan to convey the message that America is a great place to gain an education. The U.S. Department of Education and U.S. Department of State can formulate a broad campaign, in cooperation with universities, to advertise America as a place to gain an education.

Sixth, to help deal with the expense of a U.S. university education, Duke University and some other universities are setting aside resources obtained from private sources to provide financial assistance for international students, in part under the belief that providing exposure on campuses to students from different nations also benefits U.S. students. Duke's Fuqua School of Business provides low-interest loans for international students in its graduate program. A task force of educators convened by NAFSA, the Committee on Institutional Cooperation, and Indiana University recommended that universities consider developing endowments aimed at support for international students attending their schools.[87]

Finally, to the extent the United States will continue to provide financial assistance to other nations, we should consider providing part of that assistance in the form of need-based vouchers to qualified international students from those nations to study at U.S. universities. This would turn a portion of foreign aid into student aid spent in the United States for tuition and room and board. It would provide an opportunity to educate and expose individuals to America who do not possess the resources to self-fund a U.S. college education. Assistance of any kind is most effective when it is tangible and directly affects the lives of individuals. While the U.S. government funds the Fulbright Program for approximately 1,300 international students a year, the proposal here is for a broader approach that becomes part of our foreign aid packages aimed at the developing world.[88]

CONCLUSION

America remains a land of opportunity. It also remains a place where an individual can come, receive an education, and make a valuable contribution to our society. That individual may return to their native country and retain a positive impression of America as he or she rises in the ranks of business or government. That contribution may also mean staying in the United States after graduation and receiving a patent for a new technology, starting a business that creates jobs, or teaching U.S. college students at a major American university. America's legal immigration system is complex. It suffers from long waits due to inadequate annual quotas for both family- and employer-sponsored immigration. Raising those quotas would serve both the humanitarian and economic interests of the United States.

NOTES

1. *2008 Yearbook of Immigration Statistics,* Office of Immigration Statistics, Department of Homeland Security, 2009. All immigration numbers for the year 2008 are derived from this source unless otherwise noted.

2. In 2006, Congress removed the annual cap of 10,000 asylees adjusting to lawful permanent residence.

3. On the U.S. Citizenship and Immigration Services Web site, cancellation of removal is defined as "A discretionary benefit adjusting an alien's status from that of deportable alien to one lawfully admitted for permanent residence. Application for cancellation of removal is made during the course of a hearing before an immigration judge."

4. U.S. Department of State. Available at: http://travel.state.gov/visa/temp/without/without_1990.html#countries.

5. Some temporary visas, such as H-1B, allow "dual-intent," which means it is lawful to be intending to stay permanently at the time of applying for the visa.

6. http://travel.state.gov/visa/frvi/denials/denials_1361.html.

7. Ibid.

8. Victoria Duong and Lincoln Stone, "B-1 Business Visitors," in *Navigating the Fundamentals of Immigration Law: Guidance and Tips for Successful Practice, 2007–2008 Edition*, ed. Grace E. Akers (Washington, DC: American Immigration Lawyers Association, 2007), 176.

9. "Non Immigrant Visas Issued by Classification, Fiscal Years 2004–2008," U.S. Department of State, 2009. The 4 million figure includes the additional categories of B-1 and B-2 listed in the statistical table, such as "Combination B1/B2 and Border Crossing Card."

10. Susan Fortino-Brown, "Family-Sponsored Immigration," in *Navigating the Fundamentals of Immigration Law: Guidance and Tips for Successful Practice, 2007–2008 Edition*, ed. Grace E. Akers (Washington, DC: American Immigration Lawyers Association, 2007), 318. Supporting affidavits from friends may also be part of the application.

11. Interview with Greg Siskind.

12. Ibid.

13. "Temporary Benefits Employment Categories and Required Documentation," U.S. Citizenship and Immigration Services Web site.

14. "Temporary Protected Status," U.S. Citizenship and Immigration Services Web site.

15. Alex Villarreal, "US Visa Lottery Underway Despite Uncertain Future by Washington," Voice of America, October 30, 2007. An applicant can also possess two years of work experience in a field that requires two years of training. Five thousand of the 55,000 Diversity visas each year have been set aside for use under the Nicaraguan and Central American Relief Act (NACARA).

16. To a degree, those unused immigrant visas from prior years have an impact on the current backlog.

17. *Immigration Benefits*, GAO-06-20 (Washington, DC: Government Accountability Office, 2005), 43.

18. Section 202(a)(2) of the Immigration and Nationality Act.

19. The per-country limit can be exceeded up to the availability of visas in a preference category.

20. Section 202(a) of the INA.

21. Descriptions of categories taken verbatim from "How Do I Apply for Immigrant Status Based on Employment?" U.S. Citizenship and Immigration Services Web site. The first preference is allocated 28.6 percent of the annual quota, plus any numbers not needed for the fourth and fifth preference. The second preference is given 28.6 percent of the annual quota, plus any numbers not required by the first preference. Similarly, the third preference is allocated

28.6 percent of the employment-based quota, plus if there are any numbers not used by the first and second preference. The fourth and fifth preferences are allocated 7.1 percent of the quota.

22. Visa Bulletin, November 2009, U.S. Department of State.

23. Section 214(i)(1) of the Immigration and Nationality Act.

24. Section 101(a)(15)(O)(i) of the Immigration and Nationality Act.

25. Interview with Crystal Williams.

26. U.S. Department of State. *Classes of Nonimmigrants Issued Visas, Fiscal Years 1989–2008.*

27. U.S. Department of State. Available at: http://travel.state.gov/visa/temp/types/types_1286.html.

28. "Frequently Asked Questions: USCIS Announces Increased Period of Stay for Trade NAFTA Professional Workers from Canada or Mexico," USCIS, updated October 14, 2008, on the USCIS Web site.

29. U.S. Department of State. Available at: http://travel.state.gov/visa/temp/types/types_1274.html.

30. Testimony of John R. Hancock before the Subcommittee on Immigration and Claims of House Committee on the Judiciary, September 24, 1997.

31. *Policy Implications of International Graduate Students and Postdoctoral Scholars in the United States*, Committee on Science, Engineering, and Public Policy, Board on Higher Education and Workforce, Policy and Global Affairs, the National Academies (Washington, DC: National Academy of Sciences, 2005), 3.

32. Ibid., 10.

33. Portions of the research on international students in this section were commissioned by the Merage Foundations for the "Leadership Forum on Foreign Student Admission and Enrollment in U.S. Graduate Schools," held October 16 and 17, 2005, and cosponsored by the Merage Foundations and the University of California–Irvine.

34. Richard B. Freeman, "Does Globalization of the Scientific/Engineering Workforce Threaten U.S. Economic Leadership?" presented at the "Leadership Forum on Foreign Student Admission and Enrollment in U.S. Graduate Schools," held October 16 and 17, 2005, and cosponsored by the Merage Foundations and the University of California–Irvine, 8.

35. The National Science Board, *Science and Engineering Indicators 2010* (Arlington, VA: National Science Foundation, 2010), 3–50.

36. *Financial Times*, February 7, 2005.

37. Stephen Yale-Loehr, Demetrios Papademetriou, and Betsy Cooper, *Secure Borders, Open Doors: Visa Procedures in the Post September 11 Era* (Washington, DC: Migration Policy Institute, 2005), 171–172.

38. U.S. Department of State, Nonimmigrant Visa Statistics, 2001, 2003.

39. U.S. Department of State, Table XVI(B), "Nonimmigrant Visas Issued by Classification, Fiscal Years 2004–2008."

40. Ibid.

41. "Record Numbers of International Students in U.S. Higher Education," Press Release, Institute for International Education, November 16, 2009. Visa

issuance and enrollment figures do not necessarily match, since someone enrolled at a school for more than a year may have been issued a visa two or more years earlier.

42. Ibid.

43. "Statement and Recommendations on Visa Problems Harming America's Scientific, Economic, and Security Interests," June 10, 2009. Available at: http://www.ametsoc.org/sss/documents/statement_visa_problems_harming_interests.pdf.

44. Susan Lin is a composite figure used here to explain the process for international students.

45. Kyna Rubin, "China's Students: Turning Away or Staying Home," *International Educator*, Summer 2004, 10–11.

46. Victor S. Johnson, *A Visa and Immigration Policy for the Brain-Circulation Era* (Washington, DC: NAFSA, 2009), 7.

47. International students are not eligible to receive U.S. government grants (Pell Grants) or participate in the federal student loan program and generally must pay out-of-state tuition at public universities.

48. *Open Doors 2004*, Institute of International Education, Table on Primary Source of Funding by Academic Level. Available at: http://opendoors.iienetwork.org.

49. Rubin, 13.

50. Cornelius D. Scully, a former high-ranking State Department official in the Visa Office, provided helpful information on the consular interview process.

51. Working in the United States, even for a few years, can greatly enhance the future career opportunities of an international student and help repay the cost of an American education.

52. "Extension of Validity for Science Related Interagency Visa Clearances," Office of the Spokesman, U.S. Department of State, February 11, 2005. The Visa Mantis program was developed administratively by the State Department and requires interagency clearance for "visa applications for persons to study or work in certain sensitive scientific and technical fields" to "screen against the illegal transfer of technology."

53. "Annual Report of Immigrant Visa Applicants in the Family-Sponsored and Employment-Based Preferences Registered at the National Visa Center as of November 1, 2009," U.S. Department of State, Bureau of Consular Affairs, Immigrant Visa Statistics, November 2009.

54. One can estimate the additional individuals not counted in the State Department document by examining the proportion of individuals in each family preference category who are listed as adjustments, rather than "new arrivals," in Table 7 of the *2008 Yearbook of Immigration Statistics*.

55. See State Department Visa Bulletin.

56. Fortino-Brown, 315. She notes, "If the child is a natural sibling of a child who has been adopted under the age of 16, the older sibling may immigrate through adoption by the same parents before the age of 18."

57. Ibid., 311.

58. Ibid., 311. In theory, this number could be higher if the number of immediate relatives admitted in the prior fiscal year is below 254,000.

59. "Section 202 [of the Immigration and Nationality Act] prescribes that the per-country limit for preference immigrants is set at 7% of the total annual family-sponsored and employment-based preference limits," notes the State Department. December 2009 State Department Visa Bulletin.

60. Ibid. Under the law, if numbers are not needed in the fourth preference, they are added to the first preference. The third and fourth preferences could also receive additional numbers if the categories above them are not fully utilized. Since all the categories are oversubscribed, this part of the law does not have a practical impact on the annual flow.

61. Wait times for newly sponsored family immigrants are estimated based on an examination of the cutoff dates listed in the State Department Visa Bulletin.

62. This is based, in part, on cutoff dates listed in the January 2010 Visa Bulletin.

63. Fortino-Brown, 309.

64. Ibid., 326.

65. *2008 Yearbook of Immigration Statistics*, Office of Immigration Statistics, Table 6.

66. As cited in Stuart Anderson, "Muddled Masses," *Reason*, February 2000.

67. Jeffrey S. Passel, *Unauthorized Migrants: Numbers and Characteristics* (Washington, DC: Pew Hispanic Center, 2005), 24. Passel points out that this is the case "notwithstanding the continued over-representation of legal immigrants at low levels of education."

68. Ibid., 31.

69. Harriet Orcutt Duleep and Mark C. Regets, "Immigrants and Human-Capital Investment," *American Economic Review* (May 1999), 187.

70. Testimony of Jimy M. Sanders before the Senate Judiciary Committee, Subcommittee on Immigration, "Immigrant Entrepreneurs, Job Creation, and the American Dream," April 15, 1997.

71. Jonathan Bowles, *A World of Opportunity* (New York: Center for an Urban Future, 2007), 7.

72. Robert W. Fairlie, *Kauffman Index of Entrepreneurial Activity*, 1996–2008 (Kansas City, MO: Ewing Marion Kauffman Foundation, 2009), 11–13.

73. Testimony of Gary D. MacDonald, Kingston Technology, at hearing on "Immigrant Entrepreneurs, Job Creation, and the American Dream," Senate Immigration Subcommittee, April 15, 1997.

74. As cited in Anderson, "Muddled Masses."

75. Ibid.

76. *A Commission to Regulate Immigration? A Bad Idea Whose Time Should Not Come* (Arlington, VA: National Foundation for American Policy, 2009).

77. Anderson, "Muddled Masses."

78. Ibid.; George J. Borjas, *Heaven's Door* (Princeton, NJ: Princeton University Press, 1999).

79. Harriet Orcutt Duleep and Mark C. Regets, "Admission Criteria and Immigrant Earnings Profiles," *International Migration Review*, 30, no. 2 (Summer 1996), 571.

80. Ibid., 584.

81. Ibid., 586.

82. Advocates for international students do not necessarily recommend a separate standard for international graduate students vs. undergraduate students.

83. Interview with Catheryn Cotton.

84. Ibid.

85. Interview with Marlene Johnson.

86. Ibid.

87. Interview with Catheryn Cotten; *In America's Interest: Welcoming International Students, The Role of Higher Education*, NAFSA and the Committee on Institutional Cooperation, White Paper from April 21–22, 2005, symposium at Indiana University. The task force also recommended exploring longer payment schedules for such students. Marshall Kaplan, executive director of the Merage Foundations, has recommended a business and foundation fund that can provide students with financial assistance.

88. For additional recommendations for improving U.S. policies on international education, see Victor S. Johnson, *A Visa and Immigration Policy for the Brain-Circulation Era* (Washington, DC: NAFSA, 2009).

SUGGESTED READINGS

"Annual Report of Immigrant Visa Applicants in the Family-Sponsored and Employment-Based Preferences Registered at the National Visa Center as of November 1, 2009." Washington, DC: Bureau of Consular Affairs, Immigrant Visa Statistics, U.S. Department of State, 2009.

National Science Board. *Science and Engineering Indicators 2010.* Arlington, VA: National Science Foundation, 2010.

Navigating the Fundamentals of Immigration Law: Guidance and Tips for Successful Practice. Washington, DC: American Immigration Lawyers Association. (Updated annually.)

Passel, Jeffrey S. *Unauthorized Migrants: Numbers and Characteristics.* Washington, DC: Pew Hispanic Center, 2005.

2008 Yearbook of Immigration Statistics. Washington, DC: Office of Immigration Statistics, Department of Homeland Security, 2009.

U.S. Department of State Visa Bulletin. (Updated monthly.)

Four

Illegal Immigration

No issue in immigration policy ignites more controversy than illegal immigration. Choose illegal immigration as a topic and it is certain to light up the switchboard on any talk radio show. Many Americans believe, incorrectly, that most immigrants enter the United States illegally, which can skew survey results on immigration. Jason Riley, a member of the *Wall Street Journal* editorial board, has pointed out that in recent years crimes committed by illegal immigrants receive more press coverage than other similar or worse crimes committed by other people.[1]

Illegal immigration is an area where the media focusing great attention on an issue has not yielded greater understanding. In fact, based on the information they have received, it is likely many Americans have become more confused than enlightened. What are the chief causes of illegal immigration? What role do government policies play in creating or fostering the problem? And what are the best solutions? To answer these questions, it is helpful to first examine how the United States arrived at this point.

A BRIEF HISTORY OF ILLEGAL IMMIGRATION

As discussed in Chapter 1, prior to the twentieth century, individuals and families could immigrate to the United States virtually without restriction, meaning illegal immigration was not an issue. In 1882, Congress passed the Chinese Exclusion Act and later restricted immigration from Japan. But other than these restrictions, individuals could immigrate to the United States without being subjected to quotas until 1921, when restrictive immigration quotas were introduced on a temporary basis (and later broadened and made permanent in 1924). Even with new restrictions, natives of Western Hemisphere countries and their families could immigrate outside of the quotas, although they would still need to present themselves at a port of entry and meet the legal grounds of admissibility.[2]

Illegal immigration was on the minds of members of Congress in the 1920s. In the 70th Congress (1927–1929), a Senate committee passed an amendment to delete Mexico from the list of countries from the Western Hemisphere where individuals could immigrate without quota. "This action was apparently motivated by the problem of illegal entry from Mexico," writes historian E. P. Hutchinson. Facing opposition from Senators with agriculture in their states, especially sugar beets, the bill did not move on the Senate floor.[3]

The Eighteenth Amendment establishing Prohibition, which went into effect in 1920, and the new immigration restrictions passed by Congress increased the importance of border enforcement. "With the passage of this constitutional amendment and the numerical limits placed on immigration to the United States by the Immigration Acts of 1921 and 1924, border enforcement received renewed attention from the government," according to the official history of the Border Patrol.[4]

The Labor Appropriations Act of 1924 established the U.S. Border Patrol and the mission of seeking to secure the border between ports of entry. "Mounted watchmen of the U.S. Immigration Service patrolled the border in an effort to prevent illegal crossings as early as 1904, but their efforts were irregular and undertaken only when resources permitted," according to the Border Patrol. Some of the early focus was aimed at preventing illegal immigration from China. Congress authorized Mounted Guards in 1915, essentially immigration inspectors who patrolled mostly on horseback between border inspection stations.[5] The federal government did not open the first Border Patrol Academy until 1934, but by 1945 the Border Patrol employed more than 1,400 people, including civilians.[6]

With World War II requiring massive troop mobilization, a lack of manpower at home, not concerns about illegal immigration, motivated U.S. policies toward Mexico. In April 1942, the United States and Mexico signed a bilateral agreement aimed at permitting Mexicans to work in America as a way to address concerns about U.S. food production during the war. This became the Bracero program. In April 1943, Congress passed an appropriations bill (H.J. Res. 96, Public Law 45) funding various wartime programs for agriculture. The bill also established exemptions to certain immigration requirements (such as alien registration) to allow the Bracero program to be integrated with U.S. immigration law. The 1943 appropriations bill gave primary authority for regulation of the program to the Commissioner of the Immigration and Naturalization Service (INS).[7]

After World War II, concerns about illegal entry from Mexico increased, until by 1954 the Immigration and Naturalization Service believed it needed to take aggressive action. A controversial crackdown on illegal immigration in 1954, dubbed Operation Wetback, rounded up Mexican migrants (and some U.S. citizens and others in the country legally) and deported them to Mexico. INS data show a 200,000 jump in apprehensions from 885,587 in 1953 to 1,089,583 in 1954.[8] Some aspects of Operation Wetback, while a break in intensity from previous INS operations, were not dissimilar from current Border Patrol practices, such as the use of manned aircraft to alert teams on the ground as to the location of aliens. Other tactics, including "sweeps" in urban areas, would raise civil rights concerns today, although it appears that INS personnel made the vast majority of their apprehensions during Operation Wetback in rural, rather than urban areas, and primarily in Texas and California.[9]

TEMPORARY WORK VISAS EFFECTIVE IN REDUCING ILLEGAL IMMIGRATION

Today, there are few legal avenues for lesser-skilled workers to enter America, which is a primary reason for illegal immigration. The underutilized H-2A visa for seasonal agricultural workers is considered burdensome and litigation prone by growers, while employers have often used up the annual quota of H-2B temporary visas for seasonal workers in resorts, crab fishing, nurseries, and other industries. Employers generally cannot sponsor such workers for permanent residence (green cards) and, in any case, such immigrant visas for the "Other Workers" category are currently limited to only 5,000 a year.[10]

This current state of affairs is unfortunate because expanded use of temporary visas represents far and away the best way to reduce illegal immigration and prevent the deaths at the border of those seeking economic opportunity in America.

The actions of Mexican farm workers between 1953 and 1959 illustrate that allowing legal paths to work will reduce illegal immigration and save lives. "Without question, the Bracero program was . . . instrumental in ending the illegal alien problem of the mid-1940s and 1950s," wrote the Congressional Research Service.[11] In short, history shows that combining sufficient legal avenues for work and immigration enforcement can dramatically reduce illegal immigration.

The story begins shortly before the increase in immigration enforcement that took place in 1954. INS Commissioner (General) Joseph Swing preceded Operation Wetback by cultivating support among growers to replace an illegal and, therefore, unpredictable source of labor with a legal, regulated labor supply. Swing wanted growers to more heavily utilize the legal means afforded by the Bracero program. Despite the view that employers preferred hiring people here illegally, in fact, Swing received favorable press from growers and in Congress for pushing the substitution of legal for illegal workers.[12]

After the 1954 enforcement actions were combined with an increase in the use of the Bracero program, *illegal entry, as measured by INS apprehensions at the border, fell by an astonishing 95 percent between 1953 and 1959.* This demonstrated how access to legal means of entry can affect the decision-making of migrant workers.

INS apprehensions fell from the 1953 level of 885,587 to as low as 45,336 in 1959. To place the 45,336 level of apprehensions in 1959 in perspective, it would have taken the Border Patrol only about 16 days to reach that level of apprehensions in 2006.[13] To put it another way, if today illegal entry from Mexico was near the 1959 level at the height of the Bracero program, then illegal immigration from Mexico would not be considered a serious issue either in Congress or among the general public. Apprehensions are recognized as an important indicator of the illegal flow. In general, apprehension numbers drop when the flow of illegal immigration decreases.[14]

Figure 4.1 illustrates the dramatic decrease in illegal entry that accompanied the increase in legal admissions under the Bracero program. During this time period, the annual number of Mexican farm workers legally admitted more than doubled from 201,380 in 1953 to an average of 437,937 for the years 1956–1959. In addition, the number of Mexicans admitted as permanent residents (green card holders) increased from 18,454 in 1953 to an average of 42,949 between 1955 and 1959.[15]

In addition to the data, contemporaneous statements confirm the view that those on the ground understood allowing an easier path to legal entry had reduced illegal immigration. A February 1958 Border Patrol document from the El Centro (California) district states, "Should Public Law 78 be repealed or a restriction placed on the number of braceros allowed to enter the United States, we can look forward to a large increase in the number of illegal alien entrants into the United States."[16]

In April 1958, after the Mexican government asked for the removal of a large farm association in the Rio Grande Valley, the Border Patrol in Brownsville, Texas, explicitly connected preventing employers from hiring through legal means to a predictable increase in illegal migration. In objecting to the prohibition on the farm association, the Border Patrol memo explains, "It (the farm association) has about 1,700 members in the four Valley counties which it supplies braceros and has handled an estimated 35,000 braceros during the current season. Revocation of this association's certificate would result in an acute shortage of agricultural labor and offer employment to illegal entrants."[17]

FIGURE 4.1
Apprehensions and Bracero Program Admissions, 1953–1959

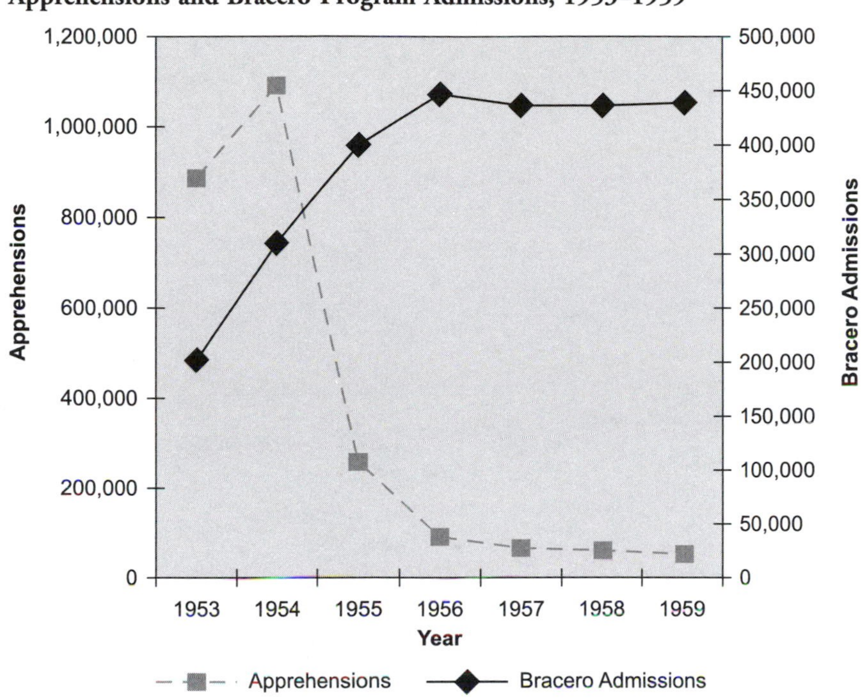

Sources: Congressional Research Service, *Temporary Worker Programs: Background and Issues*, 1980, 40; *Annual Report of the Immigration and Naturalization Service*, 1959; *INS Statistical Yearbook*, 1996.

Describing testimony before the House Committee on Agriculture by James Hennessy, executive assistant to Commissioner Swing, author Kitty Calavita writes, "While Hennessy at first insisted that INS enforcement policies be given full credit for both the reduction of illegal aliens and the subsequent expansion of the Bracero program, he was ultimately forced to admit that control of the border was in large part the consequence of an ample supply of Bracero labor." When Hennessy was asked what would happen to illegal immigration if the Bracero program ended, he replied, "We can't do the impossible, Mr. Congressman."[18]

When the Bracero program ended in December 1964, Congress began asking the INS to do the impossible—stop or significantly halt illegal immigration without the use of sufficient legal avenues to meet the demand for labor in the United States.[19]

The data are equally telling on the rise of illegal immigration after Bracero admissions ended in 1964. From 1964 to 1976, INS apprehensions increased from 86,597 to 875,915—*a more than 900 percent increase* (see Figure 4.2). Not all of this increase can be attributed to the Bracero program

FIGURE 4.2
Apprehensions after the End of the Bracero Program, 1964–1976

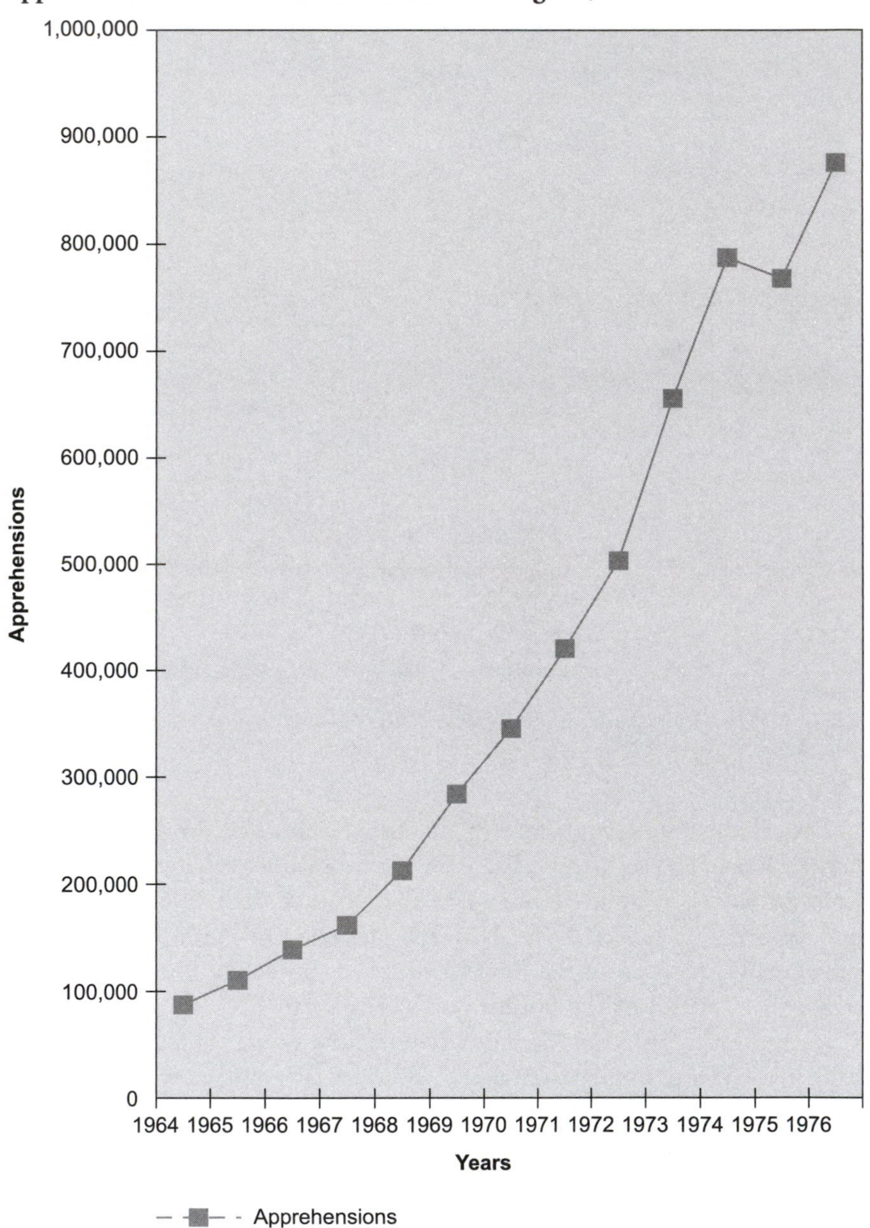

Source: INS Statistical Yearbook, 1996.

ending. The state of the Mexican economy and, importantly, the lack of legal avenues for individuals to enter legally and work in service, construction, or landscaping industries also contributed to the rise in illegal immigration. But an internal INS report found that apprehensions of adult male Mexican agricultural workers increased by 600 percent between 1965 and 1970, illustrating how terminating the Bracero program increased illegal immigration.[20] The 1970 INS annual report confirmed that the end of the Bracero program accompanied sharp rises in illegal immigration.[21]

Why did the end of the Bracero program result in vastly increased illegal immigration? Those who examined the issue only years before understood this would be a logical outcome of eliminating a reliable, legal path to entry. A 1954 House report concluded: "Reason clearly indicates that if a Mexican who wants to come to the United States for this employment can enter this country legally, with all the protection and benefits that a well-considered and well-administered employment program give him he will do so, rather than come in illegally. . . ." The report goes on to note: "If, because the program is not available or is not realistically geared to the requirements of employers or workers, the Mexican seeking employment finds it's impossible or difficult to come in legally, many of them will find their own way across the long border between the United States and Mexico and get employment where they can, under whatever wages and working conditions they are able to obtain."[22]

The data and contemporaneous analyses are so strong that it is difficult to dispute the beneficial impact the Bracero program had on limiting illegal immigration.[23] The Bracero program had flaws that we can learn from today. But the end of the Bracero program in 1964 and its curtailment in 1960 saw the beginning of the increases in illegal immigration that we see up to the present day.

IMMIGRANT DEATHS

Poverty in Mexico combined with the pull of better economic opportunities in the United States leads people to risk their lives on the journey to America. The absence of a way to enter the United States legally to work has contributed to more than 4,000 men, women, and children dying while attempting to cross to America since 1998 (see Table 4.1). The number of deaths would be even higher if not for the rescue efforts of U.S. Border Patrol agents. Just since 2005, the Border Patrol has rescued more than 10,000 migrants in areas near the southern border. In 2009 alone, the Border Patrol rescued 1,277 individuals near the southwest border.[24]

The loss of life will almost certainly continue unless more legal paths are open to work in the United States. This death toll—an average of about one

TABLE 4.1
Immigrant Deaths at the Border, 1998–2009

Year	Immigrant Deaths
1998	263
1999	249
2000	380
2001	340
2002	320
2003	338
2004	334
2005	492
2006	454
2007	398
2008	390
2009	417
TOTAL	**4,375**

Source: U.S. Border Patrol.

person a day—has occurred in the context of great pressure from Congress and executive branch officials to "control the border." The primary means of control has been to increase the size of the Border Patrol, build barriers, and deter illegal immigrants from crossing through easier terrain.

University at California–San Diego professor Wayne Cornelius writes, "The available data suggest that the current strategy of border enforcement has resulted in rechanneling flows of unauthorized migrants to more hazardous areas." He argues that the increased number of immigrant deaths is a natural result of that strategy, an approach influenced by pressure from Congress.[25]

Cornelius led a team for the Mexican Migration Field Research Program that conducted over 3,000 survey interviews with Mexican migrants in 2007 and 2008. According to the surveys, 72 percent listed purely economic reasons for immigrating illegally—higher wages and more jobs in the United States and a desire to build a house or start a business in Mexico.[26]

The surveys found the current risks do not deter most illegal immigrants: 91 percent of the migrants surveyed believed it was "very dangerous" to cross the border illegally, and 24 percent knew someone who died trying—yet still the migrants attempted to come themselves, viewing they had no viable legal ways to work in the United States.[27]

Would these individuals avail themselves of legal visas to work in America? According to the survey, 66 percent said, "Yes" to the question: "If there were a new temporary visa program for Mexican workers, like the Bracero program, would you be interested in participating?" Given that the

Bracero program carries some political baggage, it is likely the "yes" responses would have been even higher if the question were asked about a temporary work visa that allowed a person to work legally in the United States for a period of years with the ability to change employers.[28] While more than 4,000 immigrants have died trying to come to America for work since 1998, two closely examined cases have helped put names to the tragedies and illustrate the logical consequences of a policy that denies legal entry and thereby empowers and profits criminal enterprises that smuggle people into the United States.

In *The Devil's Highway*, Luis Alberto Urrea describes how in May 2001, 26 Mexican men crossed the border into the southern Arizona desert led by a coyote, a guide whose job is to lead illegal immigrants into America while avoiding detection by the Border Patrol. The coyote, known as Mendez, guided the men into brutal desert territory, the middle of what is referred to as the Devil's Highway. Mendez took wrong turns that got the group lost in the desert, but he did not want to turn back or play straight with his charges. "[The surviving victims] repeatedly asked the defendant how much further they would be required to walk. The defendant repeatedly advised them that they were within one to two hours of their destination . . . he never confessed to the members of the group that they were lost," according to official documents on the case.[29]

In fact, with several men near death, Mendez finally admitted they were lost and collected—or, some say, extorted—additional money from the men and went off with a cohort, promising to return with water for the group. He never came back and was found near death by the Border Patrol.

Describing the type of heat stroke these 24 men experienced, Urrea writes, "Dehydration has reduced all your inner streams to sluggish mudholes. Your heart pumps harder and harder to get fluid and oxygen to your organs. Empty vessels within you collapse. Your sweat runs out. . . . Your temperature redlines—you hit 105, 106, 108 degrees. . . . Your muscles, lacking water, feed on themselves. They break down and start to rot. . . . The system closes down in a series. Your kidney, your bladder, your heart."[30]

In all, 14 of the 26 men in the group died. One of them was Lorenzo Ortiz Hernandez, a father of five children ages 3 to 12. He could not support his family by growing coffee, so he decided to borrow $1,700 at 15 percent interest and take a chance at crossing illegally for an opportunity to work in America. Describing what Border Patrol agents found when they encountered Hernandez's body, Urrea writes, "Lorenzo was on his back, his eyes open to his enemy, the sun. His brown slacks were empty looking: his abdomen had fallen in. . . . It was 110 degrees before noon."[31]

The story of 73 or more illegal immigrants locked in the back of a tractor-trailer in May 2003 for a 300-mile trip to Houston also sparked consciences but no change in policies. Various middlemen (and women) arranged for a group of immigrants from Mexico and Central America to ride in the truck as a way to be smuggled into the interior of the United States. However, the air conditioner on driver Tyrone Williams's truck failed, leaving these men and women, and one child, to experience hellish conditions.

Two of the men managed to poke small holes in the truck, and the passengers sought to take turns at breathing in through these tiny passages. One 911 call was generated by a passenger with a cell phone. A passing motorist, alerted by a waving cloth from the small hole in the truck, called police. Both failed to elicit help and prevent the tragedy. By the time Tyrone Williams stopped, 19 people had died of "asphyxiation, dehydration and heat exposure as the result of being trapped inside a tractor trailer truck. Among the dead was a 5-year-old child."[32]

Throughout the trip, passengers had expressed concern for five-year-old Marco Antonio. "Please, for the sake of the child, get out of the way, let the father take the boy to the hole so he can get some fresh air," one passenger yelled. The boy was brought through the packed truck and put near the breathing holes. It did not save the boy.[33]

"The coyotes were being exclusively blamed for the deaths of the undocumented immigrants . . . in reality the responsibility was a shared one. The governments of Mexico and the United States were also partially to blame for what happened," writes Jorge Ramos, author of *Dying to Cross*. He points out that coyotes "had long since become a necessity for anyone who wanted to cross the border."[34] This is confirmed in Wayne Cornelius's survey of illegal immigrants from Oaxaca (Mexico). Cornelius found 80 percent paid a coyote to smuggle them across the border.[35]

"The coyote business had blossomed as the result of the U.S.'s very flawed immigration policies, Mexico's permanent state of economic crisis, and both countries' inability to reach any kind of immigration agreement," concludes Jorge Ramos. "If, instead of hunting down immigrants and penalizing illegal border crossings, both governments could find a way to regularize the entry of immigrants in an orderly fashion so that Mexico might provide the U.S. economy with the workers it needs, border deaths would become a thing of the past, and the countries would finally legalize something that occurs every single day, regardless of the law."[36]

ENFORCEMENT ALONE UNLIKELY TO BE EFFECTIVE IN REDUCING ILLEGAL IMMIGRATION

The evidence indicates that current policies are ineffective in addressing illegal immigration. In fact, current efforts seem to have produced the unintended consequence of swelling the illegal immigrant population. Making the United States more hazardous to enter means individuals who cross successfully stay in America rather than travel back and forth to Mexico or Central America. A great deal of circular migration that used to take place has simply stopped.

By one estimate, tougher enforcement has lengthened to nine years the average U.S. stay of a Mexican migrant; in the early 1980s, a typical Mexican migrant stayed three years.[37] Eighty-three percent of undocumented immigrants in the United States surveyed by the Mexican Migration Field Research Program said they did not return to their hometown for the annual fiesta; 61 percent had relatives who stayed in the United States due to tighter border enforcement.[38]

The number of authorized U.S. Border Patrol agents increased from 3,733 in 1990 to 14,923 by 2007. Meanwhile, the illegal immigrant population in the United States rose from 3.5 million to 11.8 million between 1990 and 2007, according to the Department of Homeland Security (see Figures 4.3 and 4.4).[39] Border Patrol levels today are far higher than at the height of the Bracero program, yet unable to reduce illegal immigration.

Two other issues related to border enforcement are important. First, even if an illegal immigrant is apprehended, it does not mean he or she will not try again. In general, after being apprehended by the Border Patrol, migrants are processed and returned to Mexico. Forty-four percent of undocumented migrants from the state of Oaxaca said they were apprehended on their most recent trip to the border. However, 97 percent of the migrants reported being eventually able to enter the United States successfully a relatively short time after being apprehended.[40] Second, rather than trekking across the border, entering illegally through a legal port of entry, such as by hiding in a vehicle, is a viable option for many illegal immigrants. Approximately 17 percent of illegal immigrants from Oaxaca had entered through a legal port of entry between 2005 and 2007.[41] This illustrates the difficulty of trying to control illegal immigration through enforcement alone.

Since 1986, it has been unlawful for U.S. employers to knowingly hire an individual unauthorized to work in the United States. There is no evidence this provision has made a significant impact on illegal immigration. Some argue that the "employer sanctions" provisions of the Immigration and Nationality Act have not been vigorously enforced. Others counter that employers are not document experts and can run afoul of civil rights laws if they too closely scrutinize the validity of documents presented to them.

One potential way around the false document and civil rights dilemmas, some argue, is to use an electronic verification system known as E-Verify. To join E-Verify, an employer must enter into a Memorandum of Understanding

FIGURE 4.3
Border Patrol Levels since 1990

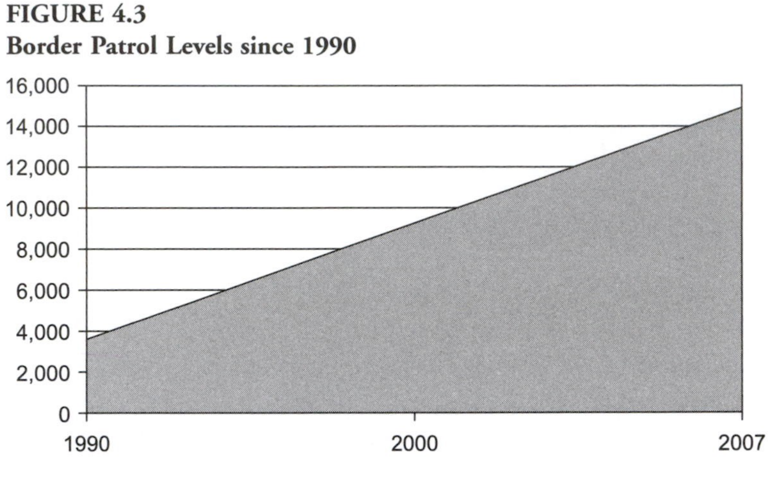

Source: U.S. Border Patrol.

FIGURE 4.4
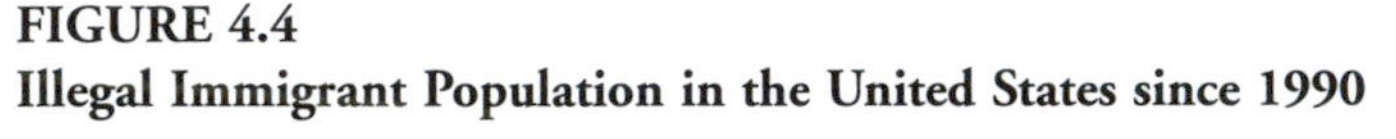
Illegal Immigrant Population in the United States since 1990

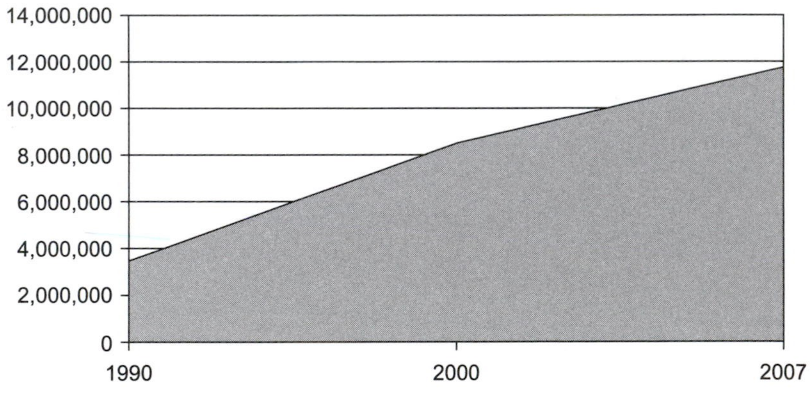

Source: Office of Immigration Statistics, Department of Homeland Security.

(MOU) with the federal government, specifically the Department of Homeland Security's (DHS) U.S. Citizenship and Immigration Services bureau and the Social Security Administration (SSA). An employer sends information on a new hire electronically to be checked against SSA and DHS databases. Efforts have increased at different levels of government to require employers to use E-Verify.[42]

There is considerable debate on several aspects of E-Verify. Currently, the system covers only a small percentage of employed individuals in the United

States. Could expansion to all or most employers occur without overwhelming the system, particularly when discrepancies in data must be checked in government files, including by hand? How large a problem are the errors in the data? Will many people be denied jobs from faulty data? Even though it is not allowed, will employers "pre-screen" applicants and thereby deny individuals the opportunity to correct possible errors in the databases that show them ineligible to work?

Leaving aside these issues, a more obvious problem with E-Verify calls into question how effective it will really be as a "magic bullet" to prevent the hiring of illegal immigrants. E-Verify cannot reliably catch identity fraud, meaning the system is unlikely to reduce illegal immigration significantly. In a 2005 report describing the Basic Pilot Program, the forerunner to E-Verify, the Government Accountability Office (GAO) stated: "the program cannot currently help employers detect identity fraud. . . . If an unauthorized worker presents valid documentation that belongs to another person authorized to work, the Basic Pilot Program may find the worker to be work-authorized. Similarly if an employee presents counterfeit documentation that contains valid information and appears authentic, the Basic Pilot Program may verify the employee as work-authorized."[43] Renaming the program E-Verify has not eliminated this problem.[44]

The bottom line is that it is difficult to argue that current enforcement measures, whether increasing the number of Border Patrol agents or expanding E-Verify, hold great prospects for success in reducing illegal immigration.

LEGALIZATION WILL NOT REDUCE ILLEGAL IMMIGRATION

Today, approximately 11 million illegal immigrants live in the United States. Whether or not to grant legal status to these individuals—or some portion of them—remains a focus of great debate. Advocates argue it is a matter of fairness, that such people have put down roots, raised U.S.-citizen children, and deserve a chance to become full members of American society. Critics say illegal immigrants have broken the law, that it's unfair to reward people here illegally, and that any "amnesty" will only encourage more people to come here without authorization.

Whatever one's opinion of legalization, even supporters cannot argue that providing legal status to those in the country illegally will reduce illegal immigration. There may be moral, economic, or security arguments in favor of legalization, but there is no logical argument that legalizing those here will discourage or prevent individuals in the future from coming here illegally, except perhaps for the spouses of current illegal immigrants. At best, legalization will have no impact on the future flow of illegal immigration. Critics argue, of course, providing legalization will lead more people to come to America illegally in the hopes of having their status also legalized at some point in the future.

The debate is over whether legalization is a good idea and if it would encourage more illegal immigration, not whether it would reduce illegal immigration. Examining the 1986 law, economists Pia M. Orrenius (Federal Reserve Bank of Dallas) and Madeline Zavodny (Federal Reserve Bank of Atlanta) wrote, "An amnesty program also does not appear to encourage illegal immigration in the long run in the hopes of another amnesty program; we do not find a significant difference between apprehensions after the [1986] IRCA amnesty expired and before the program was created." Even if critics concede that the study is correct, they might argue that the 1986 law failed to reduce or halt illegal immigration. In fact, the study concludes: "IRCA does not appear to have discouraged illegal immigration in the long run."[45] While legalization may be necessary as part of a broader compromise on immigration reform legislation, in itself it would not result in less illegal immigration in the future.

PROPOSAL TO IMPROVE U.S. BORDER SECURITY, REDUCE ILLEGAL IMMIGRATION, AND PREVENT MIGRANT DEATHS

If neither legalizing those in the United States illegally nor increasing immigration enforcement will limit migrant deaths or reduce illegal immigration, then another approach is needed. Without an alternative, Congress will remain deadlocked or, even worse, pass a bill that fails to address the core problem that drives illegal immigration—the lack of legal avenues for lesser-skilled individuals from Mexico and Central America to work in the United States. The only way that issue can be addressed is through increased use of temporary visas. To succeed, new temporary work visas must: (1) be sufficiently free of bureaucracy to be usable by employers and employees, (2) address concerns about possible exploitation, and (3) be of sufficient number to reduce illegal immigration.

The best approach is to combine fully portable work permits—not tied to a specific employer—with bilateral administrative agreements between the United States and countries that send illegal immigrants to America. This would provide labor market freedom and, therefore, protection for new workers; at the same time, it would elicit cooperation on immigration enforcement from Mexico and (eventually) other key countries.

This approach is designed to address the "future flow" of workers, reduce illegal immigration, and establish a reliable framework for improved border security and immigration enforcement. The proposal is not contingent on enacting specific enforcement measures or legalizing the status of those now in the Untied States illegally. However, as a practical matter, it is likely the proposal discussed here would only become law as part of a broader political compromise that included both some form of legalization and new enforcement measures. This proposal obviates the need for a "commission" to regulate the future flow of high- and low-skilled workers, particularly since such a commission has generally been proposed to prevent, not facilitate, employer-sponsored immigration and would thereby result in increasing both illegal immigration and deaths at the border.[46]

Often the best ideas are the least complicated. The proposal could be written to fill less than a page of the Immigration and Nationality Act. The core legislative language for such a proposal could be as follows:

Section 401

(a) In the case of an alien who is a national of a foreign state designated under subsection (b), the Secretary of Homeland Security shall authorize the alien to engage in employment in the United States and provide the alien with an 'employment authorized' endorsement or other appropriate work permit. The work permits shall have a term lasting 5 years. The alien must leave the United States after the 5-year period for a period of one year unless sponsored for an employment-based immigrant visa under section 203. An alien described here cannot remain in the United States for more than 60 days without lawful employment. Failure to leave the United States upon the completion of the 5-year period, unless otherwise eligible to remain in the United States, shall make the alien ineligible for additional work authorization under this section for a period of 6 years.

(b) Nationals of a foreign state shall only be eligible for work authorization described in (a) if the country has concluded an administrative bilateral agreement with the United States that establishes:

    (1) specific commitments to the satisfaction of the Secretary of Homeland Security and Secretary of State to assist the United States in controlling illegal immigration from that foreign state;
    (2) the annual level of work permits issued.

(c) Committee on the Judiciary of the House of Representatives and of the Senate shall be informed upon the completion of such agreements described in (b). Reports shall be issued every 6 months as to the status of these negotiations.

(d) The annual levels should be set in a manner and at a level that will replace the current illegal flow of workers from a foreign state with a legal flow.

(e) Foreign states that are the largest sources of illegal immigration to the United States should be the initial focus of these administrative agreements.

(f) A binational body should be established between the United States and each foreign state to monitor the compliance of each nation with the agreements.

(g) A nongovernmental body should be chartered to serve as an employment clearinghouse for employers in the United States and aliens described in (a). Fees assessed to aliens shall fund the nongovernmental body.

The fully portable work permits described herein would be almost identical to currently issued Employment Authorization Documents (EADs). Generally speaking, once an individual receives an Employment Authorization Document, he or she can work for any employer in the United States, enjoying the same freedom of movement in the labor market as a U.S. citizen or lawful permanent resident (green card holder). If the person is unhappy with one employer, then he or she can work for another establishment. In other words, the individual enjoys complete labor mobility.[47]

This freedom of movement directly addresses the concerns raised about temporary workers potentially being exploited by, it is alleged, being "tied" to a single employer. The best labor protection enjoyed by all Americans is the ability to leave a bad employer and work somewhere else. Good employers would have no problem with the portability aspect of these work permits since reputable employers maintain a good workforce by treating employees fairly, not by hoping to exploit people. Another advantage to this approach is procedures on temporary workers sometimes become so cumbersome that employers and employees do not avail themselves of the visas, leading to the hiring of illegal immigrants. Two examples of this happening occurred in agriculture with H-2A visas and at the tail end of the Bracero program.

The work permits would allow for health and security screening, as well as biometric documentation. Additional details can be expected to be included as part of the bilateral agreements between the United States and Mexico (and later other countries). As noted, the proposal is compatible with any other reforms Congress may choose to make on legalization or additional enforcement measures.

Some will oppose issuing these work permits because they do not want anyone coming into the country to work—legally or illegally. However, the work permits, particularly when combined with enforcement cooperation from Mexico, will be used to replace the workers who would have come in illegally. The work permits would not represent more workers but legal workers enjoying full labor market protections, rather than the flow of illegal immigrants we would continue to see without this new approach.

HOW TO DISTRIBUTE THE FULLY PORTABLE WORK PERMITS AND SET ANNUAL NUMBERS

Having established that fully portable work permits that function similar to Employment Authorization Documents would meet the primary objection raised by critics of temporary visas, the next issue is how to distribute these permits. The key is to replace the current illegal flow with a legal flow of workers. Policymakers should focus their initial attention on the countries from where most illegal immigrants come to the United States.

As noted in the sample legislative language, the best approach is for Congress to authorize the president to sign bilateral administrative agreements with Mexico, followed by El Salvador, Guatemala, Honduras, and potentially other countries, to distribute an agreed upon number of work permits annually in conjunction with additional commitments on immigration enforcement and security issues from these nations.

The work permits would help reduce illegal immigration and prevent migrant deaths, and also serve as valuable "carrots" to gain cooperation on immigration enforcement that otherwise would be politically impossible for leaders in other countries. Each year Mexico and Central American countries receive billions of dollars in remittances from their nationals working in the United States. Since these remittances represent an important source of dollars flowing into these economies, there would be a great incentive for these nations to cooperate on immigration enforcement in exchange for work permits. The agreements themselves could serve as important foreign policy tools for the president and would show the United States working in a cooperative manner on issues of importance to people in both countries.

Congress would authorize the Secretary of Homeland Security to provide work authorization (work permits) to foreign nationals of these nations within the limits agreed upon in bilateral negotiations. However, Congress would not vote on each bilateral agreement. Congress would always retain the right to revoke the authority of the Secretary of Homeland Security to issue the work authorization if it felt the authority was not being used appropriately or in the national interest.[48]

Mexico is by far the largest source country for illegal immigrants, according to the Department of Homeland Security. The estimated population of illegal immigrants from Mexico increased by an average of 220,000 per year in the United States between 2000 and 2009.[49] Overall, approximately 6.7 million of the estimated 10.8 million illegal immigrants in the United States in January 2009 were from Mexico.[50]

As of January 2009, the next largest sources of illegal immigrants to the United States were El Salvador, with 530,000 nationals residing illegally in the United States, and Guatemala, with 480,000. The average annual increase between 2000 and 2009 in the illegal immigrant population from El Salvador was 10,000, while from Guatemala it was 20,000, according to the Department of Homeland Security. For Honduras, the estimated illegal immigrant population in the United States rose from 160,000 in 2000 to 320,000 in 2009, an average of 20,000 a year (see Table 4.2).[51]

TABLE 4.2
Illegal Immigrant Population in the U.S. and Annual Average Increase, 2000–2009

Country of Birth	Estimated Population in January 2009	Average Annual Change (2000–2009)
Mexico	6,650,000	220,000
El Salvador	530,000	10,000
Guatemala	480,000	20,000
Honduras	320,000	20,000
Philippines	270,000	10,000
India	200,000	10,000
Korea	200,000	———
Ecuador	170,000	10,000
Brazil	150,000	10,000
China	120,000	10,000
Other Countries	1,650,000	40,000
All Countries	**10,750,000**	**250,000**

Source: Office of Immigration Statistics, Department of Homeland Security.

At minimum, the annual number and process for work permits should be set to correspond with the yearly gross illegal flow in recent years, but such details can be established during the course of bilateral discussions. As noted earlier, between 2000 and 2009, the number of illegal immigrants from Mexico increases, on average, by 220,000 a year. However, that number includes a drop in illegal immigration due primarily to the recent economic slowdown in the United States, since the average net number of new illegal immigrants from Mexico between 2000 and 2008 was 290,000.[52] These are net numbers in the increase of the illegal population, meaning the gross number of new Mexican illegal immigrants each year was higher. The best course would be for Congress to set the goal that the number of work permits should be established in a manner to reduce the illegal flow of workers and replace it with a legal flow. This way the United States can take into account the degree of cooperation with Mexico on immigration enforcement in establishing the annual number. In theory, the number could be adjusted over time.

MEXICO WOULD NEED TO SHARE RESPONSIBILITY FOR ILLEGAL IMMIGRATION TO THE UNITED STATES

Few Americans realize that Mexican immigration law requires its citizens to exit the country only through proper exits and with proper official documents. The relative lack of legal avenues to work in America has made it politically impossible for Mexican elected officials to enforce these provisions. The bilateral agreement with the United States as described here would fundamentally change the situation. It would put the two countries in a partnership on immigration and border security and provide tangible reasons for Mexico to enforce its own laws, which would help America control the border.

Chapter II of the General Law of Population (*Ley General de Poblacion*) of Mexico refers to migration. The relevant sections of Articles 11 and 13 establish: "The international transit of people through maritime ports, airports and borders, may only be done through the places designated for this purpose and within the established hours with the intervention of migratory authorities. . . . To enter and exit the country, nationals and foreigners must fulfill the requirements established by this law, its regulations and other applicable legislation."

Furthermore, Chapter IV of the law refers to emigration, and the relevant sections of Article 78 establish:

> People, who intend to emigrate from the country, are obligated to satisfy, among other general immigration requirements, the following:
>
> Section I. Present an ID. . . .
> Section II. Be of legal age. . . .
> Section III. Evidence, if they are Mexican, that they can fulfill the requirements to enter the country they are heading to in accordance with the immigration status they intend to hold.
> Section IV. Request from the corresponding office the necessary documents and present them to the immigration authorities at the port of exit. . . .[53]

Today, no Mexican elected official would advocate using resources to prevent Mexicans from leaving to please a U.S. congressman or president. However, in exchange for bilateral cooperation that included work permits for Mexican nationals, that would be a different story.

In his recollections on his service as Mexican foreign minister under Vicente Fox, Jorge Castañeda explained that Mexico was willing to go quite far in cooperating with U.S. immigration officials if negotiations with the Bush Administration had resulted in allowing a sufficient number of Mexicans to work legally in the United States. Without such an agreement it would be politically impossible for Mexican elected officials to empower their police authorities to limit Mexican border crossings to please U.S. officials or members of Congress.

Castañeda points out that even the Mexican opposition failed to see the commitment the Mexican government under Fox had tacitly undertaken to prevent illegal migration from Mexico in exchange for a serious, well-designed program for temporary workers. Castañeda writes,

> It was the most important concession Fox was to make to the United States during his presidency, and it will probably stand, if only because it is an absolute precondition for any immigration agreement between the two countries or for Mexican cooperation with the United States on immigration reform enacted by the U.S. Congress. Had the Mexican opposition understood at the time what Fox was promising, it would have raised hell; this had been an absolute taboo in Mexico for decades. By the time it figured it out in 2005, the commitment and its enormous significance had been assimilated at least by part of that opposition.[54]

After the September 11, 2001, terrorist attacks, bilateral talks between Mexico and the United States slowed down and eventually ended without substantial progress. Today, using the connection between work permits and a bilateral agreement on immigration enforcement issues with Mexico can result in a pact based on mutual respect, and one that can save the lives of Mexican migrants and reduce illegal immigration.

Jorge Castañeda argues that a bilateral agreement with Mexico that includes temporary visas would force the Mexican government to make difficult choices and enforce policies some might find unpopular. "For my country, such an understanding and accord requires a series of steps that until now Mexico had been unwilling to take," writes Castañeda. "The first one is to apply the law: no one should be allowed out of the country if the proper and respective procedures in the standing legislation are not complied with. If this means stopping people from leaving across the desert, so be it."[55] He points out the Fox Administration ordered patrols in the summer 2001 to impede people seeking to cross the Sonoran Desert and it helped save lives.[56]

Castañeda believes the Mexican government could provide "rewards for staying and penalties for leaving" in sending communities if people do not use the legal work permits or visas allocated as part of a bilateral agreement.[57] In addition, Mexico would secure its own southern border. "It is not simply an immigration question," notes Castañeda. "Mexico's frontier with Guatemala is mostly a nonpatrolled river, a theoretical line in the jungle, and a passageway for absolutely everything—contraband, drugs, gangs, migrants, arms, precursor chemicals—in both directions."[58]

OTHER ISSUES AND QUESTIONS ABOUT THE WORK PERMITS

While a work permit allows an individual to be employed lawfully, it does not guarantee anyone a job. Just like anyone else who possesses an Employment Authorization Document, the individual still must find an employer willing to hire the worker. The length of the work permit would be five years. It would allow an individual to travel back and forth to his or her home country. A provision can be included to require an individual who is without employment for 60 days to leave the country. Work permit holders would not be eligible for any type of welfare benefits while in the United States.

Potential work permit holders could be screened for skills likely to result in success in the U.S. labor market. Mexico has an interest in those who are most employable receiving the permits, since those individuals would be the most likely to send remittances back to the country. If the demand for the work permits exceeds the supply negotiated by the United States and Mexico, then it may be wise to issue permits on a quarterly basis. This may further temper interest in crossing illegally, since even individuals who do not receive a work permit at first know they could receive one at a later date. Increasing the number of permits can be subject to negotiation between the two countries.

What about the role of employers? There is no need for employers to file petitions for the workers, such as with other temporary visas, since an individual with a work permit can work for any employer. However, the bilateral agreement can stipulate that a system will be set up to make new holders of work permits aware of jobs in the United States. This might best be handled by a nongovernmental, nonprofit entity that would work as a clearinghouse. However, it is possible for-profit companies on either side of the border might see a role as a facilitator of worker-employer relationships.

Other issues worth clarifying: The work permits would have no connection to the North American Free Trade Agreement (NAFTA). If an individual violates the terms of his or her work permit such as by overstaying illegally, he or she could be made ineligible for future legal work permits for a period of time. The vast majority of illegal migrants do not bring family members when they cross the border illegally. Given the work permits will allow for circularity, it does not seem necessary to include family members as part of the permits.

Will individuals who receive these work permits leave upon the expiration of the term? There is no evidence that workers in current temporary visa categories, such as H-1B, H-2A, or H-2B, overstay their visas in large numbers. One reason is they wish to avail themselves in the future of those visas, enjoying the security of the safe entrance into the United States afforded by legal visas. Another reason, in the case of H-1B visas for high-skilled workers, is that individuals who wish to stay for a longer term can be sponsored for green cards (permanent residence). Individuals on H-1B visas are allowed to stay and work in the United States while they await processing for their green cards.

Currently only 5,000 green cards are allocated each year for lesser-skilled workers (10,000 after the end of a visa set-aside for certain Central Americans). If Congress is concerned about visa overstays, then clearing the existing green card backlog for the "Other Workers" category and raising that annual quota to 75,000 or higher would address the issue, since it would provide a legal avenue for employers to retain lesser-skilled workers long term. In the unlikely event as many as 6 percent of those work permit holders "overstayed" their allotted time, we would be looking at perhaps 20,000 or so individuals added to an illegal immigrant population that grew by an average of 390,000 a year from 2000 to 2008, according to the Department of Homeland Security.[59] There is no evidence that individuals who would avail themselves of the legal avenues these work permits provide would be likely to overstay the terms of the permit in significant numbers.

POLICY RECOMMENDATIONS

While in recent years poor economic conditions in the United States have reduced illegal entry to the United States, as measured by apprehensions at the border, it is unwise to assume this decrease will be a permanent phenomenon.[60] Despite the increased use of electronic verification and raids on businesses, "there is no evidence of an increase between March 2008 and March 2009 in the number of Mexicans returning home from the U.S., according to an analysis by the Pew Hispanic Center."[61] The Department of Homeland Security estimates the illegal immigrant population in the United States did fall from 11.6 million in January 2008 to 10.8 million in January 2009.[62] Improved economic conditions could reverse this trend in the future.

Strong evidence exists that the current "enforcement-only" policy has strengthened criminal gangs, providing a profitable line of business for Mexican criminal enterprises. In Phoenix, Arizona, a large proportion of kidnapping cases involve illegal immigrants smuggled into the country and then held for ransom, usually by the smuggler. Years ago, coyotes were small operators often smuggling the same illegal immigrants into the United States from one year to the next. That is no longer the case.

"Now, organized gangs own the people-smuggling trade," writes Joel Millman in a report for the *Wall Street Journal*. "According to U.S. and Mexican police, this is partly an unintended consequence of a border crackdown. Making crossings more difficult drove up their cost, attracting brutal Mexican crime rings that forced the small operators out of business."[63] Illegal immigrants have been held for weeks and beaten until a relative can pay ransom beyond the cost of any smuggling fees paid before crossing the border. "[A]s border crossings decline, gangs earn less money directly from smuggling fees than from holding some of their clients for ransom, before delivering them to their destination farther inside the U.S," writes Millman.[64]

If Congress adopted some key reforms, this problem and others would largely disappear.

First, Congress should provide fully portable work permits as part of bilateral agreements with Mexico and Central American countries. This would cut smugglers and criminal gangs out of the equation, effectively removing them from the business. If Mexican and Central American workers can come to America on a legal visa, they would have no need to employ the services of a coyote or criminal enterprise.

Second, H-2B visas, for nonagricultural, seasonal workers, should be increased. The visas in this category have been exhausted consistently during or at the start of previous fiscal years. Given the seasonal nature of the jobs, they are often difficult to fill. Blocking an increase in these visas or imposing onerous terms for compliance will not help American workers but rather harm U.S. employers and their American workers who need the additional labor to keep the businesses viable.[65]

Third, Congress should pass the AgJobs Act, which would combine reform of H-2A visas for agricultural workers with a transition of currently illegal workers into the mainstream economy. The legislation has enjoyed support from both growers and unions.

Fourth, Congress should increase the allotment of green cards (for permanent residence) for low-skilled workers well above the current level of 5,000 a year. There is no compelling reason our immigration system offers the opportunity for individuals in finance, technology, and other fields to be sponsored for permanent residence but not those in fields such as hospitality, landscaping, agriculture, and food production.

The higher relative wages offered in the United States are a primary factor in encouraging illegal immigration, leading one to conclude that greater enforcement alone is unlikely to prevent illegal immigration. Research by Gordon Hanson (University of Michigan) and Antonio Spilimbergo (International Monetary Fund) found the U.S.-Mexico wage gap is a key factor for illegal immigrants. "A reduction in the Mexican real wage or an increase in U.S. real wages leads to an increase in apprehensions in the current month. This suggests that U.S. and Mexican labor markets are tightly linked," according to Hanson and Spilimbergo.[66]

Even though it is clear the U.S. and Mexican economies are linked, current U.S. immigration policies act as if these connections can be severed simply by passing new laws or adding more personnel at the border. The United States can continue to pretend new laws in Congress can overturn the law of supply and demand, but the record of the past 50 years shows that would be a mistake.

NOTES

1. Jason L. Riley, *Let Them In* (New York: Gotham Books, 2008).

2. E. P. Hutchinson, *Legislative History of American Immigration Policy, 1798–1965* (Philadelphia: University of Pennsylvania Press, 1981), 194.

3. Ibid., 207.

4. Border Patrol History on www.CBP.gov.

5. Ibid.

6. Ibid.

7. Congressional Research Service (February 1980), "The Bracero program falls into three distinct phases: The wartime period, which extended 2 years beyond the end of World War II, until the expiration of the special authorizing legislation in 1947; the post-war transition period from 1948 until the enactment of new authorizing legislation, Public Law 78, in 1951; and the Public Law 78 period, during which the program expanded until 1960, followed by a phase-down until its termination at the end of 1964," explains the Congressional Research Service, 15.

8. *1959 INS Yearbook* and as cited in Kitty Calavita, *Inside the State* (New York: Routledge, 1992).

9. Congressional Research Service, *Temporary Worker Programs: Background and Issues*. A report prepared at the request of Senator Edward M. Kennedy, Chairman on the Judiciary, United States Senate, for the use of the Select Commission on Immigration and Refugee Policy, February 1980, 41.

10. Visa Bulletin, November 2009, U.S. Department of State: "Section 203(e) of the NACARA, as amended by Section 1(e) of Pub. L. 105-139, provides that once the Employment Third Preference Other Worker (EW) cutoff date has reached the priority date of the latest EW petition approved prior to November 19, 1997, the 10,000 EW numbers available for a fiscal year are to be reduced by up to 5,000 annually beginning in the following fiscal year. This reduction is to be made for as long as necessary to offset adjustments under the NACARA program."

11. Congressional Research Service (1980), 41.

12. The reaction of California growers, according to the head of the California Farm Placement Service, was as follows: "Employers using legally contracted Mexicans welcomed 'Operation Wetback.' It relieved them from the unfairness they had felt in adhering to the wage, housing, and other regulations governing the legal use of Mexicans, while their neighbors using wet backs [sic] were not subject to such regulations." Edward F. Hayes, Richard H. Salter, Roy Plumlee, Robert B. Lindsey, "Operation 'Wetback'—Impact on the Border States," *Employment Security Review* 22 (March 1955), 16–21, as cited in Calavita, 60.

13. *1959 INS Statistical Yearbook;* U.S. Border Patrol.

14. Congressional Research Service (1980), 36. "Despite their limitations, then, as now, INS apprehension figures are the best available indication of the degree of illegal immigration," notes the Congressional Research Service. In general, the fewer the apprehensions, the lower the flow of illegal immigration. Law enforcement, market conditions, and the availability of means of legal entry all

affect the illegal flow. Fewer apprehensions from one year to the next mean that more individuals are being deterred from entering the United States illegally. The more apprehensions, the greater the flow of illegal immigration.

15. Calavita, 218. It appears a good portion of those who received permanent visas were petitioned for by their agricultural employers, an action that was later limited by the federal government.

16. Monthly Sector Activity Reports (MSAR), El Centro, California, February 1958, Accession 63A1359, Box 3, as cited in Calavita, 83.

17. MSAR Brownsville, Texas, April 1958, Accession 63A1359, Box 4, as cited in Calavita, 84.

18. U.S. Congress, House Committee on Agriculture, Subcommittee on Equipment, Supplies, and Manpower, 1958, 450, cited in Calavita, 85.

19. INS, Calavita. In 1960, under pressure from labor unions and some members of Congress, the U.S. Department of Labor ended the "Special Program" that allowed through a streamlined process for growers to designate specific workers with whom they wished to contract. The Department of Labor's action soon led to a decline in Bracero admissions (a drop of 51 percent) and a predictable increase in illegal entry—a rise of 46 percent in apprehensions for 1961–1964 compared to 1956–1959. Annual INS apprehensions averaged 89,223 between 1961 and 1964, an increase of 46 percent over the 1956–1959 average of 61,106. Annual Bracero admissions averaged 212,750 for 1961–1964, a drop of 51 percent from the 1956–1959 average of 437,937.

20. Unpublished INS report, October 21, 1971, CO 214h, as cited in Calavita, 151.

21. U.S. Department of Justice, *Annual Report of the Immigration and Naturalization Service*, 1970, 1, as cited in Congressional Research Service (1980), 57. "Since the expiration of the Mexican Agriculture Act on December 31, 1964, the number of deportable aliens located has continued on an upward climb. For the 6-year period, FY 1965 through FY 1970, 71 percent of the 1,251,466 total deportable aliens located were of Mexican nationality. Year by year, the annual percentage of this nationality group has risen, from 50 percent in 1965 to 80 percent this year."

22. Congressional Research Service (1980), 41–42.

23. Some have argued the Bracero program established networks that helped lead to illegal immigration after the program ended. However, this notion rests on two questionable premises: 1. That no one from Mexico came into the United States to work prior to the Bracero program (in fact, many thousands did so, including to work on the railroads), and 2. Despite the enormous wage differential between the two countries, people from Mexico would not have thought of coming to work in America without the establishment of the Bracero program. Neither proposition withstands scrutiny. It was after the program ended and no alternative means to work legally was available that illegal immigration increased dramatically. Even a critic of the Bracero program, Cornell University professor Vernon Briggs, who argues that Bracero admissions later encouraged illegal migration, noted, "By the same token, however, it is simplistic to conclude that the

problem would not eventually have surfaced in the absence of the Bracero program" (Congressional Research Service (1980), 58). The evidence indicates that a reasonable enforcement deterrent at the border is necessary to enable a temporary worker program to reduce illegal immigration. One reason relatively few Mexicans initially used the Bracero program is that "the INS . . . legalized on-the-spot illegal Mexican immigrants found employed in agriculture and contracted them to their employers as braceros. During the summer of 1947 the service legalized 55,000 undocumented workers in Texas alone" (Calavita, 24).

24. U.S. Border Patrol.

25. Wayne Cornelius, "Death at the Border: The Efficacy and Unintended Consequences of U.S. Immigration Control Policy 1993–2000," *Population and Development Review* 27, no. 4 (December 2001).

26. Wayne Cornelius, *Controlling Unauthorized Immigration from Mexico: The Failure of Prevention through Deterrence and the Need for Comprehensive Reform* (San Diego: Center for Comparative Immigration Studies, University of California–San Diego, 2008), 9.

27. Ibid., 13.

28. Ibid., 10.

29. Luis Alberto Urrea, *The Devil's Highway* (New York: Little, Brown, 2005), 190.

30. Ibid., 127–129.

31. Ibid., 144–145, 174.

32. Jorge Ramos, *Dying to Cross* (New York: HarperCollins, 2005), xi.

33. Ibid., 84.

34. Ibid., 148–149.

35. Cornelius, *Controlling Unauthorized Immigration from Mexico*, 27.

36. Ramos, 149–150.

37. Eduardo Porter, "Tighter Border Yields Odd Result: More Illegals Stay," *Wall Street Journal*, October 10, 2003, 1. "Not only have U.S. policies failed to reduce the inflow of people from Mexico, they have perversely reduced the outflow to produce an unprecedented increase in the undocumented population of the United States," writes Douglas Massey. "America's unilateral effort to prevent a decades-old flow from continuing has paradoxically transformed a circular flow of Mexican workers into a settled population of families and dependents." Douglas Massey, *Backfire at the Border: Why Enforcement Without Legalization Cannot Stop Illegal Immigration*, Trade Briefing Paper No. 29 (Washington, DC: Cato Institute, Center for Trade Policy Studies, June 13, 2005), 8.

38. Cornelius, *Controlling Unauthorized Immigration from Mexico*, 34.

39. Michael Hoefer, Nancy Rytina, and Bryan C. Baker, *Estimates of the Unauthorized Immigrant Population Residing in the United States: January 2007* (Washington, DC: Office of Immigration Statistics, Department of Homeland Security, 2008), 4.

40. Cornelius, *Controlling Unauthorized Immigration from Mexico*, 22.

41. Ibid., 17.

42. The MOU for E-Verify can be found at: http://www.uscis.gov/files/nativedocuments/MOU.pdf.

43. GAO-05-813, 22–23.

44. Even though Swift & Co. was enrolled in the Basic Pilot Program it was raided as part of an identity fraud action against individual employees, which the company estimated cost it $30 to $50 million due to lost operating efficiency and the need to find new (untrained) workers. Swift was later sold to a company in Brazil. "Meatpacker Swift Sold to Brazilian Company," The DenverChannel.com, May 29, 2007. "Swift, which is privately held with publicly issued debt, initially estimated the financial impact of the raids at $30 million but has raised that estimate to as much as $50 million because it took longer than expected to return the beef plants to full production, which caused higher costs and led to lost business opportunities," reported the ABC News 7 (The DenverChannel.com).

45. Pia M. Orrenius and Madeline Zavodny, *Do Amnesty Programs Encourage Illegal Immigration? Evidence from the Immigration Reform and Control Act (IRCA)*, Federal Reserve Bank of Atlanta, Working Paper 2001-19, November 2001, 14–15.

46. See *A Commission to Regulate Immigration? A Bad Idea Whose Time Should Not Come* (Arlington, VA: National Foundation for American Policy, May 2009) at: www.nfap.com.

47. One analogy that can be used is to the work authorization granted under Temporary Protected Status (TPS). Under TPS, Congress has authorized work authorization under that status but it is the Secretary of Homeland Security that grants the work authorization to nationals of designated countries. For our purposes, the relevant aspect of TPS is it grants individuals an Employment Authorization Document that ensures labor mobility. Many human rights groups lobby for aliens in the United States to receive TPS, so clearly it is considered a good status for workers. Unlike TPS, which is for individuals inside the United States, this proposal is only for temporary workers outside the country.

48. Similarly, Congress has granted the Secretary of Homeland Security the authority to designate countries for Temporary Protected Status and issue work authorization and could change or eliminate that authority at any time. However, TPS is only for individuals inside the United States, and the bilateral agreements would only address those outside the country who wish to come in and work legally.

49. Michael Hoefer, Nancy Rytina, and Bryan C. Baker, *Estimates of the Unauthorized Immigrant Population Residing in the United States: January 2009* (Washington, DC: Office of Immigration Statistics, Department of Homeland Security, 2010), 4.

50. Ibid.

51. Ibid.

52. Michael Hoefer, Nancy Rytina, and Bryan C. Baker, *Estimates of the Unauthorized Immigrant Population Residing in the United States: January 2008* (Washington, DC: Office of Immigration Statistics, Department of Homeland Security, 2009), 4.

53. Thank you to Adriana Varela with Berry Appleman & Leiden LLP for assistance in translating the law. Also, thanks to Mexican attorney Enrique Arellano for providing a copy of the relevant sections of Mexican law.

54. Jorge Castañeda, *Ex Mex, From Migrants to Immigrants* (New York: New Press, 2007), 90.

55. Ibid., 177.

56. Ibid., 177.

57. Ibid., 177.

58. Ibid., 179.

59. Hoefer, Rytina, and Baker (2009), 4.

60. Miriam Jordan, "Illegal Immigration from Mexico Hits Lowest Level in Decade," *Wall Street Journal*, July 23, 2009.

61. Ibid.

62. Michael Hoefer, Nancy Rytina, and Bryan C. Baker (2010), 1.

63. Joel Millman, "Immigrants Become Hostages as Gangs Prey on Mexicans," *Wall Street Journal*, June 10, 2009.

64. Ibid.

65. See for example NewsChannel 8, "Maryland Crab Picker Job Fair Falls Flat: Companies Turn to Congress for Help," April 16, 2009.

66. Gordon Hanson and Antonio Spilimbergo, "Illegal Immigration, Border Enforcement, and Relative Wages: Evidence from Apprehensions at the U.S.-Mexico Border," *American Economic Review* (December 1999), 1355.

SUGGESTED READINGS

Anderson, Stuart. *The Impact of Agricultural Guest Worker Programs on Illegal Immigration*. Arlington, VA: National Foundation for American Policy, 2003.

Castañeda, Jorge. *Ex Mex: From Migrants to Immigrants.* New York: New Press, 2007.

A Commission to Regulate Immigration? A Bad Idea Whose Time Should Not Come. Arlington, VA: National Foundation for American Policy, 2009. Available at: www.nfap.com.

Cornelius, Wayne. *Controlling Unauthorized Immigration from Mexico: The Failure of Prevention through Deterrence and the Need for Comprehensive Reform.* San Diego: Center for Comparative Immigration Studies, University of California–San Diego, 2008.

Hoefer, Michael, Nancy Rytina, and Bryan C. Baker. *Estimates of the Unauthorized Immigrant Population Residing in the United States: January 2009.* Washington, DC: Office of Immigration Statistics, Department of Homeland Security, 2010.

Massey, Douglas. *Backfire at the Border: Why Enforcement without Legalization Cannot Stop Illegal Immigration.* Trade Briefing Paper No. 29. Washington, DC: Center for Trade Policy Studies, Cato Institute, 2005.

Ramos, Jorge. *Dying to Cross.* New York: HarperCollins, 2005.

Riley, Jason L. *Let Them In.* New York: Gotham Books, 2008.

Urrea, Luis Alberto. *The Devil's Highway.* New York: Little, Brown, 2005.

Five

High-Skilled Immigration and American Competitiveness

Access to high-skilled immigrants is important to the competitiveness of U.S. companies in global markets. Unfortunately, many members of Congress do not realize this—and they are the ones with the power to make the law.

The current shortcomings in the system for hiring highly educated foreign nationals inhibit or prevent talented individuals from working in the United States long term. This encourages both American businesses and foreign multinational companies to hire individuals in locations outside the United States. Unlike many other policy issues, the problems plaguing high-skill immigration can be mostly solved with a few artful strokes of the legislative pen. The solutions are straightforward: raise the quotas, streamline the process, and focus enforcement on real problems.

Moving more resources outside the United States if Congress fails to liberalize rules on high-skill immigration is not an idle threat. There are more than 23,000 affiliates of 2,500 U.S. companies already in operation abroad.[1] Expanding existing facilities or building new ones is easy to imagine, even if that is not the first choice of employers. Microsoft, for example, opened a facility in Canada at least in part due to U.S. immigration restrictions. In contrast to U.S. policies, Canadian officials have actively sought to encourage foreign nationals educated in the United States to work in Canada. *Maclean's* magazine described it as "stealing from Uncle Sam," after the publication obtained a document from the Canadian consulate in Los Angeles that read, in part, "Significant numbers of high quality economic class immigrants are being gleaned from this territory . . . this office regularly engages in promotion and recruitment efforts to exploit this talent."[2]

Even smaller companies are more a part of the global economy than ever before. Today, it is possible to post on one of several Web sites the specifications for a technology project and allow bids to come in from all over the world.[3] In many cases, the geographic location in which the work is performed is not a factor.

Policy toward employment-based immigration is often mired in accusations that companies ignore U.S. citizens in the recruitment process, even though in nearly all businesses in the United States the vast majority of employees are Americans. In reality, the issue is not companies hiring foreign nationals instead of Americans. The issue is that when companies recruit on college campuses, they find a high proportion of students in important disciplines are foreign nationals.

In 2007, U.S. universities awarded about half of master's degrees and 73 percent of PhDs in electrical engineering to foreign nationals, according to the National Science Foundation.[4] Patents produced by foreign nationals are indicators that international students completing their studies not only make up a large proportion of new potential entrants to the labor market but also end up producing important innovations.

As Tables 5.1 and 5.2 show, a substantial percentage of fulltime graduate students at U.S. universities in important fields are foreign nationals on student visas. Such visas do not allow an individual to stay and work in the United States long term. To work for years in the United States, an international student generally would need an H-1B visa.

In computer sciences, statistics and economics, international students made up 58 to 60 percent of the fulltime graduate students on U.S. campuses in 2006.[5] The proportion of international students in graduate programs in mathematics (39 percent), chemistry (41 percent), and physics

TABLE 5.1
What Employers Find on U.S. Campuses: Percentage of Foreign Nationals in U.S. Graduate School Programs in Selected Fields, 2006

Field	Percent of Fulltime Graduate Students with Foreign Student Visas	Total Fulltime Graduate Students with Foreign Student Visas
Statistics	60.8%	1,960
Economics (except agricultural)	59.6%	5,966
Computer Sciences	58.4%	16,801
Cardiology	50.0%	16
Physics	45.9%	5,707
Chemistry	40.7%	7,712
Mathematics/Applied Mathematics	39.4%	4,862
Pharmaceutical Sciences	36.8%	1,650
Radiology	31.5%	58

Source: National Science Foundation/Division of Science Resources Statistics, *Survey of Graduate Students and Postdoctorates in Science and Engineering*. Tables 18 and 21 of Graduate Students and Postdoctorates in Science and Engineering: Fall 2006.

TABLE 5.2
Percentage of Foreign Nationals in U.S. Engineering Programs, 2006

Field	Percent Fulltime Graduate Students with Foreign Student Visas	Fulltime Graduate Students with Foreign Student Visas
Petroleum Engineering	83.9%	543
Electrical Engineering	68.2%	18,683
Mining Engineering	56.9%	103
Agricultural Engineering	56.6%	505
Industrial Engineering	56.5%	3,625
Mechanical Engineering	52.4%	6,640
Chemical Engineering	52.1%	3,241
Metall./Matl. Engineering	51.7%	2,390
Engineering Science	48.0%	795
Engineering (other)	44.6%	1,830
Civil Engineering	42.5%	5,554
Aerospace Engineering	39.3%	1,327
Biomedical Engineering	34.4%	1,948
Nuclear Engineering	33.0%	300
ENGINEERING (TOTAL)	**54.1%**	**47,484**

Source: National Science Foundation/Division of Science Resources Statistics, *Survey of Graduate Students and Postdoctorates in Science and Engineering*. Tables 18 and 21 of Graduate Students and Postdoctorates in Science and Engineering: Fall 2006.

(46 percent) is also significant. In graduate level engineering programs in the United States, 47,484 of the 87,818 full-time students (54 percent) were in the United States on temporary student visas in 2006.[6] As discussed in Chapter 9, there is little evidence that international students "crowd out" Americans. Rather, a case can be made that their presence on U.S. campuses helps keep many graduate-level science and engineering programs in operation by providing universities with a sufficient base of students.

When an employer recruits at a U.S. college and finds an outstanding international student, a company can file for him or her to be on OPT (Optional Practical Training) for 12 months, with the possibility of an extension for an additional 17 months.[7] At some point in that process, the individual could be hired on an H-1B visa, if one is available.[8] If the individual was educated outside the country or OPT is not appropriate or the best option for that person, the employer would generally attempt to hire them directly in H-1B status.[9]

THE DIVISION BETWEEN TEMPORARY STATUS AND PERMANENT RESIDENCE

The visas that allow highly educated foreign-born individuals to work in the United States can be divided into two categories—temporary and permanent. Green card holders can stay here permanently (unless they commit a crime or an offense subjecting them to deportation).[10] Given a choice, workers seeking to stay more than a year in the Untied States would prefer permanent residence (a green card). Due to low quotas for employment-based green cards, that choice is not always available to the worker or the employer. Temporary visas, such as H-1B or L-1, allow individuals to stay in the United States only so long as they maintain their immigration status. That includes staying employed at a sponsoring (or "petitioning") employer. If the employer goes out of business, the temporary visa holder generally needs to quickly find a new employer or leave the country to avoid being present unlawfully.

TEMPORARY VISAS: THE RECENT HISTORY

H-1Bs visas are central to retaining skilled talent in America; otherwise skilled foreign nationals, particularly graduates of U.S. universities, generally could not work or remain in the United States. A key reason for this, as discussed later in the chapter, is that the current wait for employer-sponsored green cards (used to stay permanently) is 6 to 20 years, a time frame unrealistic for hiring new employees.

H-1B visas are temporary visas that allow foreign nationals to work in the United States on short-term projects or while being sponsored for a green card. The visas generally are good for up to six years (with a renewal after three years). Contrary to popular impression, Congress did not "create" an H-1B visa program in 1990. Prior to 1990, going back to the 1950s, H-1s generally could enter the United States to work if they did not intend to stay permanently.

Congress changed the law in 1990, redesignated the category H-1B, and allowed "dual intent," which meant H-1B visa holders could intend to become permanent residents (green card recipients). Most importantly, lawmakers put in place an annual limit of 65,000.

The key legislative issue involving H-1Bs has been the low annual quota, which has meant for several months at a time employers generally could not hire skilled foreign nationals to work in the United States. As early as 1997, the 65,000 annual limit established by Congress only seven years earlier proved to be insufficient to meet demand. From FY 1997 to FY 2010, employers exhausted the supply of H-1B visas every year, except when the ceiling was temporarily increased for the years 2001 to 2003.

In late 2004, Congress approved an exemption of 20,000 from the annual cap for foreign nationals who receive an advanced degree from a U.S. university. (Congress had earlier approved an exemption from the 65,000 numerical limit for those hired by universities and nonprofit or government research institutes.) But with each revision have come greater regulation and scrutiny for employers and, starting in 1998, high and escalating fees for hiring H-1B professionals. For example, a training and scholarship fee, which Congress began at $500 in 1998, soon escalated to a $1,500 fee on each new petition (and the first renewal of H-1B status).[11] In addition, companies must pay a $500 anti-fraud fee.

The mandated scholarship and training fees U.S. companies pay for each H-1B professional hired equalled more than $2 billion from 1999 through FY 2010.[12] Since 1999, the H-1B fees paid by companies have funded more than 50,000 scholarships (up to $10,000 each) for U.S. students in math and science through the National Science Foundation, as well as hands-on science programs for 158,000 elementary, middle, and high school students and 4,700 teachers. More than 55,000 U.S. workers have received training, with additional Americans trained annually via grants made to states and localities.[13]

Some argue that companies should not be permitted to hire international students and other foreign nationals on skilled visas unless employers do more to support education. It is argued companies will not have any incentive to improve U.S. education if they can hire foreign nationals. But U.S. companies already have a great incentive to improve education, since nearly all of their employees are educated in American schools. In addition, U.S. businesses pay over $91 billion a year in state and local taxes directed toward public education. Companies such as Intel, Oracle, Microsoft, and others also make substantial charitable contributions to aid education in the United States. The Gates Foundation alone, funded by Microsoft stock, has contributed $3 billion to U.S. public education since 1999. Elected officials, not companies, are responsible for local, state, and federal education policy. Changes to our schools, even if the right ones are adopted, would take years to have a major impact on overall student performance.

THE COMPLAINTS OF CRITICS IN CONTEXT

A key premise of critics is that companies hire H-1B professionals to the exclusion of Americans. But in 2008, a typical year, the number of new H-1B visa holders in the United States accounted for only 0.07 percent of the U.S. labor force. Including those petitions exempt from counting against the H-1B quota, a total of 107,686 new H-1B petitions were approved by USCIS in FY 2008. That compares to the U.S. civilian labor force of 154.6 million in 2008.[14]

Contrary to assertions that H-1B visa holders are not highly skilled, official data for FY 2008 show 57 percent of recent H-1B professionals earned a master's degree or higher, according to the Department of Homeland

Security. Forty-one percent earned a master's degree, 11 percent earned a PhD, and 5 percent a professional degree.[15]

A large variety of businesses and organizations in America, including public school systems, hire H-1B professionals every year. In FY 2009, 27,288 different employers hired at least one individual on a new H-1B petition, according to USCIS. Contrary to the popular impression, 96 percent of these employers (26,304 of 27,288) hired ten or fewer individuals on a new H-1B petition. U.S. employers who hired between one and ten new H-1B visa holders utilized 52 percent of the new H-1B petitions in FY 2009. A total of 18,747 employers, or 69 percent, hired only one foreign national on a new H-1B petition.[16]

U.S. workers account for 85 percent to 99 percent of the workforce of nearly all companies that utilize H-1B visa holders. We know this since any businesses with more than 15 percent of their workforce on H-1B visas are considered "H-1B dependent" under the law and must adhere to a stricter set of labor rules (relatively few companies fall into this designation). Still, Senator Charles Grassley (R-IA) has stated, "Unfortunately, the H-1B program is so popular, it is now replacing the U.S. labor force rather than supplementing it."[17] There does not appear to be any basis for such a statement.[18]

The current annual level of H-1Bs is about the same level as in 1990, even though the U.S. gross domestic product has risen by 64 percent (from $8.5 trillion to $14 trillion) over the past two decades, and the demand for skilled labor, particularly in technical fields, has increased. The size of the U.S. labor force has also risen considerably, and the pace of technological change, such as the ubiquity of the Internet, has become significant since the H-1B quota was first established.

Some have argued against increasing the H-1B quota by asserting (incorrectly) that Indian companies use the majority of the annual allotment of new H-1B petitions. While it is true Indian businesses were conspicuous among the top 10 users of H-1Bs in FY 2008 (and in previous years), they represent only a fraction of total H-1B use. Moreover, these numbers have dropped significantly since 2006.

Seeking to undermine support for H-1B visas in general, critics have tended to leave the impression that Indian technology companies use far more H-1B visas than they actually do. USCIS data show that in FY 2009, less than 6 percent of new H-1B petitions went to Indian technology companies. Identifying 25 India-based firms, one finds that Indian companies utilized fewer than 5,000 (4,809) new H-1B visas in FY 2009. Moreover, tracking these same companies over time, one finds that the number of new H-1B visas utilized by Indian technology firms fell by 70 percent between FY 2006 and FY 2009. Pointing out such data is not intended to accept the premise of some critics that H-1B visa holders are "taking American jobs." To the extent that Indian (and non-Indian) companies performing information technology service work allow U.S. businesses to focus on core functions, run more efficiently, and enhance shareholder wealth, U.S. companies can hire more people in the long run by becoming more profitable.[19]

CHEAP LABOR? THE DATA SUGGEST OTHERWISE

There is not much evidence that foreign nationals working on H-1B visas are vastly underpaid as a group. A study by Madeline Zavodny, a research economist at the Federal Reserve Bank of Atlanta, called into question the assertion that widespread underpayment of H-1B professionals exists. Zavodny found, "H-1B workers [also] do not appear to depress contemporaneous earnings growth." As to unemployment, the study concluded that the entry of H-1B computer programmers does "not appear to have an adverse impact on contemporaneous unemployment rates." The study also noted that some results "do suggest a positive relationship between the number of LCA [Labor Condition] applications and the unemployment rate a year later." Zavodny concluded: "None of the results suggest that an influx of H-1Bs as proxied by Labor Condition Applications filed relative to total IT employment, lower contemporaneous average earnings. Indeed, many of the results indicate a positive, statistically significant relationship." This would mean H-1B employment is actually associated with better job conditions for natives, according to the study, which could be because H-1B professionals are complementary to native professionals.[20]

A 2009 study by University of Maryland researchers Sunil Mithas and Henry C. Lucas Jr. found foreign-born professionals in information technology (IT) actually earned more than their native counterparts. "Contrary to the popular belief that foreign workers are a cheap source of labor for U.S. firms, we find that after controlling for their human capital attributes, foreign IT professionals (those without U.S. citizenship and those with H-1B or other work visas) earn a salary premium when compared with IT professionals with U.S. citizenship," wrote Mithas and Lucas. "Firms pay a premium not for the education of non-US citizens, but for their IT skills as reflected in their IT experience."[21] The study examined the skills and compensation of over 50,000 IT professionals in the United States between 2000 and 2005. Similar to Zavodny, Mithas and Lucas conclude, "This result implies complementarity among American and foreign IT professionals and supports the view that high-skill immigration can potentially make everyone (i.e., American as well as foreign workers) better off."[22]

Some have complained that prevailing wage requirements do not accurately reflect the market wage for professionals. Critics have even sought to use prevailing wage data filed by employers with the Department of Labor (DOL) to argue that employers underpay H-1B visa holders.[23] The problem is the wage data maintained by the Department of Labor are simply listings of the minimum an employer must pay an H-1B professional for a particular job. That means the prevailing wage data do not necessarily reflect the salaries actually paid to H-1B professionals.

The data showing what an employer pays an H-1B visa holder are contained on the I-129 forms filed with U.S. Citizenship and Immigration Services. Unlike the prevailing wage data at DOL, the forms filed with USCIS are not normally available to the public. To examine this issue, the National Foundation for American Policy asked a law firm to select a random sample of H-1B cases from among its client base. They represented different occupations, but the vast majority of the H-1Bs were in high technology fields. Among the 100 randomly selected cases, *the average actual wage was more than 22 percent higher than the prevailing wage.*[24]

MOVING AWAY FROM A ZERO-SUM VIEW OF THE WORLD

One reason so much emotion swirls around high-skill immigration issues is many people assume if a foreign national fills a job, then that means an American who could have filled that job is out of luck. Yet the flow of jobs in an economy and even within a company is much more dynamic than allowed for in such a simple one-for-one, zero-sum analysis of employment.

In a widely cited study, the National Foundation for American Policy found evidence H-1B visa holders are associated with increases in employment at U.S. technology companies in the Standard and Poor's (S&P) 500. Some criticized the study, in part, because public statements citing the research did not carefully couch the conclusions in the same language used in the study. That led to the impression the analysis had concluded the hiring of each H-1B visa holder "caused" the hiring of additional Americans.[25]

The study stated that correlation is not the same as causation. However, making inferences based on association is common in much significant research, such as that showing a connection between higher levels of education and higher wages. The study found an association between companies filing for H-1B visa holders and later increases in employment at these technology companies. At minimum, the study's findings disputed the notion that "cheaper" H-1Bs were leading to fewer Americans employed in these companies.

The findings were consistent with information from tech companies on the dynamic process of job creation, and the results held up in estimates with different controls and subsets of firms. One reason the study has been widely cited is it reflects the real world experiences of tech companies in hiring highly skilled foreign-born professionals and international graduate students from U.S. universities. In addition to citing the research, Bill Gates noted Microsoft's own internal findings that H-1Bs lead to increased complementary employment: "Microsoft has found that for every H-1B hire we make, we add on average four additional employees to support them in various capacities."[26] That is similar to the finding in the National Foundation for American Policy research. Discussions with executives at eBay and other tech companies revealed the same experiences. It is common sense to job creators that hiring talented individuals leads to growth and innovation.

THE CASE OF GOOGLE

Google is considered one of the world's most innovative companies. Based in Mountain View, California, the company has transformed Internet commerce and advertising, as well as the way many people utilize information on the Internet. Although the company is American, founded by Larry Page and Russian-born immigrant Sergey Brin (see Table 5.3), those who lead the firm concede it would not be the same company if it did not hire, in addition to Americans, many outstanding individuals born outside the United States.

"Google's hiring process is rigorous, and we make great efforts to uncover the most talented employees we can find. Often times, many of these exceptional employees were born here in the United States and have spent their whole lives here. But in other cases, the most talented software engineer or product manager we can find happens to have been born elsewhere," according to Laszlo Bock, Vice-President for People Operations at Google. "As a result, Google depends on programs like the H-1B visa for highly skilled workers."[27]

In testimony before the House Judiciary Subcommittee on Immigration, Laszlo Bock stated that about 8 percent of Google's U.S.-based employees are working on H-1B temporary visas from over 80 different countries. "So, while nine out of ten of our employees are citizens or permanent residents, our need to find the specialized skills required to run our business successfully requires us to look at candidates from around the globe—many of whom are already in the U.S. studying at one of our great universities," said Bock. "It is no stretch to say that without these employees, we might not be able to develop future revolutionary products like the next Gmail or Google Earth."[28]

At the hearing, Bock shared two examples of H-1B visa holders at Google:

Orkut Buyukkokten was born in Konya, Turkey, and later received his PhD in computer science from Stanford University. He joined Google as a software engineer in 2002 through the H-1B visa program. Every engineer at Google is allotted what we call "20 percent time," giving them the freedom to spend one day a week pursuing whatever projects interest them. In his 20 percent time, Orkut developed and programmed a new social networking service, which Google later launched publicly and dubbed—you guessed it—"orkut." Today, orkut—the web service—has tens of millions of users worldwide, and is so popular in Brazil that Orkut—the person—was treated as a celebrity on a recent visit there. After spending four years in the U.S. on an H-1B visa, Orkut recently received his green card for permanent residency.

Krishna Bharat joined Google even earlier, in 1999, and also through the H-1B program. A native of India, he received his PhD from Georgia Tech in human computer interaction. His work on Web search at DEC Systems Research Center and at Google earned him several patents, and he is a noted authority on search engine technology. Krishna was one of the chief creators of Google News, our service that aggregates more than 4,500 English-language news Web sites around the world. Today, Krishna serves as Google's principal scientist, and he, too, has received his green card for permanent residency.

Without Orkut and Krishna—and many, many other employees—Google would not be able to offer innovative and useful new products to our users. Immigration laws that enable us to attract and retain highly skilled workers, regardless of their country of origin, make that possible.[29]

As Bock pointed out in his testimony, Google does not hire foreign nationals instead of Americans, but *in addition* to them. "We believe that it is in the best interests of the United States to welcome into our workforce talented individuals who happen to have been born elsewhere, rather than send them back to their countries of origin," said Bock. "But this doesn't mean we don't recruit here in the U.S., or that American workers are being left behind. To the contrary, we are creating jobs here in the U.S. every day."

Google more than doubled employment from 5,700 to 12,200 between 2004 and 2007. At times the company has added 500 employees each month, although it, too, was affected by the slowdown in the economy in 2008 and 2009.[30] Bock noted:

But we're not the only ones recruiting talented engineers, scientists, and mathematicians. The fact is that we are in a fierce worldwide competition for top talent unlike ever before. As companies in India, China, and other countries step up efforts to attract highly skilled employees, the United States must continue to focus on attracting and retaining these great minds. . . . As a global company, Google is fortunate to be able to have employees work for us in other countries if they are not allowed to stay in the U.S. It is vital to have a local presence in other countries, to help tailor our products and services for our international users.

However, many of our core products are created and improved here in the U.S., and we believe that worker satisfaction is higher when employees can work

TABLE 5.3
Selected Immigrant-Founded Companies (Publicly Traded)

Company	Immigrant Founder/ Co-Founder	Employees	Industry
Intel	Andy Grove—Hungary	83,900 (2008)	Semiconductor
Solectron	Winston Chen—Taiwan	53,000 (2005)*	Electronics manufacturing
Sanmina-SCI	Jure Sola—Bosnia Milan Mandaric—Croatia	38,602 (2009)	Bare printed circuit board manufacturing
Sun Microsystems	Andreas Bechtolsheim—Germany Vinod Khosla—India	29,000 (2009)	Electronic computer manufacturing
Google	Sergey Brin—Russia	20,222 (2008)	Web search portals
eBay	Pierre Omidyar—France	16,200 (2008)	Electronic auctions
Yahoo!	Jerry Yang—Taiwan	13,600 (2008)	Web search portals
Life Time Fitness	Bahram Akradi—Iran	16,700 (2008)	Fitness and rec. sports centers
Tetra Tech	Henri Hodara—France	10,000 (2009)	Engineering services
UTStarcom	Ying Wu—China	4,400 (2008)	Telephone apparatus manufacturing

*Solectron was acquired by Flextronics International in October 2007.
Source: Stuart Anderson and Michaela Platzer, *American Made: The Impact of Immigrant Entrepreneurs and Professionals on U.S. Competitiveness* (Arlington, VA: National Venture Capital Association, November 2006), 32; Company 10-K filings and Hoover's. Employment numbers, which are worldwide totals, updated to 2008 or 2009 as indicated.

in the location they prefer. Being able to have H-1B visa holders remain in the U.S., building our products and expanding our business, also translates into more jobs and greater economic growth here at home. . . . America's edge in the world economy depends on the ability of U.S. companies to innovate and create the next generation of must-have products and services. And that ability to innovate and create, in turn, depends on having the best and brightest workers.[31]

FLUCTUATIONS IN H-1B USE

The fluctuations in H-1B use call into question the argument that employers hire H-1B visa holders for "cheap labor." One presumes that keeping costs low is even more important when times are tough, yet instead of increases in H-1B use when the economy has slowed (i.e., to save money on alleged "cheaper workers") we've seen decreases in applications by employers (see Table 5.4).

TABLE 5.4
H-1B Visas Issued Against the CAP by Year

Year	CAP*	#Issued	#Unused
1992	65,000	48,600	16,400
1993	65,000	61,600	3,400
1994	65,000	60,300	4,700
1995	65,000	54,200	10,800
1996	65,000	55,100	9,900
1997	65,000	65,000	0
1998	65,000	65,000	0
1999	115,000	115,000	0
2000	115,000	115,000	0
2001	195,000	163,600	31,400
2002	195,000	79,100	115,900
2003	195,000	78,000	117,000
2004	65,000	65,000	0
2005	65,000	65,000	0
2006	65,000	65,000	0
2007	65,000	65,000	0
2008	65,000	65,000	0
2009	65,000	65,000	0
2010	65,000	65,000	0

*Does not include exemptions from the cap. Exemptions from the annual cap include those hired by universities and non-profit research institutes and 20,000 individuals who received a master's degree or higher from a U.S. university.
Source: Department of Homeland Security; National Foundation for American Policy.

The labor market and economic conditions have determined the use of H-1B visas. In FY 2002 and 2003, legislation set the H-1B annual cap at 195,000. However, approximately 230,000 visas in those two years went unused because economic conditions and employer needs lagged. Similarly, in FY 2010, the quota for H-1Bs remained unfilled at the start of the fiscal year (and for months into the fiscal year), even though in FY 2009 the demand was so high that the application process stopped months before the fiscal year started. In that year, the immigration agency distributed the over-subscribed visas via a lottery system.

THE LAW REQUIRES COMPARABLE WAGES AND THE OPPORTUNITY TO FIND A NEW EMPLOYER

Under the law, when hiring an H-1B professional, companies must pay *the higher* of the prevailing wage or actual wage paid to "all other individuals with similar experience and qualifications for the specific employment in question."[32] Companies must also comply with a complex series of rules related to, among other things, the placement of employees at off-site facilities. For example, if an H-1B petition is filed for an employee to work in Pittsburgh and then the company needs to send the person to work for a client in San Francisco, the employer generally would need to have filed a separate labor condition application (LCA) with the U.S. Department of Labor (specifying the employer will pay wages at least those paid to similar U.S. workers in that geographic area).[33]

While the Department of Labor is unlikely to catch all underpayment of wages, the better protection for both H-1B professionals and other workers is the freedom to change employers and the competition for their services. Additional measures that could be introduced into law or regulations to increase labor mobility among skilled foreign nationals should be encouraged. Still, a myth has been perpetuated that H-1B visa holders are "indentured servants." This is far from the truth. A sampling of U.S. employers and immigration lawyers found that individuals on H-1B visas change companies frequently. A number of S&P 500 companies related that the majority of their H-1B hires first worked for other employers. H-1B visa holders are individuals who understand the marketplace, exchange information with others in the field, and are highly sought by employers. In fact, Congress made it easier for those in H-1B status to change jobs by allowing movement to another employer before all paperwork is completed. "When the economy is good, someone on an H-1B can usually get a new job in a few weeks," said Warren Leiden, partner, Berry Appleman & Leiden LLP.[34] In other words, even if a company hired someone for less than the market wage initially, it is unlikely such a situation would persist.

Data from the Department of Homeland Security show that in FY 2008 more H-1B applications were approved for "continuing" employment than for initial employment. While continuing employment also includes H-1B professionals receiving an "extension" to stay at the same employer for an additional three years, anecdotal evidence indicates that many "continuing" employment petitions involve an H-1B visa holder changing to a new employer.[35]

Critics do not explain why H-1B professionals who are said to be underpaid would remain en masse with their employers when they could seek higher wages with competing firms. To the extent H-1B visa holders are reluctant to change jobs after beginning an application for a green card, the solution is to provide more employment-based immigrant visas and eliminate the current green card backlog. But the power to do that rests squarely in the hands of members of Congress, including Congressional critics of H-1B visas.

HIGH FEES PAID BY EMPLOYERS UNDERMINE UNDERPAYMENT ALLEGATIONS

Those arguing companies are hiring foreign nationals as "cheap labor" ignore an important ingredient in the immigration process—substantial legal and government fees paid by employers. To hire a foreign national on an H-1B visa and to sponsor him or her for permanent residence involves a substantial investment for employers. In addition, the fees paid do not take into account the staff time for human resources personnel or the lack of certainty in the process. Businesses run on predictability, and not knowing whether the government will approve an application is a type of hiring "tax" just as much as any government-imposed fee.

Attorney fees for an H-1B visa range from $1,800 to $2,500 (or higher), according to the American Council on International Personnel. Government fees also add up quickly: $1,500 for an education/training fee that goes mostly toward scholarships for American students; $500 for an anti-fraud fee; $1,000 premium processing if an employer needs timely adjudication; and, if the case involves processing outside the United States, visa fees are $131, and other fees related to visa issuance/reciprocity could be up to $800. In total, government and legal fees for an H-1B visa holder can range between $4,120 and $6,751.

That is only the start of the fees. After three years, if an employer wishes to renew H-1B status for the employee (filing an extension), then the costs cited previously would need to be repeated. In addition, if the employee on an H-1B has one or more dependents (an H-4 visa), then another $931 to $1,581 could be spent on various government and legal fees.

These expenses do not include another $12,135 to $23,270 in estimated costs associated with an employer sponsoring a foreign national for permanent residence (a green card), according to the American Council on International Personnel.[36] Legal fees alone for this burdensome process typically exceed $10,000. Costs to satisfy the government's requirement to document advertising and recruitment for "labor certification," a process to demonstrate a lack of qualified Americans for the position, can range from $500 to $8,000.[37]

The combined H-1B and green card costs for employers can range from over $20,000 to over $35,000.[38] And this estimate does not include other costs that may arise in the process, such as needing to file for family members as part of the green card application or filing for more than one extension. It also does not take into account an employer's staff time devoted to the process even if an outside immigration counsel is used.

Related to this, an examination of the typical back wages owed to the relatively small number of employers the Department of Labor finds each year to be in violation of the H-1B law yields an interesting result—the average amount of back wages owed in these cases is no more than what employers usually pay in H-1B legal and government fees. The National Foundation for American Policy examined all Department of Labor final agency actions between 1992 and 2004 against companies investigated for violations of the H-1B rules. Yet even in this highly stratified sample—employers where suspicion of abuse was present—the average amount of back wages owed to an H-1B employee was only $5,919. In many cases, that would be less than the amount that U.S. employers pay in H-1B legal and government-imposed fees.[39] These figures cast doubt on allegations of widespread significant underpayment of H-1B professionals.

The argument that foreign nationals are only hired because they will work more cheaply implies that those born outside the United States have nothing to offer U.S. employers except a willingness to work for little money, a questionable assertion. But for critics, the contention that H-1B visa holders are paid less than comparable Americans is, in essence, the only plausible argument that can be made against employers. Otherwise, one would need to concede the foreign nationals being hired are at least as talented as their American counterparts. That means no matter how much evidence to the contrary, critics will never abandon the claim that foreign nationals are only hired because they work more cheaply.

The irony is if companies simply wanted to obtain services based only on the cheapest wages, then U.S. companies would move all of their work outside the United States, since wage rates are lower in most countries around the world. The fact that does not happen shows the issue is more complex than foreign nationals being hired only because, as it is alleged, they will work more cheaply.

FRAUD ALLEGATIONS AND H-1Bs

In September 2008, U.S. Citizenship and Immigration Services released an *H-1B Benefit Fraud and Compliance Assessment.*[40] USCIS's Benefit Fraud and Compliance Assessment Program drew a sample of 246 cases from a total of 96,827 "approved, denied, or pending petitions."[41] To verify compliance, USCIS sent Fraud Detection and National Security (FDNS) Immigration Officers to visit all 246 employers and conduct interviews with the petitioning employer and, when possible, the beneficiary. Follow-up interviews and visits were conducted on a case-by-case basis.

The most important distinction made in the USCIS report was the division between companies with less than $10 million in annual revenue and businesses with more than $10 million. (A division based on employee size found similar differences.) Additional data would likely show even a starker contrast between alleged compliance and non-compliance based on the size of business and its revenues. Still, even the modest separation of companies above and below $10 million in annual revenues illuminates the issue.[42]

The bottom line finding of the USCIS report is that there is little evidence of widespread abuse among companies with more than $10 million in annual gross income (revenues). Only 7 percent of companies with more than $10 million in annual revenues (8 cases) were found to involve fraud or technical violations. USCIS did not provide a breakdown of those 8 cases (how many were fraud vs. technical violations). However, if it maintained the same 2:1 ratio of fraud to technical violation cited overall in the report, then that would be about 5 cases of suspected fraud out of 113 cases, or only about 4 percent.

Critics of H-1Bs have focused most of their ire at well-known, larger U.S. technology companies and Indian-based consulting firms. Both categories would have much more than $10 million in annual revenue and more than 25 employees. In the USCIS report, companies with less than $10 million in annual revenue had a 41 percent violation rate, compared to a 7 percent rate for companies with greater than $10 million in revenue. The USCIS analysis reported that 54 percent of companies with 25 or fewer employees had fraud or technical violations in their sample, compared to 11 percent for businesses with 26 or more employees.[43]

An aspect of the USCIS report that officials concede raised thorny issues is determining whether to categorize a finding at a particular employer "fraud" or a "technical violation." While USCIS deserves credit for making these distinctions, were this the "real world" and not a baseline analysis designed primarily for internal purposes, a federal agency could not simply declare a company committed fraud and that would be the end of the matter.

A case in which fraud may be present would first be referred for prosecution, at which time an employer would have the ability to defend itself against any allegations. Therefore, it is possible at least some of the cases USCIS categorized as fraud for the purposes of the report would not withstand a defense put on by an employer in an impartial setting. As discussed later in this chapter, USCIS has responded to its report and Congressional criticism by authorizing a large number of random on-site audits of employers of H-1B visa holders.

One ironic twist in the USCIS efforts to investigate whether U.S. companies are paying the proper prevailing wage to employees came in October 2009, when the U.S. Department of Labor announced it had concluded that workers at the USCIS Vermont Service Center had not been paid the correct prevailing wage. "The U.S. Department of Labor has recovered more than $1.4 million in back wages for 237 employees of Computer Sciences Corp., a contractor for the U.S. Department of Homeland Security's U.S. Citizenship and Immigration Services Vermont Service Center at various locations in St. Albans and Essex Junction, Vt.," according to a DOL press release.[44]

EMPLOYMENT-BASED GREEN CARD QUOTAS LEAD TO DECADE-LONG WAITS

One fact dominates all others in the discussion over employment-based green cards—the wait times are long due to the low annual quotas (only 140,000 green cards for the employees sponsored and their dependents) and the per-country limits. A reasonable estimate is that Indians filing in 2010 for employment-based immigrant visas will wait 12 years or more to gain permanent residence (a green card). In fact, on paper, the wait time for Indian professionals sponsored in the third preference could be as long as 20 years, although, in practice, such long potential waits would likely encourage individuals over time to abandon their applications or discourage filings in the first place.

In the past, scientists, engineers, and others from India have represented half of the skilled professionals that U.S. companies have sponsored for employment. If wait times of this magnitude persist, companies and foreign-born professionals say this will cause many skilled people to leave the country and seek better long-term opportunities elsewhere. Given the pace of technological change and the relatively short window of opportunity to build careers, expecting skilled professionals to remain in holding patterns for 12 to 20 years is unrealistic.

Skilled individuals born in India whose U.S. employers file for them in 2010 are unlikely to receive employment-based green cards before the year 2022 or, in some cases, potentially even 2029. To put this in perspective, children today in kindergarten may graduate from college by the time Indians who file new applications for an employment-based immigrant visa would receive a green card.[45]

The key reason wait times are much longer for skilled immigrants from India than for other countries is the per-country limits, which allow only a certain number of employment-based immigrants from any one country to gain permanent residence in a year. The per-country limit affects Indians, but mostly not nationals from other countries because about half of H-1B visas have gone to Indian professionals in recent years and these H-1B visa holders are the prime candidates to be sponsored for a green card. One can estimate a wait of at least six or seven years for potential immigrants filing in 2010 in the third preference for all countries except India, China, Mexico, and the Philippines, based on an analysis of the State Department Visa Bulletin.

The process for employer-sponsored immigrants can be time consuming and expensive. Most employer-sponsored immigrants are in the second or third preference and generally require labor certification. This involves "testing" the labor market through advertising, job postings, and other government-approved recruitment mechanisms. More people immigrate in the third preference category than in the first or second preference of the employment-based immigration system.[46]

The law permits individuals to remain lawfully in H-1B status beyond six years if, for example, a valid petition is pending for an employment-based green card (although there are restrictions on this). Although permitted to wait in the United States, the immigration process places such individuals in a precarious situation. If a foreign national's employer experiences layoffs or goes out of business, the individual may have to start the green card process over again. If he or she cannot find another employer in a timely manner, the foreign national would be unable to remain legally in the United States. A pending green card application also may mean an individual cannot be promoted, since it could invalidate prior filings with the federal government. Moreover, people with pending green card applications are likely to be hesitant to change employers or to become entrepreneurs. Often their spouses cannot work.

Without action by Congress to raise or exempt individuals from these quotas and eliminate the per-country limit for employer-sponsored immigrants, America is likely to continue losing talented individuals unable or unwilling to endure such extraordinarily long waits to become lawful permanent residents. Congress has not raised the statutory level for employment-based green card quotas since 1990. Although legislative support has existed for providing more green cards for skilled immigrants, any attempt to liberalize employment-based green card quotas has been tied to efforts to pass comprehensive immigration reform legislation, efforts that failed in 2006 and 2007 and were not attempted in 2008 or 2009.

LOOKING AHEAD

There are at least four actions Congress can take that will significantly reduce wait times and provide substantial relief to employers and skilled immigrants:

First, Congress can exempt from the green card quotas immigrants with a master's degree or higher from a U.S. university in a science, technology, engineering, or math field. This provision has been included in past legislation by Rep. Zoe Lofgren (D-CA). Congress could expand this measure to go beyond only degrees in those fields or to include individuals who received a PhD in a technical field from abroad. Research has shown that those who receive their degree abroad not only arrive in the United States with substantial human capital, garnered without any U.S. expense, but also may be among the finest in their fields.[47]

Second, the new law could count only the principal employment-based immigrants, not their dependents, against the 140,000 annual employment-based quota. One reason for the large green card backlog is that annual H-1B temporary visa quotas count only the principal recipient of an H-1B visa, whereas about half of the 140,000 quota for employment-based immigrant visas is utilized by the dependents (spouse and/or children) of the sponsored immigrant. In addition, Congress could raise the 140,000 annual quota to a much higher level.

Third, lawmakers could provide additional green card relief by including numbers previously allocated by Congress that were not utilized in prior years, such as due to agency processing delays.

Fourth, Congress could eliminate the per-country limit on employment-based immigrants. This policy recommendation was included in a past bill by Representative Lofgren and Rep. Bob Goodlatte (R-VA). Failing to eliminate the per-country limit could result in skilled immigrants from India continuing to endure long waits even if other legislative changes are made.

In practice, the per-country limit under current law takes the employment-based immigration system away from a "first come, first served" approach to one that favors people from less-populated countries (since countries with small populations will not reach the per-country limits). Does the United States have an interest in favoring immigrants from countries with smaller populations? There is no reason to think we do. Under the current system, an employer could file for labor certification for three engineers on the same day—one from Denmark, one from Syria, and one from India. Because the per-country limit would restrict the number of skilled immigrants from India in a year, the engineers born in Denmark and Syria would receive their green cards potentially years before the engineer from India. This would be unfair and serve no policy purpose.

Eliminating the per-country limit for employment-based immigration would not prevent individuals born in other countries from gaining green cards. There is no per-country limit for H-1B visas, and skilled professionals from a variety of countries gain access to those visas on an annual basis. Approximately half of the annual H-1B quota have gone to professionals from India in recent years, with the remainder going to nationals of China, Canada, the United Kingdom, and other countries.[48] The new policy would put in place a first come, first served approach most people would find fair, not prevent individuals from different countries from gaining skill-based green cards.[49]

Congress can eliminate the per-country limit for employment-based immigrants without changing the limit for family based immigrants. The purpose of the per-country limits for family based categories seems different than for employment. In fact, it appears the only reason the per-country limits exist for employment is they were carried over to the employment-based system with little thought about the difference between the categories. In the family categories, the purpose is to prevent one or a few countries from crowding out individuals from other countries. In the employment-based categories, U.S. employers are hiring based on merit, without regard to race, religion, or nationality. In fact, it is a moral and legal hallmark in America that hiring be accomplished without regard to such factors. Ironically, if U.S. companies decided among themselves to offer green cards to only a certain number of Indians or Chinese in a given year, then they would face both public and legal scorn. However, in essence, the U.S. government is mandating that type of a policy for U.S. companies.

Liberalizing rules for green cards is less controversial than other proposed immigration reforms. For example, the Semiconductor Industry Association and the Institute of Electrical and Electronics Engineers-USA (IEEE-USA) have both asked Congress to exempt "foreign professionals with advanced degrees in STEM (science, technology, engineering, and math) fields from U.S. universities" from the annual employment-based green card quota and to streamline the path from international student to permanent resident.[50]

WAYS TO REDUCE FRAUD AND INCREASE COMPLIANCE

U.S. Citizenship and Immigration Services has taken unprecedented steps in an effort to ensure compliance with the rules on H-1B visas by undertaking site visits to cover potentially a majority of the employers that hire skilled foreign nationals. The site visits are selected at random and provide deterrence given the large proportion of companies that could receive such audits, note agency officials.[51] According to a November 2009 announcement, the immigration agency has planned to conduct up to 25,000 on-site inspections. To put that number in perspective, in FY 2008, 24,692 different employers hired at least one individual on a new H-1B petition, with 16,130 of these employers hiring only one person on a new H-1B petition.[52]

Few, if any, government oversight efforts have involved onsite visits of this magnitude. Despite this, it is likely critics in Congress will continue with their various proposals to restrict the use of H-1B visas.

In a letter to H-1B critic Sen. Charles Grassley, Alejandro Mayorkas, Director of U.S. Citizenship and Immigration Services, wrote, "[The inspection program determines] whether the location of employment actually exists and if a beneficiary is employed at the location specified, performing the duties as described, and paid the salary as identified in the petition." The agency has also hired Dun and Bradstreet to verify information it receives from companies.[53] Mayorkas is a former federal prosecutor.

Congress, USCIS, and the Department of Labor can implement additional reforms that would limit fraud and help protect both H-1B professionals and, potentially, American professionals by, among other things, empowering H-1B visa holders to blow the whistle on bad employers.

The best way to eliminate H-1B visa fraud is to empower the potential victims of such fraud—the H-1B visa holders. To the extent the current legal regime is insufficient to protect H-1B professionals, it can result in individuals being taken advantage of, which harms the H-1B visa holder and, potentially, American workers.

Even if the typical H-1B visa holder is not an indentured servant, as critics allege, situations can arise that leave an individual vulnerable to exploitation. One example highlighted on the Web site of Immigration Voice, an organization of H-1B visa holders and green card holders focusing on employment-based immigration reforms, involved a professional who entered the United States in the previous four months but had not been paid. He planned to leave the country because his employer did not have work for him as promised.[54] (Such an employer has acted illegally, since it is explicitly against the law to "bench" or place someone in a nonproductive capacity and not pay the individual.)

In this case, the H-1B professional asked what would happen to him if his employer terminated him and he did not have another job. Also, if he did not have a pay stub, he wondered how he could prove he had been working in H-1B status.

Greg Siskind, a partner with the law firm of Siskind Susser, based in Memphis, Tennessee, points out that individuals facing such circumstances have incentives not to report their employer if they feel the potential loss of their legal status. "While an H-1B employee has the right to switch employers and begin work upon filing an H-1B with a new employer rather than waiting for approval, you need to prove you were in status when you filed," said Siskind. "So if the current employer is not paying anything, the worker is stuck."[55]

To address these and other situations, a number of measures can be taken that would enhance protections for H-1B visa holders and, indirectly, U.S. professionals:

First, Congress, USCIS, and DOL should explicitly protect the immigration status of any H-1B visa holder who files a complaint alleging a violation by his employer. Whistleblower protections exist under current law.

However, these provisions are not widely known, carry a degree of ambiguity, and are virtually unpublicized by the Department of Labor and U.S. Citizenship and Immigration Services.[56]

More explicit language by Congress can be combined with effective action by government agencies to protect the immigration status of whistleblowers. This should not require an employer to pay a salary to an individual simply because he or she filed a complaint that is pending, since that can easily be abused. And there should be discouragement in the law or regulations regarding the filing of frivolous claims. However, making it clear that an H-1B visa holder who files a complaint can stay in the United States in H-1B status (and seek other employment) while a complaint is adjudicated would increase protections for these individuals and the integrity of the H-1B visa process. "Explicitly protecting the immigration status of H-1B visa holders who blow the whistle on bad employers will solve the problems many Members of Congress seek to address without imposing provisions that will harm innovation and keep out talent," said Aman Kapoor, president of Immigration Voice and a former H-1B visa holder.[57]

Second, a process should be in place for an H-1B visa holder to file for private arbitration, if necessary, to retrieve disputed wages owed. Such a dispute may not rise to the level of a formal complaint, or perhaps an individual feels uncomfortable contacting federal authorities over a private wage issue. While government bureaucrats are not universally loved in America, they are loathed in other nations. The right to arbitration of a wage dispute, which could also carry protection of immigration status, would help provide greater employee-employer balance for a group of people concerned with their immigration status in the United States.

Third would be to increase employment-based green card quotas as discussed elsewhere in this chapter. The possibility one would need to restart the process with a new employer can limit the mobility of someone in H-1B status, which would make them less likely to complain. While most employers only want people to work for them who wish to be there, some employers could take advantage of a situation created by Congress not increasing the quotas for employment-based green cards.

Fourth, all H-1B visa holders should receive the key documents relevant to their case and H-1B status. This includes a copy of the labor condition application, which carries wage information and, for example, the I-797 approval notice. USCIS and the Department of Labor should seek to ensure H-1B visa holders are receiving the documentation they are entitled to, as well as information related to protection of immigration status and how to file complaints.

Fifth, USCIS can continue its administrative efforts to combat fraud. The agency has already used the report to increase scrutiny of companies that fall within certain characteristics. This has taken place in the form of providing more explicit guidance to adjudicators in the service centers that adjudicate H-1B petitions, as well as increased site visits.

Sixth, Congress should avoid enacting measures that would be so restrictive as to encourage U.S. employers to hire skilled foreign nationals abroad rather than in the United States. Two such actions would be to apply "recruitment" and "nondisplacement" attestations to all U.S. employers. In 2009, after Congress imposed new requirements (attestations) related to "recruitment" and "non-displacement" on U.S. financial institutions that received bailout funds, Bank of America, viewing the new H-1B restrictions too difficult to comply with, rescinded job offers to 50 international graduate students; other banks responded by hiring graduates and placing them in offices abroad.

Some explanation is needed to appreciate the problems with these attestations. Back in 1998, after much debate and consideration, Congress enacted measures that would impose certain attestations on past willful violators and companies with more than 15 percent of H-1Bs on their workforce, so-called "H-1B dependent" companies. Congress specifically imposed the attestations on only willful violators and H-1B "dependent" companies (though 15 percent may be too low a threshold for dependency) because it believed such measures would be exceedingly difficult for fast-moving tech companies to comply with, given the broad scope the Department of Labor would apply to inherently ambiguous terms like "essentially equivalent" jobs.

In essence, the nondisplacement attestation requires companies to attest they will not lay off a U.S. worker within a certain time period of hiring an H-1B professional for a job. Current law states that an H-1B dependent company or past willful violator must attest that "the employer did not displace and will not displace a United States worker employed by the employer within the period beginning 90 days before and ending 90 days after the date of filing of any visa petition supported by the application."[58]

While there is little evidence that U.S. companies are firing Americans to hire H-1B professionals in their places, the problem for employers arises from the legal ambiguities surrounding the statute and regulations. An analysis of the current statute by the law firm of Paul Hastings helps explain the problem: "Employers must prove that job departures are voluntary and are not 'constructive discharges'; they must demonstrate when discharges are performance related; they must demonstrate the nature of a contract whose ending results in personnel changes; they must demonstrate when offers of different jobs within the same company are bona fide; they have to demonstrate (according to a highly subjective DOL regulatory standard) whether two jobs are "essentially equivalent," requiring analysis of the job requirements, the typical characteristics of employees performing those jobs, etc.; they must assess and document what are relevant 'areas of employment' for the displacement analysis; they must assess and document issues of 'direct' versus 'secondary' displacement; and far more."[59]

There is no evidence of a need to expand the scope or application of the nondisplacement attestation. In the days of flexible job functions and multiple locations such a provision can cause a general counsel to conclude his or her company may be unlikely to be in compliance if they hire any H-1B professionals. The safer alternative would be to expand outside the United States rather than risk such legal liability.

Current law already addresses the main concerns of critics. Under Section 413 of the American Competitiveness and Workforce Improvement Act (passed in 1998), a company found committing a "willful" violation of the law regulating the proper wages for H-1B visa holders and displacing a U.S. worker is barred for three years from hiring any foreign nationals in the United States and faces up to a $35,000 fine per violation.[60]

Another measure critics would like to enact is to expand a "recruitment" attestation to all employers, rather than applying it only to willful violators and "H-1B-dependent" companies as under current law. This is not a small matter. In 1998, the H-1B visa bill was held up for approximately six months over the recruitment (and nondisplacement) attestation. A compromise was reached to impose the two attestations on a smaller segment of employers—primarily those with more than 15 percent of their workforce on H-1B visas—not on all companies that hire skilled foreign-born professionals, scientists, and researchers.

Under current law, those companies to which the recruitment attestation applies must attest when petitioning for an H-1B visa holder that the employer "has taken good faith steps to recruit, in the United States using procedures that meet industry-wide standards . . . [and] has offered the job to any United States worker who applies and is equally or better qualified for the job. . . ."[61]

Such an attestation when applied to all employers could deter companies from hiring a foreign national even when he or she is the best person for a job. "The main problem with imposing a new recruitment attestation on all employers is not that companies are not recruiting U.S. workers—they obviously are—it's the enormous time and effort of satisfying the Labor Department's inevitable bureaucratic requirements and *being exposed to the legal risk of failing to do so after the fact in a later audit,*" said Warren Leiden, partner, Berry Appleman & Leiden LLP.[62]

The real problem with critics is that their solutions are essentially thinly disguised efforts to prevent employers from obtaining H-1B visas for any skilled foreign nationals, not really an attempt to address abuse. If one is concerned with companies committing fraud, then strict new requirements would not impact businesses that already ignore the current rules but rather would affect those who attempt to obey the law.

A worrisome aspect of current immigration policy is its impact on outstanding international students and other temporary visa holders who end up leaving the United States and taking their skills with them. A March 2009 report from Duke University and University of California–Berkeley, *Losing the World's Best and Brightest: America's New Immigrant Entrepreneurs, Part V*, surveyed more than 1,200 international students.[63] The research shows it is no longer a given that outstanding international students, researchers, and professionals will want to stay and work in America or, equally important, believe they will be able to make their careers here.

According to the survey results, "The vast majority of foreign students, and 85 percent of Indians and Chinese and 72 percent of Europeans are concerned about obtaining work visas" in the United States.[64] This relates primarily to the problems in recent years in obtaining H-1B temporary visas, due to the supply being exhausted before or during a fiscal year. Generally speaking, an international student will be unable to work long term in the United States without such a visa.

A relatively high proportion of students also expressed anxiety about being able to obtain a green card to remain permanently in the United States. Fifty-five percent of Chinese, 53 percent of Europeans, and 38 percent of Indian students said they were concerned about being able to obtain permanent residence.[65] These percentages are perhaps surprising given green card sponsorship is further on the time horizon for most students. "It is only after working here for a while that students fall in love with America and decide to stay permanently," said Vivek Wadhwa, lead author of the study and director of research, Center for Entrepreneurship and Research Commercialization and exec in residence, Pratt School of Engineering, Duke University. "When they come here, the vast majority plan to go back home—that is what they tell their friends and relatives, and they have emotional bonds to their home countries. This changes with time."[66]

The problem facing skilled foreign nationals, employers, and the U.S. economy is current law does not match the aspirations of these individuals or allow the country to harness their abilities. One result is many outstanding foreign nationals see potentially brighter futures in their home countries, leaving America vulnerable to losing a pool of talent that has helped spur jobs, growth, and innovation inside the United States. Today, highly educated professionals are faced with many options. If the United States wishes to encourage more of these professionals to choose a career in America, then it is important to provide a more open legal regime for skilled immigrants.

NOTES

1. Raymond J. Mataloni Jr., "U.S. Multinational Companies: Operations in 2006," in *Survey of Current Business* 88, no. 11 (2008): table 17.2, 43, cited in Daniel Griswold, *Mad about Trade* (Washington, DC: Cato Institute, 2009), 98–99.

2. Charlie Gillis and Colin Campbell, "Stealing Talent from Uncle Sam," *Maclean's*, November 10, 2009.

3. One example is www.elance.com.

4. Tabulations of the NSF-NIH Survey of Graduate Students and Postdoctorates in S&E performed using the National Science Foundation's Webcaspar data tool, available at: http://webcaspar.nsf.gov.

5. National Science Foundation/Division of Science Resources Statistics, *Survey of Graduate Students and Postdoctorates in Science and Engineering*. Tables 18 and 21 of Graduate Students and Postdoctorates in Science and Engineering: Fall 2006.

6. Ibid.

7. http://www.dhs.gov/xnews/releases/pr_1207334008610.shtm.

8. In many years the supply of H-1B visas has been exhausted before the end of the fiscal year. It has been necessary in certain years to distribute H-1B visas by lottery due to more applications being received than the allotted quota before the start of a fiscal year.

9. Today, since they have no appropriate temporary visa category, new foreign nurses generally must wait six years or more to begin working, shutting many out of the United States.

10. It is also possible the U.S. government could view an individual as abandoning their permanent residence status.

11. The "L-1 Visa and H-1B Visa Reform Act," passed in November 2004, raised the training and scholarship fee again to $1,500. The November 2004 legislation also adjusted the division of the fees as follows: 50 percent to National Science Foundation scholarships for U.S. undergraduate and graduate students in science and math; 30 percent to Department of Labor training programs for U.S. workers; 10 percent to the National Science Foundation for K–12 math and science programs; 5 percent to the Department of Labor for processing; 5 percent to the Department of Homeland Security for processing.

12. The fee figures are derived from data from the Department of Homeland Security, *U.S. Businesses Contribute over $91 Billion a Year in Taxes to Fund Public Education; Company-Paid H-1B Scholarship and Training Fees Approach $2 Billion since 1999* (Arlington, VA: National Foundation for American Policy, 2007), available at: http://www.nfap.com/pdf/0507brief-business-immigration.pdf. The research staff of

the National Taxpayers Union pointed out two relevant studies and the relevant figures on taxes from the Tax Foundation.

13. See *U.S. Businesses Pay over $91 Billion a Year in Taxes to Support Education*, National Foundation for American Policy; FY 2010 National Science Foundation Budget Request to Congress, EHR-20-21.

14. Bureau of Labor Statistics, U.S. Department of Labor; USCIS.

15. *Characteristics of Specialty Occupational Workers (H-1B): Fiscal Year 2008*, Department of Homeland Security, May 1, 2009, 9.

16. The data discussed here come from the U.S. Citizenship and Immigration Services list of FY 2009 employers and H-1B initial beneficiaries.

17. Floor statement of Senator Charles Grassley, November 5, 2007.

18. Given the current H-1B quota and the size of the U.S. workforce (approximately 154 million), it would take H-1B visa holders about 1,445 years to equal the size of, or "replace," the U.S. labor force.

19. Analysis of USCIS data. Also see *H-1B Visas by the Numbers: 2010 and Beyond*, National Foundation for American Policy, March 2010, 1.

20. Madeline Zavodny, "The H-1B Program and Its Effects on Information Technology Workers," Federal Reserve Bank of Atlanta, *Economic Review*, Third Quarter 2003.

21. S. Mithas and H. C. Lucas, "Are Foreign IT Workers Cheaper? United States' Visa Policies and Compensation of Information Technology Professionals," Working Paper (College Park: Smith School of Business, University of Maryland, 2009), 1.

22. Ibid., 29.

23. For a more detailed discussion of the wage issues, see *H-1B Professionals and Wages: Setting the Record Straight* (Arlington, VA: National Foundation for American Policy, 2006). Under Section 212(n)(1) of the Immigration and Nationality Act, an employer hiring an individual in H-1B status must pay at least "the actual wage level paid by the employer to all other individuals with similar experience and qualifications for the specific employment in question" or "the prevailing wage level for the occupational classification in the area of employment, *whichever is greater* . . ." Therefore, relying solely on prevailing wage data is inappropriate. Available at: www.nfap.com.

24. Ibid. While it is possible cases from a different law firm could yield somewhat different results, this law firm served a diverse client base that appears typical of the employers petitioning for H-1B professionals. This is not meant to be definitive proof that actual wages are always, on average, 22 percent higher than prevailing wages. However, it, along with other evidence, does show that analyses utilizing prevailing wage data to claim H-1B professionals are underpaid are not reliable.

25. *H-1B Visas and Job Creation* (Arlington, VA: National Foundation for American Policy, 2008). While the study acknowledged that H-1B applications could indicate broader hiring, the analysis controlled for the overall business climate and found little change in the result that H-1B professionals are associated with increased hiring at large technology companies.

26. Written Testimony of William H. Gates, Chairman, Microsoft Corporation and Co-Chair, Bill and Melinda Gates Foundation, before the Committee on Science and Technology United States House of Representatives, March 12, 2008, 14.

27. Testimony of Laszlo Bock before the House Judiciary Subcommittee on Immigration, Citizenship, Refugees, Border Security, and International Law, June 6, 2007.

28. Ibid.

29. Ibid.

30. Ibid., Google.

31. Ibid.

32. Section 212(n)(1) of the Immigration and Nationality Act.

33. The first step in the process for employers is obtaining certification from the Department of Labor by filing (and gaining approval of) a labor condition application (LCA) that contains H-1B wage and job information. The next step is to apply for an I-129 petition with U.S. Citizenship and Immigration Services.

34. Interview with Warren Leiden.

35. *Characteristics of Specialty Occupational Workers (H-1B): Fiscal Year 2008.* See Table 4A. In FY 2008, 166,917 petitions were approved for "continuing" employment and 109,335 for "initial" employment.

36. American Council on International Personnel.

37. Advertising costs can vary significantly depending on the location, dates, and length of ads required to fulfill the obligations of labor certification, according to the American Council on International Personnel and the companies it surveyed.

38. American Council on International Personnel.

39. Calculation by National Foundation for American Policy from Department of Labor data. Over the course of more than a dozen years, the cumulative total of back wages owed was approximately $19 million. Placed in the context of, at the time, a $12 trillion U.S. economy, this figure is not large. The National Foundation for American Policy requested but did not receive individual case data for later years.

40. U.S. Citizenship and Immigration Services released an *H-1B Benefit Fraud and Compliance Assessment* in September 2008. The report was drafted by the Office of Fraud Detection and National Security, which is a division of the National Security and Records Directorate.

41. *H-1B Benefit Fraud and Compliance Assessment*, 4.

42. USCIS would not provide additional data that might give more information on violations at different levels of annual revenue and employees. USCIS said it would not provide such information out of concern that statistically the sample became less reliable with fewer employers within a particular revenue strata.

43. Ibid., 14.

44. "U.S. Labor Department Recovers More Than $1.4 Million in Back Wages for 237 Contract Employees of USCIS Vermont Service Center," Press Release, Wage and Hour Division, U.S. Department of Labor, October 8, 2009.

45. The analysis relies on government data, independent analysis, and consultation with government officials. The estimates were formulated by examining recent use of H-1B visas, analyzing cutoff dates in the State Department Visa Bulletin, and tabulating data on annual green card use by skilled immigrants. It is possible to estimate the number of Indians who have started the process for an employment-based immigrant visa. A relevant beginning point is the cutoff date listed in the December 2009 Visa Bulletin for Indians, which in the third preference is May 1, 2001. That cutoff date means only labor certification and/or applications for green cards filed prior to May 1, 2001, were being processed by December 2009. From FY 2001 to 2009, approximately 508,000 Indians received initial employment on H-1B temporary visas. The number of Indians who received initial employment on an H-1B visa for FY 2001 through FY 2008 is detailed in reports by USCIS and the Department of Homeland Security. (For the actual number of Indians who received an H-1B for initial employment for FY 2001 through FY 2008, see the report *Characteristics of Specialty Occupation Workers (H-1B)*, Office of Immigration Statistics, Department of Homeland Security and U.S. Citizenship and Immigration Services for those years. One can estimate the FY 2009 number based on earlier usage.)

If one assumes half of the 508,000 Indians with new H-1Bs during this time period possessed employers who began the process for permanent residence on their behalf, then it would leave us with 254,000. Half is a reasonable estimate, since the stay rates for Indians five years after receiving a PhD from a U.S. university are 85 percent and a majority of H-1B visa holders possess a master's degree or higher; see Michael G. Finn, *Stay Rates of Foreign Doctorate Recipients from U.S. Universities, 2005* (Oak Ridge, TN: Oak Ridge Institute for Science and Education, 2007), Table 7, available at: http://orise.orau.gov/sep/files/stayrate07.pdf; and *Characteristics of Specialty Occupation Workers (H-1B): Fiscal Year 2008.* "Based on my experience and interaction with other H-1B visa holders, estimating half of Indian H-1Bs have been sponsored for a green card could even be conservative, since it's likely to be more than half," said Aman Kapoor, president of Immigration Voice, in an interview. "Also, Indians get sponsored for green cards from L-1 and J-1 visas."

Although this calculation would yield 254,000 "principals" from India who received an H-1B visa and at least began the process for an employment-based immigrant visa, that number does not include dependents (spouses and minor children). The State Department estimates that, on average, each principal has 1.1 dependents, adding another 279,400 individuals. This would bring the estimated total to 533,400.

If one divides 533,400 by 23,816, which is the average number of Indians who received employment-based immigrant visas each year from 2006 to 2008, we find it could take more than 20 years to clear the cases for Indians who started the process for employment-based immigration after the May 1, 2001, cutoff date.

The estimate of the Indian professionals (and dependents) waiting for employment-based green cards does not include anyone from India sponsored for an employment-based immigrant visa who has worked on a different temporary visa, such as an

L-1 or J-1. On the other hand, the wait in the second preference for Indians would be less than in the third preference. If one wants to be even more conservative and estimate that such long waits will discourage individuals from filing or that perhaps fewer individuals have filed for employment-based immigrant visas than the estimates herein, then one can reduce the projected wait by one-third. That would still yield a wait of 12 years or more for Indians filing in 2010 for employment-based immigrant visas.

46. Cases can fall into the third preference even if the sponsored immigrant has an advanced degree. If a job does not require a master's degree, it would be a third preference case despite the applicant having a master's degree, notes attorney Greg Siskind. After completing the first phase of the immigration process, labor certification, in the second stage an employer must file Form I-140, along with the approved labor certification, to U.S. Citizenship and Immigration Services. The I-140 is also referred to as a "petition." The third phase of the process is generally filing an application for adjustment of status, also known as Form I-485. Adjustment of status means the person can stay inside the country and transition from a temporary status, such as H-1B, to a permanent status, such as an employment-based immigrant. As part of the process, the foreign national undergoes medical, criminal, and other background checks.

47. Paula E. Stephan and Sharon G. Levin, "Exceptional Contributions to U.S. Science by the Foreign-Born and Foreign-Educated," *Population Research and Policy Review* 20 (2001): 59, 75.

48. For FY 2001 through FY 2008, see the report *Characteristics of Specialty Occupation Workers (H-1B)*, Office of Immigration Statistics, Department of Homeland Security and U.S. Citizenship and Immigration Services for those years. For FY 2005 and earlier, Indians received 49 percent or fewer of the H-1Bs issued for initial employment. For FY 2006 to FY 2008, the proportion has been between 54 and 56 percent.

49. It is difficult to predict the precise impact on the distribution of employment-based green cards in the initial years after eliminating the per-country limit, since it is likely such a change in the law would be accompanied by other legislative changes. For example, if the skilled immigrant backlogs were eliminated entirely, then the country distribution of green cards for employment-based immigration would likely be similar to that which we have seen for H-1B visas.

50. http://www.sia-online.org/galleries/default-file/SIA-IEEE-USA_Letters.pdf.

51. Discussions with USCIS personnel.

52. The data discussed here are from the U.S. Citizenship and Immigration Services list of FY 2008 employers and H-1B initial beneficiaries.

53. Patrick Thibodeau, "Feds Plan 25,000 On-Site H-1B Inspections," *ComputerWorld*, November 17, 2009.

54. Posted on Immigration Voice Forum, February 19, 2009.

55. Interview with Greg Siskind.

56. Section 212(t)[first](3)(C)(v) of the INA. The law states: "The Secretary of Labor and Secretary of Homeland Security shall devise a process under which a nonimmigrant under section 101(a)(15)(H)(i)(B1) or 101(a)(15)(E)(iii) who files

a complaint regarding a violation of clause (iv) and is otherwise eligible to remain and work in the United States may be allowed to seek other appropriate employment in the United States for a period not to exceed the maximum period of stay authorized for such nonimmigrant classification."

57. Interview with Aman Kapoor.

58. Section 412 of the American Competitiveness and Workforce Improvement Act, passed in 1998. The statute defines displacement as follows: "The employer is considered to 'displace' a United States worker from a job if the employer lays off the worker from a job that is essentially the equivalent of the job for which the nonimmigrant or nonimmigrants is or are sought." (Nonimmigrants are temporary visa holders, such as those on H-1B visas, and do not have the right to stay in the country permanently without becoming lawful permanent residents.)

59. Analysis provided by Paul Hastings.

60. Section 413 of the American Competitiveness and Workforce Improvement Act.

61. Section 412 of the American Competitiveness and Workforce Improvement Act. In addition, the attestation states the employer must offer "compensation that is at least as great as that required to be offered to H-1B nonimmigrants under subparagraph (A), United States workers for the job for which the nonimmigrant or nonimmigrants is or are sought; and (II) has offered the job to any United States worker who applies and is equally or better qualified for the job for which the nonimmigrant or nonimmigrants is or are sought."

62. Interview with Warren Leiden. Emphasis added.

63. Vivek Wadhwa, AnnaLee Saxenian, Richard Freeman, and Alex Salkever, *Losing the World's Best and Brightest: America's New Immigrant Entrepreneurs, Part Five* (Kansas City, MO: Duke University, University of California–Berkeley, and Ewing Marion Kauffman Foundation, 2009).

64. Ibid., 3.

65. Ibid., 3.

66. Interview with Vivek Wadhwa.

SUGGESTED READINGS

Characteristics of Specialty Occupational Workers (H-1B): Fiscal Year 2008. Washington, DC: Department of Homeland Security, 2009.

Chellaraj, Gnanaraj, Keith E. Maskus, and Aaditya Mattoo. "The Contribution of Skilled Immigration and International Graduate Students to U.S. Innovation." Policy Research Working Paper Series. Washington, DC: World Bank, 2005.

Mithas, S., and H. C. Lucas. "Are Foreign IT Workers Cheaper? United States' Visa Policies and Compensation of Information Technology Professionals." Working Paper. College Park: Smith School of Business, University of Maryland, 2009.

Wadhwa, Vivek, AnnaLee Saxenian, Richard Freeman, and Alex Salkever. *Losing the World's Best and Brightest: America's New Immigrant Entrepreneurs, Part*

Five. Kansas City, MO: Duke University, University of California–Berkeley, and Ewing Marion Kauffman Foundation, 2009.

Zavodny, Madeline. "The H-1B Program and Its Effects on Information Technology Workers." *Economic Review*, third quarter 2003. Atlanta: Federal Reserve Bank of Atlanta, 2003.

Six

Refugees and Asylees

While *refugee* is often used in the popular sense of the word, in legal terms there are only two ways to become a refugee to the United States. One way is for those outside the country to be interviewed by U.S. officials and admitted to America as part of the annual flow of refugees, which is set by the Secretary of State and President in consultation with Congress. The second way is for an individual inside the United States to be granted asylum. For immigration purposes, the difference between an *asylee* and a *refugee* is an asylee seeks protection while in the United States and a refugee is outside of U.S. borders and generally must go through the U.S. refugee admissions process. In both cases, an individual must meet the legal definition of a refugee.

Immigration law defines a *refugee* as "any person who is outside any country of such person's nationality . . . and who is unable or unwilling to return to, and is unable or unwilling to avail himself or herself of the protection of, that country because of persecution or a well-founded fear of persecution on account of race, religion, nationality, membership in a particular social group, or political opinion. . . ."[1]

"Fear of persecution" is not easy to define, but Tito Munoz has a good way of explaining it. Munoz once contrasted his life in the peasant movement in Colombia, where family members were murdered for their part in the movement, to his life as a local Latino outreach volunteer for the Republican Party in Virginia. "Here it's easy. You can talk about what you believe and you can participate in politics and they don't kill you."[2]

The concept of America as a land where one can practice one's religion or express unpopular political opinions took hold from the country's founding. In 1776, Thomas Paine wrote in *Common Sense* that America was "the asylum for the persecuted lovers of civil and religious liberty from every part of Europe."[3] In 1783, George Washington wrote, "The bosom of America is open to receive not only the Opulent and respectable Stranger, but the oppressed and persecuted of all Nations and Religions."[4]

While the receptivity to refugees has changed in different periods of U.S. history, the motivations of those seeking refuge have remained the same. "Almost every decade since 1607 has given America a fresh quota of political and religious refugees, and even those who came primarily to improve their material lot have not been unmindful of America's other attractions," notes one historian.[5] Until the twentieth century, America did not possess separate laws on refugees, so it is difficult to classify those coming here during those earlier years as motivated primarily by fear of persecution in their homeland as opposed to a desire for greater economic opportunity.

It is natural to expect those who have sought political and religious liberty to view economic freedom as part of America's attraction. In seventeenth-, eighteenth-, and nineteenth-century Europe, the legal and political structures restricted who could acquire the primary means of gaining wealth—land ownership. Throughout history, persecuted religious and ethnic minorities have been limited in their ability to earn a living to support a family.

The immigration of Russian Jews epitomizes the combination of broader economic and human rights concerns that impel immigrants. A year after the 1881 assassination of Tsar Alexander II, Russia's "May Laws" not only restricted Jewish religious activity but also denied employment and schooling opportunities to many Jews. Russian immigration to America rose from only 5,000 in 1880 to 258,000 a year by 1907.[6]

Modern-day Cuba is a more recent example. One may argue that many fleeing Cuba have sought greater economic opportunity in the United States. However, in a country where it can be against the law to raise private capital and start a successful business—something millions of Americans aspire to do—it is not easy to separate the desire for economic freedom from the hope of fleeing the political tyranny that makes economic freedom for individuals impossible to achieve. Advocating political and economic freedom is a surefire way to find oneself imprisoned in Cuba or other countries with a communist leadership.

THE HISTORY OF U.S. POLICIES TOWARD REFUGEES: THE PLIGHT OF JEWISH REFUGEES

Prior to the 1920s, no need existed for a separate U.S. refugee policy, since individuals could immigrate to the United States without numerical limits. Immigration officials did not inquire if an individual fled persecution. Unfortunately for Jews seeking refuge from fascism in the 1930s, U.S. immigration policies at that time became the most restrictive in the nation's history.

The key dilemma that confronted Jews in Europe was that many nations, not only America, maintained restrictive immigration policies. Few places permitted permanent refuge for Jews. In 1939, illegal immigration of Jews into Palestine increased substantially because the British government placed a low annual quota on the number of Jews who could immigrate to Palestine. Arab approval was required to increase the quota.[7]

The inability of Jews to leave and find safe havens due to the unwillingness of governments to accept Jewish refugees contributed to the almost complete elimination of European Jewry, scholars now believe. "The overall picture clearly shows that the original policy was to force the Jews to leave," writes David S. Wyman, author of *Paper Walls*. "The shift to extermination came only after the emigration method had failed, a failure in large part due to lack of countries open to refugees."[8]

In addition to restrictive quotas, a crucial roadblock that hindered potential immigrants to the United States was the definition of "public charge" as interpreted by U.S. government officials. Starting in 1930, the Hoover Administration—in an action continued by President Roosevelt's Administration—began to interpret "public charge" (an inability to support yourself or your family) in a way that blocked those seeking to escape anti-Semitism. The few exceptions were generally intellectuals and researchers, such as Albert Einstein, hired by academic institutions. David S. Wyman notes that before the Great Depression, the public charge portion of the Immigration Act of 1917 did not prevent individuals from immigrating, since it was assumed arriving immigrants could work to earn their keep. "Under the new interpretation the government assumed that, because of the depression, a newcomer would probably not be able to find employment. Consequently, in order to satisfy the . . . law, an intending immigrant had either to possess enough money to support himself without a job, or he had to produce affidavits showing that relatives or friends in the United States would provide for him if he found no work," notes Wyman.[9]

The Roosevelt Administration maintained the restrictive interpretation of "public charge." But in 1935, the State Department directed its consular officers to provide those refugees seeking to escape Germany "the most considerate attention and the most generous and favorable treatment under the laws." However, it still became difficult to obtain a visa. A further encouragement for a more liberal interpretation resulted in increases in immigration from Germany in both 1936 and 1937. Still, the numbers were small—5,436 in 1935, 6,538 in 1936, and 11,648 in 1937.[10]

"Looking at Roosevelt's reactions over the full sweep of 1938 to 1945, one can trace a pattern of decreasing sensitivity toward the plight of the European Jews," writes Wyman. "In 1942, the year he learned that the extermination of the Jews was under way, Roosevelt completely abandoned the issue to the State Department . . . even though he knew the State Department's policy was one of avoidance—indeed, obstruction—of rescue."[11]

While anti-Semitism was prevalent in the American public and a factor in the political failure to open the doors wider to Jewish refugees, at least equally harmful was the view toward Jews and immigrants held by high-ranking State Department officials. In 1941, Assistant Secretary of State Breckinridge Long wrote in his diary about a telegram he received from Laurence A. Steinhardt, U.S. ambassador to the Soviet Union: "He said the general type of intending immigrant was just the same as the criminal Jews who crowd our police court dockets in New York. . . . I think he is right—not as regards the Russian and Polish Jew alone but the lower level of all that Slav population of Eastern Europe and Western Asia."[12]

Long and his staff worked to tighten already restrictive immigration policies by placing as many bureaucratic obstacles as possible into the paths of refugees. In a June 26, 1940 memorandum that left no doubt of the goal of State Department policy, Long wrote: "We can delay and effectively stop for a temporary period of indefinite length the number of immigrants into the United States. We could do this by simply advising our consuls to put every obstacle in the way and to require additional evidence and to resort to various administrative advices which would postpone and postpone and postpone the granting of the visas."[13]

One can understand how the obstacles placed in the path of Jewish refugees fleeing death or persecution both historically and in the 1930s and 1940s resulted in immigration policy becoming a prominent part of the founding documents of Israel.[14] After World War II, many governments still did not want to accept the immigration of Jews who had survived the Holocaust. Many European countries were in a poor economic condition to accept many refugees, while the U.S. Congress remained controlled by restrictionist legislators who opposed allowing in Jews in large numbers.

President Harry Truman asked Congress for a bill to bring Jewish refugees to America, after an investigation of displaced Jews held at U.S. Army facilities and Great Britain's refusal to raise the quotas in Palestine showed the status quo was untenable. "The resulting report chronicled shocking mistreatment of the already abused refugees and recommended that the gates of Palestine be opened wide for resettlement," according to Leonard Dinnerstein in *America and the Survivors of the Holocaust*. "The first act passed in 1948—dubbed by one critic 'the most anti-Semitic law in U.S. history'—actually favored those who had collaborated with Hitler over many of the persecuted East European Jews. Only in 1950, after Israel had become a state and most of the refugees had gone there, was a revised bill eliminating the anti-Semitic features of the earlier legislation passed by Congress."[15]

A chief culprit was Senator Pat McCarran (D-NV), who used various legislative maneuvers to pass the mostly restrictive 1948 Act. In addition, he pressured government officials in the issuance of visas and, through delays, almost blocked the more permissive legislation in 1950. Only approximately 16 percent of those who gained entry to the United States as displaced persons between 1948 and 1952 were Jewish, according to Dinnerstein, who notes, "McCarran's numerous tricks and ploys were effective. Jews who might otherwise have chosen the United States as their place of resettlement went to Israel or to whatever other nation would have them."[16]

REFUGEES FROM COMMUNISM

After dealing with refugees from World War II, the next test of U.S. policies came in how to help those who escaped from communist countries. Given the Cold War, it makes sense that U.S. policy turned in this direction.

The Hungarian Revolution of 1956 was short lived. Soviet tanks rolled into Budapest, crushing hopes and creating thousands of refugees. That the United States bore some responsibility to help these refugees became clearer after recriminations that American broadcasts in Europe encouraged the belief America would intervene to assist the Hungarians. Without American military intervention, Hungarians had no chance to stand against the invading Soviet troops. President Eisenhower took steps to eventually admit 38,000 Hungarian refugees, most of whom had fled to Austria.[17]

Until 1980, whether a refuge came from a communist country was a central question for refugees seeking admission to the United States. "Both the Refugee Escape Act of 1957 and the Immigration Act of 1965 defined refugees as people fleeing communism or communist-dominated lands, and in practice this rather loose definition served as a yardstick for admission," explained historian Maldwyn Allen Jones.[18]

In 1959, after Fidel Castro seized power in Cuba, he did not allow people to vote in free and fair elections. That did not stop Cubans from voting with their feet. Within two years, 100,000 or more Cubans came to the United States to escape the Castro regime. Unlike other refugees who had been officially screened prior to coming to America, "the Cubans simply came—by commercial airline when they could get permission to leave, illegally by small boat or raft when they could not," notes David W. Haines.[19]

Between October 1962 and 1965, after the Cuban Missile Crisis ended, refugees from Cuba continued to arrive by small boat or raft, since Fidel Castro had banned civilian air travel from Cuba to the United States. In September 1965, Castro reversed course and opened a port for Cubans to travel by sea, declaring, "Now it will be known who is at fault if someone drowns trying to reach the American paradise, the Yanqui paradise. That for the well-prepared imperialist. Let's see what they say or do." In response, President Lyndon Johnson announced upon signing the Immigration Act of 1965 at the Statue of Liberty: "I declare this afternoon to the people of Cuba that those who seek refuge here in America will find it. The dedication of America to our traditions as an asylum for the oppressed is going to be upheld."[20]

After a few months of Cubans resuming dangerous trips to America by sea, the United States and Cuba reached a Memorandum of Understanding that allowed for direct flights. From December 1965 until the flights ended in April 1973, approximately 265,000 Cubans resettled in America, many reuniting with relatives.[21]

Congress needed to pass new legislation to ensure that Cubans who arrived here possessed an immigration status. Otherwise, the Cubans would be here illegally or at least would not be lawful permanent residents able eventually to pursue U.S. citizenship. Most of the Cubans had been "paroled" into the United States under the Attorney General's authority. That made it legal for them to stay in America but left them in limbo.

In 1966, Congress passed the Cuban Adjustment Act, which allowed Cubans physically present in America for one year or more to become lawful permanent residents. "What distinguishes the Cuban Adjustment Act from all other acts that adjust parolees and humanitarian entrants to permanent residents is that it did not have a cutoff date," notes a Congressional Research Service analysis. "As a result, aliens from Cuba who enter the United States today are eligible to apply for an adjustment of status after a year in this country at the discretion of the Attorney General [now the Secretary of Homeland Security], an opportunity that no other group or nationality has under the Immigration and Nationality Act."[22]

This crucial distinction in U.S. law is the reason Cubans have been treated differently than Haitians, which engenders controversy to this day. The Mariel boatlift in 1980 brought approximately 125,000 Cubans and 25,000 Haitians to America in dangerous treks across the sea. An analysis performed by the Reagan Administration declared that the Cubans generally were eligible to become lawful permanent residents due to the Cuban Adjustment Act. The Haitians were not eligible, nor could most meet the definition of refugee under the law (individualized persecution). It became necessary to include special provisions in the 1986 Immigration Reform and Control Act to allow the Haitians and certain Cubans to adjust to permanent residence status.[23]

Today, when Haitians are discovered coming ashore, they are generally placed in detention while awaiting an individual asylum hearing. Meanwhile, a Cuban found landing on shore would usually be allowed to remain free because the provisions of the Cuban Adjustment Act conferring lawful permanent residence within a year would become operative before proceedings against the individual could be completed. In 1998, as part of a larger bill, Congress passed the Haitian Refugee Immigration Fairness Act, which allowed Haitians paroled into the country or who filed asylum claims prior to December 31, 1995, to become lawful permanent residents.[24] As a result of the devastation caused by the January 2010 earthquake, Haitians already in the United States became eligible to apply for Temporary Protected Status (TPS), which would allow them to avoid deportation and gain eligibility to work while in that status.

In August 1994, when Fidel Castro appeared ready to allow a new wave of Cuban immigrants to exit for America by sea, the Clinton Administration announced a change of policy: the United States would repatriate to Cuba—rather than bring to America—Cubans interdicted at sea. The United States entered into new agreements with Cuba in 1994 and 1995 that established an annual allotment of approximately 20,000 Cubans a year under the U.S. refugee system. "As a consequence of the migration agreements and interdiction policy, a 'wet foot/dry foot' practice toward Cuban migrants has evolved," notes the Congressional Research Service. "Put simply, Cubans who do not reach the shore, i.e., dry land, are returned to Cuba unless they cite fears of persecution. Those Cubans who successfully reach the shore are inspected for entry by INS [now Homeland Security] and generally permitted to stay in the United States and adjust under the Cuban Adjustment Act after one year."[25]

Elian Gonzalez, a five-year-old Cuban child found at sea, came to America in November 1999. It appears the U.S. Coast Guard brought Elian ashore in contravention of the normal policy of repatriating to Cuba individuals intercepted at sea. Concern for the child's health may have been the overriding factor in contravening the policy.[26] The ensuing controversy created headlines internationally, pitting Elian's Florida-based relatives, who sought custody and asylum for the boy, against Elian's father, who remained in Cuba. Elian's mother's death at sea while attempting to bring the boy to freedom added poignancy to the story. In the end, after Attorney General Janet Reno and federal courts decided in favor of the boy's father, armed INS agents raided the home of Elian Gonzalez's relatives and took the boy into custody, returning him to Cuba.

THE VIETNAM WAR AND ITS AFTERMATH

All wars leave a legacy. The most enduring legacy of the Vietnam War is the uprooting of more than a half a million people who resettled in the United States as refugees. After U.S. troops pulled out of Vietnam, the

South Vietnamese government collapsed and communist troops took over the country. The U.S. military managed to airlift many, but not all, of those who faced persecution for having worked for, or cooperated with, America and its South Vietnamese ally.

The United States set up processing centers at a handful of military bases in California and elsewhere and enlisted the help of refugee resettlement agencies. In the first wave, in 1975, approximately 130,000 were settled in America. Congress also passed legislation to facilitate the refugee processing and settlement for Southeast Asia refugees.[27]

Refugees from Vietnam, Laos, and Cambodia, fleeing primarily to Thailand and Malaysia, often made perilous journeys across the South China Sea. The refugees traveled in overcrowded boats and braved pirates and other dangers. In 1980, the United States accepted 166,700 refugees from the region.[28] Refugee admissions from Southeast Asia continued through the 1990s and beyond, and eventually included in-country processing with the permission of the Vietnamese government.

The other major refugee program that dominated U.S. policies in the 1980s and 1990s involved the Soviet Union and the aftermath of its collapse. The story of Soviet Jews fighting for their right to immigrate to a land where they could practice their religion without fear of persecution is one of bravery and sacrifice. Individuals like Natan Sharansky, now an elected official in Israel, were willing to endure imprisonment (or worse) for the cause.

Jews in Israel and the United States made significant financial sacrifices to ensure Soviet Jews could begin a new life outside their place of birth. In 1977, for example, the Jewish community in the United States raised money to settle 6,800 refugees from the Soviet Union in America. Between 1965 and 1994, the Hebrew Immigrant Aid Society (HIAS) helped over 322,000 Soviet Jews settle in the United States.[29]

"Were it not for the Hebrew Immigrant Aid Society, there might be no Google," wrote Stephanie Strom in the *New York Times*. "Thirty years ago today, Sergey Brin, a 6-year-old Soviet boy facing an uncertain future, arrived in the United States with the help of the society. Now Mr. Brin, the billionaire co-founder of Google, is giving $1 million to the society, widely known as HIAS, which helped his family escape anti-Semitism in the Soviet Union and establish itself here." In an interview, Sergey Brin said, "I would have never had the kinds of opportunities I've had here in the Soviet Union, or even in Russia today."[30]

The right of Jews and other religious minorities to emigrate became a topic at U.S.-Soviet Summit meetings. The Nixon Administration's behind-the-scenes diplomacy helped increase Jewish emigration from 13,022 in 1971, to 34,733 in 1973. Soviet Jewish emigration also became a part of U.S. trade policy. In 1974, Senator Henry "Scoop" Jackson, Rep. Charles

Vanik and others believed if the United States explicitly tied Soviet policies on Jewish emigration to whether Soviet-made goods received Most-Favored-Nation trade status (essentially the same status enjoyed by other countries), then the USSR would open its door wider to allow religious minorities to leave. Despite its good intentions, this judgment proved to be incorrect. Like any world power, the Soviet Union did not wish to be publicly chastised or threatened. Jewish emigration fell by 62 percent between 1973 and 1975. In 1978, when overall U.S.-Soviet relations improved, the numbers rose dramatically. However, Jewish emigration fell again to less than 1,000 annually in the early 1980s due to an overall souring in relations brought upon primarily by the Soviet invasion of Afghanistan.[31]

After the breakup of the Soviet Union, religious minorities threatened in the new environment could still apply for interviews to determine if they qualified as refugees. Legislative language by Senator Frank Lautenberg had long made it somewhat easier for individuals from the USSR to meet the definition of refugee. Between 1990 and 1995, more than 275,000 people from the (former) USSR were admitted to the United States as refugees and became lawful permanent residents.[32] Overall, approximately 40 percent of refugees came from Ukraine, 24 percent from Russia, and the remainder from Byelorussia and other republics.[33]

THE 1980 REFUGEE ACT AND THE CURRENT REFUGEE PROCESS

The Refugee Act of 1980 codified and updated policies that had become ad hoc in response to various international events. The United States adopted the United Nations definition of a refugee and ensured refugee protection would go beyond those persecuted by communist governments. Congress also established formal mechanisms for setting the annual refugee admission level and resettling refugees, with the help of voluntary agencies, once they arrived in America.[34]

"The Refugee Act of 1980 requires annual consultations by the Administration with Congress to determine refugee admission numbers for the fiscal year," notes the Refugee Council USA. "In practice, overall admission levels are tacitly set during the Congressional [and Administration] budget and appropriations process, which usually occurs earlier in the year, before the consultation process. After the consultations are concluded, the President announces the admission ceilings for the coming year (referred to as the Presidential Determination). Until the Presidential Determination is issued, there is no authority to admit refugees into the U.S. Changes in the ceilings may be made during the year, either regionally or overall, in consultation with Congress."[35]

According to the Department of State, refugees from 65 nationalities gained admission to the United States in 2008. Refugee admission levels exceeded 60,000 in FY 2008, the highest since 2002, when the aftermath of the September 11, 2001, terrorist attacks led to enhanced screening procedures that limited refugee admissions. In 2008, approximately 14,000 refugees came from Iraq, and another nearly 9,000 from Africa, including Burundi, Somalia, Liberia, and Sudan. In a document submitted to Congress, the State Department recommended a ceiling of 80,000 refugees for FY 2010, including 15,500 for Africa, 17,000 for East Asia, and 35,000 for the Near East/South Asia (including Iraqis associated with the United States).

An individual must pass an individual screening to determine if he or she meets the legal definition of refugee. Refugee officers from the Refugee Affairs Division of U.S. Citizenship and Immigration Services, a part of the Department of Homeland Security, conduct the interviews. Individuals detailed from other parts of the immigration service also participate in processing refugees. In FY 2007, refugee officers traveled to 69 countries and undertook "more than 200 circuit rides to interview 67,606 individuals for refugee resettlement in the U.S."[36]

ASYLUM

Robin Williams's character sought it in *Moscow on the Hudson*. Famed ballet star Mikhail Baryshnikov received it both in real life and in the Hollywood movie *White Nights*. Sometimes even a Cuban baseball player may pursue it. The "it" is asylum, also known more popularly as "political asylum."

Asylum is often the most personal of immigration procedures, requiring an individual to concede there is little or no chance he can return to safety in his native land. It also can compel individuals to reveal the most intimate details of their lives to strangers. This means overcoming cultural taboos on privacy. Failure to overcome these cultural traditions can result in individuals being deported back into the hands of their persecutors.

An "affirmative" asylum application is when an individual files with immigration authorities (in the Department of Homeland Security) without having first been detained for possible removal from the country. In other words, a person comes forward and files an application, which is usually mailed with supporting documents. In such instances, immigration authorities contact the individual, and an asylum officer hears the case. An asylum officer may decide not to approve the asylum application—perhaps because the officer did not find the claimant credible or believed the alleged persecution did not meet the legal definition. The asylum officer would send the asylum applicant a notice that the case was referred to an immigration judge.

An immigration judge is also the person who hears an asylum case when a foreign national asks for asylum while in government custody. This is a defense against removal from the country. Immigration judges are located within the U.S. Department of Justice in the Executive Office for Immigration Review (EOIR).[37] Under reforms made in the 1990s, asylum applicants who are not in detention cannot obtain permission to work in the United States while their applications are pending.[38]

The true-life story of David Ngaruri Kenney, related in the book *Asylum Denied*, which he coauthored with Georgetown University law professor Philip G. Schrag, explains the asylum process better than any textbook. Kenney's journey to where he is today came only after experiencing a series of twists and misfortunes nearly rivaling the title character of Voltaire's *Candide*.

Born in Kenya, David's older brothers forcibly evicted him and his younger siblings after the death of their father and the absence of his mentally ill mother. David eventually managed to earn a meager living as a tea farmer. Unfortunately, like many countries saddled with corrupt and arbitrary leaders, farmers found their ability to sustain themselves, never mind prosper, hampered by the government's policies.

When Kenyan tea farmers in his region joined together to object to the policies, David became an accidental leader. He found himself speaking to a large crowd and developed into an organizer of a boycott to protest government farming policies. He also learned firsthand that criticizing the Kenyan government can be dangerous.

One evening, security officers arrested David and brought him into the forest. They put a gun to his forehead and threatened to shoot him. They did not. Instead, the police threw him into a small cell, a type of pit, and stripped him naked.

In darkness, with no windows and no clothing, cold water began to fill the tiny cell. "The water level started to rise. It came up to my knees, my waist, and then my chest," recalled David. "I thought that my jailers were going to drown me, because the walls reached above my head. I had no way to climb higher to escape the rising water."[39]

After several months in solitary confinement, authorities released him after imposing strict conditions on his public activities. Also, the boycott committee was required to put up a large bond. Despite the police surveillance, David managed to form a friendship with young Americans from the Peace Corps.

A salient physical characteristic affected David's future—he stood over seven feet tall. Although he had never played basketball, the Americans convinced David he could go to the United States and be free if he was a promising basketball player. In what would be a montage in a typical

American movie, David secretly left his hometown to train as a basketball player for a few weeks to impress a visiting coach from the University of Colorado. The coach saw enough promise that he told David he could help him if he scored high enough on his SAT (Scholastic Aptitude Test).

David eventually gained entrance to a community college in America but found he was more interested in his classes than the local coach liked, and the young man's college basketball career ended before it started. David figured out how to earn money investing in the stock market and gained entrance to the University of San Francisco.

Before completing his studies, David faced a dilemma. His little brother had been arrested on trumped up charges organized by David's older brothers. He knew it would be dangerous to return to his old village, and he would face a renewal of restrictions on his public activities, as well as police surveillance. Despite concerns for returning to Kenya, he felt compelled to make the trip, believing it was the only way to save his little brother. Though noble and successful in its purpose—his brother was eventually set free—the trip proved pivotal during his asylum case.

In May 2000, faced with the end of his studies, he decided that applying for asylum would be his only option to remain safely in America. Under the law, an individual usually must file for asylum within one year of entering the United States. However, the Department of Homeland Security exempts those, like David, who hold student visas when applying for asylum. Under a stricter interpretation of the law, no matter how much David had been tortured or feared future persecution, he would have been forbidden to even apply for asylum. In 1996, a major legislative effort was undertaken to prevent Congress from making asylum laws too restrictive. Ironically for David, the man who led that legislative effort was Philip G. Schrag, the director of a Georgetown University legal clinic that helps asylum applicants and a man who played a critical role in David's life.[40]

David's decision to prepare his asylum application without the aid of an attorney was his first mistake. If anyone can imagine defending yourself from a civil lawsuit or against criminal prosecution without an attorney, then it's easy to understand how even a capable person, particularly a foreigner, would fall short when representing himself in something as complex as proving a fear of persecution. "In retrospect, I should have found a lawyer to prepare me for this interview and to accompany me to the appointment, but I didn't think I would need a lawyer," recalled David. "It simply never occurred to me that the American government would doubt my story."[41]

Data show asylum applicants like David who are not in detention when filing their cases are about three times more likely to win their case for asylum in immigration court if represented by an attorney than those without legal representation (39 percent vs. 14 percent).[42] For those filing for asylum while in detention, an attorney makes it six times more likely they'll win their case.[43]

David did not prepare himself well for the asylum officer's probing questions. He did not possess documents from Kenya that could corroborate his story, such as arrest records, statements from witnesses, or evidence that a tea boycott even took place, never mind that he helped lead it and faced persecution as a result. Moreover, psychologically, he was unprepared to describe the humiliation and torture he faced at the hands of his captors. Asylum officers typically consult country reports on human rights prepared by the U.S. Department of State. But even though the tea boycott and rallies were important events for people in that community, it was not large enough to warrant inclusion in the State Department's human rights report on Kenya. Given the inadequate job David performed representing himself, it is not surprising he received a notice in the mail weeks later informing him his application was not approved. His case was referred to an immigration judge for possible deportation.

While researching law schools, David discovered Georgetown University operated a law clinic that could help him. Even though law students, rather than experienced attorneys, perform most of the work, the clinic's success rate in asylum cases has been an impressive 85 percent.[44] The difference between David's original application and what the law students prepared was night and day. David's initial application ran about 30 or so pages, while the documents prepared and filed by the law students exceeded 500 pages. The students tracked down hard-to-find documentation inside Kenya to corroborate David's story and gathered affidavits from 12 people supporting his claims of persecution. In addition, their efforts persuaded him to see a counselor, and for the first time he was able to tell his story about the torture. The sessions with the counselor also proved to be a breakthrough for his personal well-being.

David soon faced his day in court. In the immigration court, one judge would decide his fate. An attorney representing the immigration service (at that time it was still the INS) opposed the grant of asylum. While this element of the adversarial process is preserved from U.S. criminal procedures, asylum hearings are less rigid in rules of evidence and in what attorneys on both sides can say in court. With the help of the Georgetown University law students Bernie Huang and Dave Herzog, the immigration judge had no trouble believing the essentials of David's story. In a closing statement, Dave Herzog likened his client's tea boycott to America's own history and the Boston Tea Party: "[A] group of frustrated farmers in the Central Province of Kenya grew outraged by President Moi's eagerness to grow rich at their expense. These farmers were led not by Benjamin Franklin and Thomas Paine but by David Wachira Ngarurih. His Boston Harbor was the Kerugoya Moi

Stadium and his message was the same: let the people dictate the course of their own lives."[45]

Immigration judge Joan Churchill ruled that although she believed David's story, he did not qualify as a refugee because of a technicality—he had voluntarily returned to his village for two months to help his younger brother out of his legal troubles. The judge argued David could not fear persecution if he had returned to his home country of his own accord. Judge Churchill had used a similar reasoning to deny another asylum applicant who had put himself at risk by going home to help a family member. In that case, the full Board of Immigration Appeals rejected her reasoning but did not make it a precedent decision. In a bit of irony, the INS Basic Law Manual published by the Department of Justice included a hypothetical case in which asylum should be granted that matched the set of facts in David's case.

Philip Schrag appealed David's case first to the Board of Immigration Appeals, which many believed was performing less-than-thorough reviews in the face of Attorney General John Ashcroft's mandate to reduce the case backlog while lowering the number of judges to review cases. Then, Schrag filed an appeal before the 4th Circuit Court of Appeals in Richmond. That court also ruled against David. His asylum claim was at an end.[46]

In a study on the asylum process called *Refugee Roulette*, researchers found great disparity in the granting of asylum from one immigration judge to another. In other words, in addition to whether or not an individual is represented by an attorney, the other most significant factor in the granting of asylum is who hears the case. The study found, for example, that "in Miami, Colombians before one judge were granted asylum at a rate of 5%, while those who appeared before another judge, with an 88% grant rate, were almost eighteen times more likely to win asylum."[47]

LOOKING AHEAD

Americans may recall hearing about the case of the *St. Louis*, a ship filled with Jewish refugees from Europe that was denied entry to a U.S. port in 1939. Of the 620 passengers on the ship who were forced to return to Europe, 254 died in France, Belgium, and the Netherlands during the Holocaust. "Most of these people were murdered in the killing centers of Auschwitz and Sobibor; the rest died in internment camps, in hiding or attempting to evade the Nazis," according to researchers Sarah A. Ogilvie and Scott Miller.[48]

The U.S. president, in consultation with Congress, has the authority to raise the recent annual refugee levels of approximately 70,000 a year. Doing so would be consistent with America's post-World War II policy of helping victims of persecution find a durable solution. Refugee Council USA has recommended a series of reforms to help modernize the refugee admissions process to identify those most in need of protection: "Over the past thirty years the program has become increasingly complex and multifaceted. The U.S. has shifted from working to resettle refugees from a limited number of geographical regions to almost every region of the world. Access to the program, registration, collection of bio-data, medical clearances, and security screening procedures has become more complicated and cumbersome. These obstacles often lead to years of delay, lack of family reunification, or denials to bona fide refugees in need of U.S. protection."[49]

In the area of asylum, Philip Schrag has recommended at least three reforms that would ensure improved protection for legitimate asylum seekers. First, he proposes the federal government should "provide regular training for immigration judges and for the judges of the U.S. courts of appeals." Second, he recommends ensuring legal representation for asylum applicants with help of federal resources, something now prohibited by federal law. Unlike in criminal cases, there is no right to an attorney in immigration cases, even though the stakes may be just as high as in many criminal prosecutions. Absent federal funding, providing more funding for legal clinics through foundations and other private sources would help ensure that victims of human rights abuses have access to attorneys. Schrag's third recommendation is to restore the appeals process by ensuring the Board of Immigration Appeals (BIA) serves as a "genuine appellate body." Related to this, he recommends moving the BIA out of the Department of Justice and making it an independent agency.[50]

While nothing as dramatic as a ship appearing off the U.S. coast filled with hundreds of refugees may be happening today, on a regular basis individuals fleeing persecution are seeking protection both inside and outside the United States. Reasonable reforms can be made to ensure that such individuals receive both the process and protection they deserve.

NOTES

1. INA Section 101(a)(42)(A). The legal definition allows a person inside his or her country or a person with no nationality to be declared a refugee if they meet the other definitions. Also, "a person who has been forced to abort a pregnancy or to undergo involuntary sterilization, or who has been persecuted for failure or refusal to undergo such a procedure or for other resistance to a coercive population control program, shall be deemed to have been persecuted on account of political opinion." But a refugee does not include anyone "who ordered, incited, assisted, or otherwise participated in the persecution of any person on

account of race, religion, nationality, membership in a particular social group, or political opinion."

2. Mary Katharine Ham, "Tito the (Party) Builder," *The Weekly Standard,* March, 9, 2009, 16.

3. As cited in Maldwyn Allen Jones, *American Immigration* (Chicago: University of Chicago Press, 1992), 67.

4. Ibid., 67.

5. Ibid., 4.

6. Ibid., 173

7. David S. Wyman, *Paper Walls: America and the Refugee Crisis, 1938–1941* (New York: Pantheon Books), 37.

8. Ibid., 35.

9. Ibid., 3–4.

10. Ibid., 5, 226.

11. Ibid., x.

12. Ibid., 146.

13. Ibid., 173.

14. For a discussion of this issue and the importance of immigration to Israel more generally, see Dan Senor and Saul Singer, *Start-Up Nation* (New York: Twelve, 2009), to which I contributed background research utilized by the authors, some of which is reproduced in this book on immigration.

15. Leonard Dinnerstein, *America and the Survivors of the Holocaust* (New York: Columbia University Press, 1982), intro.

16. Ibid., 251. Approximately 100,000 Jews came to the United States as displaced persons after World War II under a separate Truman Directive, issued in 1945, and the 1948 and 1950 legislation.

17. David W. Haines, ed., *Refugees in America in the 1990s* (Westport, CT: Greenwood Press, 1996), 5–6.

18. Jones, 278.

19. Haines, 7.

20. Ibid., 9–10.

21. Ibid., 10.

22. Memorandum to Senate Committee on the Judiciary Subcommittee on Immigration from Ruth Ellen Wasem, "U.S. Policies on Cuban Migration Before and After the Mariel Boatlift," Congressional Research Service, July 9, 2001, 2–3.

23. Ibid., 3.

24. Memorandum to Senate Judiciary Committee Subcommittee on Immigration from Ruth Ellen Wasem, "Haitian Migration to the United States: Brief History and Policy Analysis," Congressional Research Service, July 10, 2001, 4.

25. Memorandum to Senate Judiciary Committee Subcommittee on Immigration from Ruth Ellen Wasem, Congressional Research Service, "Policy Aftermath of the Elian Gonzalez Case," July 10, 2001, 2.

26. Ibid., 2–3.

27. Haines, 10–11.

28. Ibid., 11–12.

29. Ibid., 283.

30. Stephanie Strom, "Billionaire Aids Charity That Aided Him," *New York Times,* October 25, 2009.

31. Stuart Anderson, "Stop the Sanctions Game," *Journal of Commerce*, July 23, 1996.

32. *1996 Yearbook of Immigration Statistics*, Immigration and Naturalization Service, October 1997, Table 25.

33. Haines, 283–284.

34. Ibid., 13.

35. The Refugee Council USA Web site explains the refugee admission and funding process. Available at: http://www.rcusa.org.

36. Refugee Affairs Division, U.S. Citizenship and Immigration Services.

37. David L. Cleveland, "Asylum and Withholding of Removal," *Navigating the Fundamentals of Immigration Law: Guidance and Tips for Successful Practice, 2007–2008 Edition*, ed. Grace E. Akers (Washington, DC: American Immigration Lawyers Association, 2007), 404.

38. The exception is if the government does not act on an application within 180 days, notes Philip G. Schrag. An asylum applicant is also not allowed to work during the appeals process, even if an application is denied within 180 days.

39. David Ngaruri Kenney and Philip G. Schrag, *Asylum Denied* (Berkeley: University of California Press, 2008), 9–10.

40. The history of the battle over asylum policy is told in Philip G. Schrag, *A Well-Founded Fear: The Congressional Battle to Save Political Asylum in the United States* (New York: Routledge, 2000).

41. Kenney and Schrag, 90.

42. Ibid., 315.

43. Ibid., 315.

44. Ibid., 100.

45. Ibid., 160.

46. David married an American who stood by him through his legal proceedings and appeals. Because he had gambled and not departed the country, he could have been barred from re-entering the United States for 10 years, despite his marriage. He lives in the Washington, DC, area with his wife and child. He has completed a degree in law and has become an American citizen.

47. Jaya Ramji-Nogales, Andrew I. Schoenholtz, and Phillip G. Schrag, *Stanford Law Review* 60, no. 2 (2007), 399.

48. Sarah A. Ogilvie and Scott Miller, *Refuge Denied: The St. Louis Passengers and the Holocaust* (Madison: University of Wisconsin Press, 2006), 174–175; Kenney and Schrag, 1.

49. "The U.S. Refugee Admissions and Resettlement Program at a Crossroads: Recommendations by Refugee Council USA," Refugee Council USA, 2009. Available at: http://www.rcusa.org.

50. Kenney and Schrag, 314–317.

SUGGESTED READINGS

Haines, David W., ed. *Refugees in America in the 1990s*. Westport, CT: Greenwood Press, 1996.

Kenney, David Ngaruri, and Philip G. Schrag. *Asylum Denied.* Berkeley: University of California Press, 2008.

The U.S. Refugee Admissions and Resettlement Program at a Crossroads: Recommendations by Refugee Council USA. Washington, DC: Refugee Council USA, 2009. Available at: http://www.rcusa.org.

Wyman, David S. *Paper Walls: America and the Refugee Crisis, 1938–1941.* New York: Pantheon Books, 1985.

Seven

The Economic Debate over Immigration

The fallacy that drives most discussions of the impact of immigration on natives is that only a fixed economic pie and a fixed number of jobs exist, so any newcomer must take away jobs or wealth from natives. Mark J. Perry, a professor of economics and finance in the School of Management at the Flint campus of the University of Michigan, disputes this notion: "There is no fixed pie or fixed number of jobs, so there is no way for immigrants to take away jobs from Americans. Immigrants expand the economic pie."[1]

In explaining the results of a study finding no evidence that immigration increases state unemployment levels, economists Richard Vedder, Lowell Gallaway, and Stephen Moore elaborated on how immigrants can both fill and create jobs in the economy:

> First, immigrants may expand the demand for goods and services through their consumption. Second, immigrants may contribute to output through the investment of savings they bring with them. Third, immigrants have high rates of entrepreneurship which may lead to the creation of new jobs for U.S. workers. Fourth, immigrants may fill vital niches in the low and high skilled ends of the labor market, thus creating subsidiary job opportunities for Americans. Fifth, immigrants may contribute to economies of scale in production and the growth of markets.[2]

The debate over the impact of immigration on U.S. workers and the American economy has intensified in recent years.[3] Economists and policy analysts using competing methodologies have come to different conclusions. In many ways, examining immigration solely for its impact on specific categories of native workers fails to account for the larger economic perspective of the nation. For example, immigrants are crucial to labor force growth in the United States, which plays a role in overall economic growth. "Growth in the native population has been in decline since the 1970s, so immigrant workers have filled in, providing half of the growth in the U.S. labor force since 1990."[4]

William Beach, director of the Center for Data Analysis at the Heritage Foundation, and James Sherk, an analyst at the Center, note that the importance of immigrants, in their view, is not simply because they increase the number of workers but because of the "deepening in the division of labor." As Beach and Sherk explain: "New workers (whether straight out of school or straight from across the border) enable established workers to do new things and give businesses opportunities to create new value for customers. To paraphrase [economist] Adam Smith, new workers encourage greater specialization by existing workers because the new workers take the lower-paying jobs. Then a more specialized work force provides opportunities for businesses to develop new production processes and better products."

Beach and Sherk compare a large city that can employ many medical specialists to a small town that can only support a general practitioner. "No matter how well the town's doctor could do if he focused just on treating cancer victims, the town's economy cannot support so narrowly tailored an expert. The city, however, has hospitals staffed with specialists in virtually every field, each of whom can do a better job than a GP at treating the diseases they have focused their energies on fighting. Immigration works in the same way," write Beach and Sherk. "By expanding the size of the labor force, immigration allows American workers to increase their degree of specialization and become more productive, earning higher wages. That same specialization also permits businesses to apply their capital in new and more productive ways, expanding economic growth."[5]

THE BIG PICTURE

Pia Orrenius, a senior economist at the Federal Reserve Bank of Dallas who served on the President's Council of Economic Advisers from 2004 to 2005, has provided a clear explanation of how a dynamic approach to the issue of immigration leads one to conclude there is relatively little negative impact, if any, on native workers:

> Market forces on both the demand and supply sides also mitigate the labor market impact of immigration. With an influx of immigrants, the return on capital rises, spurring investment. Firms also increase production of labor-intensive goods, further dampening any adverse effects on low-skilled native workers. Meanwhile, existing workers, like firms, respond rationally to immigration. Natives and previous immigrants move, upgrade their skills or switch jobs in response to immigrant influxes, much as they do in response to broader market forces, such as the rising skill premium. These responses reduce immigration's negative impact. And as

consumers we all benefit from the greater output and lower prices of many goods and services resulting from an immigrant workforce.

Orrenius notes, "It should not be surprising that most studies find immigrants have little effect on average wages. New immigrants are more likely to compete with each other and with earlier immigrants than with native-born workers. Those just arriving in the U.S. are not close substitutes for U.S. workers, because they typically lack the language skills, educational background and institutional know-how of native-born workers. As immigrants gain this human capital over time they become more substitutable for native workers—but they also become more productive."[6]

In June 2006, more than 500 economists of varying political perspectives, including five Nobel Prize winners, signed a letter to President George W. Bush and members of Congress declaring the consensus among economists is that immigrants are a positive force in America. The letter stated:

> Throughout our history as an immigrant nation, those who were already here have worried about the impact of newcomers. Yet, over time, immigrants have become part of a richer America, richer both economically and culturally. . . . Immigrants do not take American jobs. The American economy can create as many jobs as there are workers willing to work so long as labor markets remain free, flexible and open to all workers on an equal basis. . . . While a small percentage of native-born Americans may be harmed by immigration, vastly more Americans benefit from the contributions that immigrants make to our economy, including lower consumer prices. As with trade in goods and services, the gains from immigration outweigh the losses. . . . We must not forget that the gains to immigrants coming to the United States are immense. Immigration is the greatest anti-poverty program ever devised. The American dream is a reality for many immigrants who not only increase their own living standards but who also send billions of dollars of their money back to their families in their home countries—a form of truly effective foreign aid.

The letter concludes, "America is a generous and open country and these qualities make America a beacon to the world. We should not let exaggerated fears dim that beacon."[7]

It is easy to miss this broader picture if one concentrates, as many do, solely on the more narrow issue of the impact of immigration on small segments of the U.S. native-born workforce. In a paper for the Washington, DC–based Immigration Policy Center, economist Giovanni Peri, explains, "The United States has the enormous international advantage of being able to attract talent in science, technology, and engineering from all over the world to its most prestigious institutions. . . . The country is certainly better off by having the whole world as a potential supplier of highly talented individuals rather than only the native-born."[8]

Peri describes why his research shows a gain from immigration to native-born Americans with a college degree:

> The relatively large positive effect of immigrants on the wages of native-born workers with a college degree or more is driven by the fact that creative, innovative, and complex professions benefit particularly from the complementarities brought by foreign-born scientists, engineers, and other highly skilled workers. A team of engineers may have greater productivity than an engineer working in isolation, implying that a foreign-born engineer may increase the productivity of native-born team members. Moreover, the analysis in this paper probably does not capture the largest share of the positive effects brought by foreign-born professionals. Technological and scientific innovation is the acknowledged engine of U.S. economic growth and human talent is the main input in generating this growth.[9]

Foreign graduate students, particularly those who study science or engineering, are indeed a boon to the U.S. economy and education system. They are critical to America's technological leadership in the world economy. "Foreign students, skilled immigrants, and doctorates in science and engineering play a major role in driving scientific innovation in the United States," according to a study by Keith Maskus, an economist at the University of Colorado; Aaditya Mattoo, lead economist at the World Bank's Development Economics Group; and Gnanaraj Chellaraj, a consultant to the World Bank. Their research found that for every 100 international students who receive science or engineering PhDs from American universities, the nation gains 62 future patent applications.[10]

In conducting their research, Maskus, Mattoo, and Chellaraj found that "increases in the presence of foreign graduate students have a positive and significant impact on future U.S. patent applications and grants awarded to both firms and universities."[11] One of the issues the economists examined, which they answered in the affirmative, is "the possibility that skilled migrants may generate dynamic gains through increasing innovation." One reason this issue is important to policy discussions is such gains would aid future productivity and increase real wages for natives. "Put differently, in a dynamic context immigration of skilled workers would be complementary to local skills, rather than substitutes for them," note Maskus, Mattoo, and Chellaraj. "Thus, more realistic theory suggests that skilled migration would support rising aggregate real incomes in the long run."[12] The bottom line conclusion, the researchers note, is that "reducing foreign students by tighter enforcement of visa restraints could reduce innovative activity significantly" in the United States.

Do international students "crowd out" Americans who wish to attend college? The authors dispute as "questionable" a contention by Harvard economist George Borjas that suggests U.S. domestic and foreign graduate students are highly substitutable. The authors argue that results from international tests "indicate that the native U.S. student pool for engineering and science programs is likely to be limited due to lower math and science achievement." Pointing to research by Richard Freeman, Maskus, Mattoo, and Chellaraj are not asserting that Americans are not as smart as potential foreign graduate students, but point to data over the last three decades showing, "The number of PhDs granted to undergraduates of U.S. institutions, most of whom were U.S. citizens, did not change much during this period, while there was a substantial growth in the number of foreign bachelor's graduates obtaining U.S. doctorates. Thus the change in proportion is mostly due to the expansion of PhD programs, with a majority of the new slots being taken for foreign students rather than through substitution."[13]

JOBS

As noted earlier, much of the anxiety over immigration appears to stem from a belief that new entrants to the labor force compete with existing workers for a fixed number of jobs. However, it is easy to forget that people work today in companies and industries that did not even exist in the early 1990s. Within sectors, jobs increase or decrease from year to year based on product demand and other factors. "When I was involved in creating the first Internet browser in 1993, I can tell you how many Internet jobs there were, there were 200. I can tell you how many there are now, there's two million now," said Marc Andreessen, a founder of Netscape.[14]

Job creation through immigrant entrepreneurship receives little attention in most immigration policy discussions. Indian and Chinese entrepreneurs appear to have founded nearly one-third of Silicon Valley's technology companies, according to research by University of California–Berkeley professor Annalee Saxenian. She writes, "Silicon Valley's new foreign-born entrepreneurs are highly educated professionals in dynamic and technologically sophisticated industries. And they have been extremely successful. . . . By 2000, these companies collectively accounted for more than $19.5 billion in sales and 72,839 jobs."[15] (See Chapter 2 for a further discussion of immigrant entrepreneurship.)

The enormous churning of jobs in the economy is another often overlooked phenomenon. While nobody wishes anyone to lose a job, it is a common occurrence in America. As Dallas Federal Reserve Bank economist W. Michael Cox and his colleague Richard Alm have explained, "New Bureau of Labor Statistics data covering the past decade show that job losses seem as common as sport utility vehicles on the highways. Annual job loss ranged from a low of 27 million in 1993 to a high of 35.4 million in 2001. Even in 2000, when the unemployment rate hit its lowest point of the 1990s expansion, 33 million jobs were eliminated." Cox and Alm further note, "The flip side is that, according to the labor bureau's figures, annual job gains ranged from 29.6 million in 1993 to 35.6 million in 1999. Day in and day out, workers quit their jobs or get fired, then move on to new positions. Companies start up, fail, downsize, upsize and fill the vacancies of those who left."[16]

Looking more broadly at U.S. Department of Labor data, between 1992 and 2006, an average of 32.1 million jobs were created and 30.4 million were eliminated each year, notes the Cato Institute's Daniel Griswold. This created an average annual net gain of 1.7 million jobs between 1992 and 2006, a time period that saw steady or increased levels of both legal and illegal immigration to the United States.[17]

While it is understandable why individuals come before Congress and plead to prevent competition for their company or employment category, the experience in countries with highly regulated labor markets is that attempts to limit competition do far more harm than good. As a way of illustrating the premise that a "fixed" number of jobs does not exist in the U.S. economy, it is useful to examine immigration's impact on a micro-level, as the *Washington Post* did in an article about a popular local restaurant. "We would not exist without immigrant labor," said Ashok Bajaj, owner of the Oval Room, a Washington, DC, restaurant. "If the laws change, the entire economics of the restaurant industry would change, too." Bajaj, a New Delhi native who moved here from London in 1988, told the *Post* he was willing to invest a million dollars in DC "because of the availability of labor at attractive prices." More than two-thirds of the restaurant's employees are immigrants. "If those workers in the Washington area hadn't been available, Bajaj said, he probably would have opened the restaurant somewhere else, perhaps in London, Sydney or New York."

The story goes on to note:

> A wide range of other businesses profit from the restaurant industry's immigrant labor. Thursday morning, the bread guy dropped off $32.75 worth of ciabatta and other items. Restaurant supplier Adams-Burch pulled up with $79.20 worth of brandy snifters. Keany Produce pushed $97.10 worth of arugula and other produce down the long, dim corridor to the kitchen, and the delivery guy from Samuels & Son unloaded $305.26 worth of salmon, cod and other seafood. The booming restaurant business in Washington has rippled through to Philadelphia-based Samuels, which has been around since the 1920s. It has expanded from about 25 employees a decade ago to 150 today on the strength of the increasing numbers of high-end restaurants. Those are union jobs paying $12 to $19 an hour, and Samuel D'Angelo, the company president, figures that about 75 percent of his workforce was born in the United States.

However, D'Angelo adds, "If there weren't all these immigrants out there to staff these white-tablecloth restaurants, things wouldn't have progressed the way they have in the last five or 10 years."[18]

RESEARCH ON IMMIGRATION

The most influential economist arguing that immigrants have a negative impact on U.S. workers is Harvard University's George Borjas. Many news articles and commentators have cited his research, which concludes that since 1980, immigration has reduced the wages of native high school dropouts by approximately 8 percent.[19] "The immigrant influx of the 1980s and 1990s lowered the wage of most native workers, particularly of those workers at the bottom and top of the education distribution," write Borjas and his co-researcher Lawrence Katz, an economist at Harvard University and the National Bureau of Economic Research. "The wage fell by 8.2 percent for high school dropouts and 3.8 percent for college graduates."

One of the criticisms of Borjas's approach is that the numbers he cites are derived from a "static" analysis. A static analysis generally does not take into account additional actions that may take place in response to a particular event. For example, in the case of immigration, the availability of additional workers may increase investment. Taking into account such additional actions would require a "dynamic" analysis. "As emphasized above, these simulations assume the capital stock is constant so that the results summarized [above] represent the short-run impact of immigration. An alternative simulation would measure the impacts under the assumption that the capital stock adjusts completely to the increased labor supply," according to Borjas and Katz. "As expected, the labor market impact of immigration is muted in the long-run, as capital adjusts to the increased workforce. In fact, there's barely a change in the wage of the typical worker."[20] The long-run Borjas-Katz analysis shows a 4.8 percent wage decline for native high school dropouts. "The increase in the capital stock, however, completely removes the wage loss suffered by college graduates."[21] This more "dynamic" approach has received less attention in the media than the approach showing larger possible wage effects. Borjas deserves credit for acknowledging his critics by including this long-run scenario in his research.

THE OTHER SIDE OF THE DEBATE

In recent years, George Borjas has attracted critics of his approach to analyzing immigration. One of the most notable critics is University of California–Berkeley, economist David Card, who writes, "Overall, evidence that immigrants have harmed the opportunities of less educated natives is scant."[22] George Mason University economist Tyler Cowen and analyst Daniel Rothschild conclude, "Most economists have sided with Card."[23]

Card performed pioneering research on immigration when he examined the economic impact of the Mariel boatlift on Miami residents. In 1980, Cuban leader Fidel Castro decided to allow wholesale immigration from Cuba to the United States. This exodus from Cuba boosted the labor force in the Miami area by 7 percent in a short period of time. An estimated 125,000 Cubans departed from Mariel to the United States, half of whom settled permanently in Miami. Yet after Card conducted a detailed analysis of the Mariel boatlift's impact, he found, "First, the Mariel immigration had essentially no effect on the wages or employment outcomes of non-Cuban workers in the Miami labor market. Second, and perhaps even more surprising, the Mariel immigration had no strong effect on the wages of other Cubans."[24] The implicit conclusions from Card's study are that the Mariel Cubans were not perfect substitutes for Miami workers, and that the new people spent money on goods and services and encouraged increased investment, all of which created additional employment opportunities.

In a more recent paper, Card again found that any negative impact on U.S. workers is limited. "New evidence from the 2000 Census re-confirms the main lesson of earlier studies: Although immigration has a strong effect on relative supplies of different skill groups, local labor market outcomes of low skilled natives are not much affected by the relative supply shocks," writes Card. "Recent evidence on the response of local industry structure to immigration-induced supply shocks shows that the absorption of unskilled immigrants takes place within industries in high-immigrant cities, rather than between industries, as implied by simple trade models."[25]

An important issue among researchers is whether to adopt the traditional approach of examining immigration's impact within cities or regions or to employ the method of George Borjas, who uses a "national" approach. Under a national approach, one would examine wages among workers in the nation as whole, rather than examining their wages within cities.

David Card implicitly criticizes Borjas for perhaps seeking out a model that ensures finding the negative impact on natives that Borjas believed would be found if the only right approach was used. As noted, rather than examining cities, Borjas's approach is to use a nationwide approach that, among other things, assumes workers move out of local areas in response to the entry of immigrants, meaning the negative results would only show up examining national—rather than local—data. "As the evidence has accumulated over the past two decades that local labor market outcomes are only weakly correlated with immigrant densities, some analysts have argued that the cross-city research design is inherently compromised by intercity mobility of people, goods, and services," writes Card. "Underlying this argument is the belief that labor market competition posed by immigration *has* to affect native opportunities, so if we don't find an impact, the research design *must* be flawed."[26]

Card makes three important points in rebutting Borjas on the impact of immigration on native high school dropouts. First, Card notes that even though new immigrants in recent decades have added to the supply of dropouts, "the overall fraction of dropouts in urban areas fell from 24.3 percent in 1980 to 17.7 percent in 2000." Second, Card disputes the premise that natives leave areas where immigrants go to work and avoid immigration's impacts, questioning a central reason cited by Borjas for utilizing a "national" model. Card looked at the effects of immigration inflows on native migration rates between 1980 and 1990 and found that native mobility had virtually no effect on the impact of immigration on native workers.[27]

Third, Card notes that if the Borjas-Katz approach was correct, then "the presence of immigrants in the U.S. labor market should have raised the wage premium for high school graduates relative to dropouts . . . in the absence of other factors." In other words, having a high school diploma should have become more valuable when compared to dropping out of school. But according to Card, that is not what happened. His research shows that the wage gap between dropouts and high school graduates essentially has been constant since 1980.[28]

Another critic of Borjas's approach is Diana Furchtgott-Roth, director of the Hudson Institute's Center for Employment Policy and the chief economist at the U.S. Department of Labor from 2003 to 2005. "Foreign-born workers complement rather than substitute for native-born workers because they have a different pattern of education and skills. . . . So how does Mr. Borjas get his results? Mr. Borjas assumes that immigrants and native-born Americans are perfect substitutes, and that physical capital is fixed and doesn't vary with additional immigration. Mr. Borjas measures immigration's effect on wages assuming that no other changes take place in the economy," writes Furchtgott-Roth.[29]

In addition to the impact of immigrants on native high school dropouts, an area that inspires much controversy is whether newly arriving immigrants harm the employment prospects of black Americans. The 1997 National Academy of Sciences report *The New Americans* looked at this issue and concluded, "While some have suspected that blacks suffer disproportionately from the inflow of low-skilled immigrants, none of the available evidence suggests that they have been particularly hard-hit on a national level. Some have lost their jobs, especially in places where immigrants are concentrated. But the majority of blacks live elsewhere, and their economic fortunes are tied largely to other factors."[30]

Evidence on the likely limited impact of low-skilled immigrants on natives has come in a study by economists Adriana Kugler (University of Houston) and Mutlu Yuksel (IZA—Institute for the Study of Labor). Kugler and Yuksel focused on the impact of the large migration of young, less-skilled men from Central America who came to the United States in the late 1990s in response to the devastation of Hurricane Mitch. Similar to other research, they found no evidence that natives moved out or, in their words, "adjusted" in response to the new flow of immigrants to Southern states. However, the economists provided a new wrinkle by controlling for migration to other states by earlier immigrants. The result? "[R]ecent Latin American immigrants have no effects on native wages and employment but reduce the employment of earlier Latin American immigrants."[31]

RESEARCH BY GIOVANNI PERI

In the past few years, many economists and commentators have cited research performed by economists Gianmarco I. P. Ottaviano (University of Bologna) and Giovanni Peri (University of California–Davis). "It turns out empirically and theoretically that immigration, as we have known it during the nineties, had a sizeable beneficial effect on wages of U.S. born workers," concluded Gianmarco and Peri.[32]

The economists explain that a key reason this increase in wages occurred was "because U.S.-born and foreign-born workers are not perfectly substitutable even when they have similar observable skills. Workers born, raised, and partly educated in foreign environments are not identical to U.S.-born and raised workers. Such differences that we may call the diversity of foreign-born, is the basis for the gains from immigration that accrue to U.S.-born workers. Even a small amount of differences that translates in a relatively high elasticity of substitution between U.S. and foreign-born workers (between 4 and 7 percent) is enough to generate the average wage gains."[33]

In an analysis published by the Immigration Policy Center, Giovanni Peri found much different results than George Borjas. Peri found that immigration increased the real wages of U.S. native-born workers as a whole by approximately 1 percent between 1990 and 2000, compared to the Borjas and Katz study that found a 1.3 percent decline. And rather than the 7 to 8 percent decline in real wages for native high school dropouts found in the Borjas-Katz research, Peri's analysis shows only a 1.2 percent decline for such workers between 1990 and 2000.[34]

Peri explains that while he used a "national" (as opposed to the cities) analysis, his research differs from Borjas's by "(1) accounting for the different occupational distribution of native and foreign-born workers within the same educational group (which more accurately gauges the 'complementary' effects of immigration); (2) allowing investments to follow opportunities (with the presence of more workers stimulating the creation of new businesses); and (3) calculating the overall effect of immigrants on natives' wages (factoring in the 'complementary' distribution of foreign-born workers across occupations and educational groups)."[35]

Using this approach is why Peri's findings differ from those of Borjas: "Because immigrants stimulate investment, have skill sets and educational levels that complement those of natives, and do not compete for the same jobs as most natives, this analysis finds that immigration increased the average wages of all native-born workers in the 1990s except those who did not have a high-school diploma (whereas the traditional Borjas approach finds a decrease among workers in all educational groups). Even for native-born workers without a high-school diploma, the decline in wages from immigration was much smaller than the Borjas approach suggests."[36]

In another research paper, Peri examined the impact of immigration on state employment and productivity, concluding: "We find no evidence that immigrants crowded-out employment and hours worked by natives. At the same time we find robust evidence that they increased total factor productivity." His results suggested immigrants encouraged specialization and other benefits. "Combining these effects, an increase in employment in a U.S state of 1 percent due to immigrants produced an increase in income per worker of 0.5 percent in that state."[37]

THE ECONOMIC BENEFITS OF IMMIGRATION REFORM

Contrary to public perceptions, increasing the flow of less-skilled foreign workers can be positive for Americans, particularly if these workers are admitted through an orderly and legal system. A 2009 study for the Cato Institute by Peter Dixon and Maureen Rimmer, both with the Centre of Policy Studies at Monash University in Australia, compared various scenarios and concluded U.S. households would gain approximately $260 billion a year with the right policies on immigration.[38]

What are these policies? Utilizing an economic model developed for the U.S. International Trade Commission, Dixon and Rimmer compared an increase in border enforcement—basically a continuation of current U.S. policies—to a new legal regime that permitted widespread use of legal temporary visas to replace the current illegal flow. The result is that an increase in border enforcement such that the supply of illegal immigrants is reduced by 28.6 percent leads to a cost of $80 billion a year for U.S. households. A similar reduction in U.S. household welfare can be seen if stepped-up internal enforcement reduced illegal immigration and shifted employer costs to paying for less-productive activities related to complying with the law.

In contrast, a policy that made liberal use of temporary visas, similar to using portable work permits as discussed in Chapter 4, would result in a "welfare gain for U.S. households . . . equivalent to 1.19 percent of the Gross National Product, or $170 billion." Additional gains to U.S. households, the researchers suggest, could come from implementing a visa tax. Dixon and Rimmer write, "This [policy] would eliminate smugglers' fees and other costs faced by illegal immigrants. It would also allow immigrants (now guest workers rather than illegals) to have higher productivity. Both effects create a surplus gain for the economy by raising the value of immigrant labor relative to the wage necessary to attract it. This surplus can then be extracted for the benefit of U.S. households."[39]

In answer to follow-up questions on the study, Peter Dixon conceded his study may have overestimated any public costs from temporary visa holders and that it is likely such costs would be much lower than indicated in the paper. That is because most temporary visa holders would be primarily able-bodied men in their 20s and perhaps 30s who pay taxes on their earnings, utilize few public resources, and in many cases may only stay in the United States for three to six years. This means the benefits of a more liberalized regime of temporary visas may be even greater than originally estimated by Dixon and Rimmer.[40]

Would this increase in temporary visas lead to more unemployment for American workers? Dixon and Rimmer say it would not: "Among other key findings is that additional low-skilled immigration would not increase the unemployment rates of low-skilled U.S. workers. While our modeling suggests that there would be reductions in the number of jobs for U.S. workers in low-skilled occupations, this does not mean that unemployment rates for these U.S. workers would rise. With increases in low-skilled immigration, the U.S. economy would expand, creating more jobs in higher-skilled areas. Over time, some U.S. workers now in low-paying jobs would move up the occupational ladder, actually reducing the wage pressure on low-skilled U.S. workers who remain in low-skilled jobs."[41]

A key reason why immigration is beneficial is it encourages a more productive use of human capital in the U.S. economy. "If you have high-skilled natives doing low-productivity jobs, it's a fundamental misallocation of labor and a big inefficiency," according to Pia Orrenius of the Federal Reserve Bank of Dallas. "And it makes people—natives—worse off."[42] As Dixon and Rimmer note, pointing to the benefits of an increased use of temporary visas, "The presence of more guest workers in lower-skilled, lower-paying occupations encourages Americans to seek employment in occupations where they can be more productive."[43]

NATIONAL ACADEMY OF SCIENCES REPORT AND FISCAL IMPACTS

Released in 1997, a report by the National Academy of Sciences (technically the National Research Council) continues to play a role in the debate over the economic impact of immigrants. Chaired by Jim Smith of the Rand Corporation, the panel of economists, demographers, and sociologists came to a consensus of sorts on immigration.

In its release of the study, the National Academy of Sciences (NAS) declared, "Immigration benefits the U.S. economy overall and has little negative effect on the income and job opportunities of most native-born Americans." Some of the details in the report are worth examining.

In explaining the benefits to the economy, panel chair Jim Smith stated in Congressional testimony, "Due to the immigrants who arrived since 1980, Total Gross National Product is about 200 billion dollars higher each year and native born Americans gain around 10 billion dollars each year."[44] In response to a question, Smith stated the number could be higher if the study had included economies of scale that could come from immigration and goods and services that would not have been produced domestically without immigrants. In addition, Smith pointed out no dollar amounts were placed on the contributions made by outstanding immigrants, such as top scientists, researchers or Nobel Prize-caliber foreign-born.[45]

Examining the report, one finds that the value created by immigrant entrepreneurs or the niches filled in the workplace by immigrants with different skills than natives were not included in the $10 billion figure. Smith also noted the $10 billion does not capture the full value of the contribution: "The $10 billion gain is an annual figure. If we discount that stream of yearly gains by a real interest rate of 3 percent, the net present value of the gains from those immigrants who arrived since 1980 would be $333 billion."[46]

For the labor market impact of immigrants on natives, the National Academy of Sciences largely utilized the model developed by George Borjas. Given the subsequent criticisms of Borjas's work and the research of Giovanni Peri, one wonders whether a similar panel today would rely on Borjas's model. Still, even then, the NAS study concluded, "The evidence points to the conclusion that immigration has had a relatively small adverse impact on the wage and employment opportunities of competing native groups."[47] The study found native high school dropouts may have experienced a drop in wages of 5 percent due to competing with immigrants. In response to a question, Jim Smith said even that 5 percent figure would be lower if one removed illegal immigrants from the equation, since illegal immigrants are more likely to lack a high school education. He added that even if America stopped all legal immigration of unskilled workers, the likely result would be an increase in illegal immigrants seeking to fill that gap.[48]

The National Academy of Sciences report also weighed in on the fiscal impact of immigration. "According to the report, over the long run an additional immigrant and all descendants would actually save the taxpayers $80,000," testified NAS panel member Ronald D. Lee, a professor of demography at the University of California–Berkeley.[49] The report noted that most immigrants arrive with their education already paid for and impose no added costs on many things they pay taxes to support, such as national defense.[50] He pointed out the NAS report found the fiscal impact of immigrants depends largely on education: "Immigrants who arrive with less than high school cost $10,000; those with high school contribute $50,000; those with more than high school contribute $200,000. Averaging over age and education gives +$80,000." Other factors can affect the impact as well. Lee noted, "A 30-year-old with less than high school education arriving alone would have a negative fiscal impact. However, together with a 12-year-old child, the combined fiscal impact of the two would be positive."[51]

The NAS study's findings on the fiscal impact on states have produced some misunderstanding. Given America's tax structure, where most tax dollars are sent to the federal government, particularly to support entitlement programs like Social Security and Medicare, it makes sense that the impact of immigrants would be more positive at the federal level than the state level. And that is what the NAS panel found, stating that, at least under a static model, immigrants were a fiscal burden to states, while they were a fiscal boon to the federal government.

A major problem with the NAS findings on states is that a dynamic model was used for the overall fiscal contributions of immigrants but a static model was produced, at least for illustrative purposes, for some states. The static model showed a relatively heavy cost of immigrants for taxpayers in California and New Jersey.

Ronald Lee rejected the use of the static model in assessing the fiscal impact of immigrants: "News accounts of the Panel's report have emphasized different numbers, which indicate that immigrant households imposed large net costs each year," testified Lee. "But these numbers do not best represent the Panel's findings, and should not be used for assessing the consequences of immigration policies."[52] The problem, Lee found, was that calculating annual numbers requires a model that counts the native-born children of immigrants as "costs" created by immigrant households when those children are in school but fails to include the taxes those children pay once they grow up and enter the workforce.

This raises an obvious question: What would the panel have found if it performed a dynamic analysis for individual states, taking into account the native-born children of immigrants as future workers and taxpayers? In response to questions, Lee said certain assumptions would need to be made, but that under a dynamic model "it appears highly likely that only for California would there be a negative net present value of an immigrant. For other states, the result would be positive." He added, "If only legal immigrants were counted in the calculation, then surely the result of the calculation for California would be more positive—that is closer to break even, or possibly greater than break even."[53]

A December 2006 report by the Texas Comptroller of Public Accounts utilized a mostly dynamic analysis that factored in economic activity by illegal immigrants. The report found illegal immigrants have produced a positive effect on the Texas economy and state budget, concluding: "The Comptroller's office estimates the absence of the estimated 1.4 million undocumented immigrants in Texas in fiscal 2005 would have been a loss to our Gross State Product of $17.7 billion. Also, the Comptroller's office estimates that state revenues collected from undocumented immigrants exceed what the state spent on services, with the difference being $424.7 million."[54]

IMMIGRANTS AND SOCIAL SECURITY

Social Security is a part of the fiscal equation where there is little disagreement that immigrants are helpful to the United States. Social Security benefits to current retirees are funded primarily out of the taxes paid by today's workers. For that reason, additional workers are extremely beneficial to America's "pay as you go" system. Immigrants typically arrive near the start of their working years and may contribute to the system for up to four decades before receiving any benefits.

Legal immigrants and their descendants make important positive contributions to America's Social Security system. Higher levels of legal immigration would benefit Social Security. However, increased taxes, benefits cutbacks, or some combination of the two would be necessary to prevent the worsening in the solvency of the Social Security trust fund caused by reductions in legal immigration. Policy makers considering changes to either Social Security or America's legal immigration system should be aware of the positive impact that legal immigrants have on Social Security.

A 2005 report from the National Foundation for American Policy found, "Over the next 50 years, new legal immigrants entering the United States will provide a net benefit of $407 billion in present value to America's Social Security system, according to official Social Security Administration data." The report concluded, "Maintaining or increasing current levels of legal immigration significantly aids the Social Security system, while imposing an immigration moratorium or reducing legal immigration would worsen the solvency of Social Security, harm taxpayers, and increase the size of the long-range actuarial deficit of the Social Security trust fund, according to data and an analysis from the Social Security Administration (SSA) Office of the Chief Actuary."[55]

A moratorium on legal immigrants entering the country would harm the Social Security system by ballooning the size of the actuarial deficit by almost one-third—31 percent—over a 50-year period, the report found. To compensate for the loss of revenue caused by a moratorium would require increasing Social Security taxes on Americans by $407 billion in present value over 50 years and $346 billion over 75 years. Such a tax increase would cost an American earning $60,000 in 2004 more than $1,860 in higher payroll taxes over the next 10 years. Even smaller reductions in legal immigration would increase the actuarial deficit and would need higher taxes or reductions in benefits to make up for the lost revenue.[56]

In contrast, increases in legal immigration would provide a significant boost to Social Security. The size of the actuarial deficit would be *reduced* over 50 years by 10 percent if legal immigration increased 33 percent (an additional 264,000 immigrants a year). A 33 percent increase in legal immigration would increase revenues to Social Security by a present value of $138 billion over 50 years and $121 billion over 75 years. (While not the focus of the study, it should be noted that the Social Security Administration actuaries have concluded illegal immigrants are also beneficial to the Social Security system, since they enter at young ages and, unless paid off the books, pay FICA payroll taxes.)

A final word on fiscal impacts is in order. In recent years, it has become popular and, at times necessary, to examine the worth of immigration based on the potential fiscal impact of a particular policy. However, such an approach by itself can overlook the noneconomic benefit of policies that promote greater economic freedom. Even in an economic sense, it can lead to the false impression that an individual's total worth to society is only as a taxpayer who can help support government spending in Washington, DC, or in the state legislature.

The economy and the federal (or state) budget are two different things. If U.S. tax rates were reduced such that all Americans paid exactly $5,000 a year, it would not mean that Apple founder Steve Jobs and a local cashier have an equal impact on the economy because they now pay the same amount in taxes. Starting a business, producing innovations, working to satisfy consumer needs, making other workers more productive, and spending and investing the fruits of one's labor can all produce a positive impact on the economy whether or not they are reflected in annual tax payments to the federal government.

CONCLUSION

The immigration issue remains complex, as evidenced by how results differ on its impact depending on the chosen methodology. It appears immigrants increase specialization in the economy, enhance the nation's productive capacity, and aid innovation in the United States. The best evidence suggests that immigrants improve their own lot and that of their children by coming to America and exert little adverse impact on natives.

While much of the debate over immigration focuses on the economic impact, it is sometimes important to step back and look at the bigger picture. In a hearing to discuss the findings of the 1997 National Academy of Sciences report, then Senate Immigration Chair Spencer Abraham stated, "While the economic case for immigration is important, it does not capture all that is important about immigration policy. Much about immigration is embodied in the freedom for people to seek a better life for themselves and their children. The freedom for families to reunite. The freedom to hire individuals who will help American companies grow and compete. And the freedom to live in a land where we do not persecute people based on their religious beliefs or the color of their skin but judge them solely by the content of their character."[57]

NOTES

1. Interview with Mark J. Perry.
2. Richard Vedder, Lowell Gallaway, and Stephen Moore, *Immigration and Unemployment: New Evidence* (Arlington, VA: Alexis de Tocqueville Institution, 1994), 2, as cited in Stuart Anderson, *Employment-Based Immigration and High Technology* (Washington, DC: Empower America, 1996), 66.
3. Portions of this chapter originally appeared in research the author produced for the Merage Foundations and is used with thanks and permission.
4. Patrice Hill, "How Immigrants Make Economy Grow," *Washington Times*, May 1, 2006.
5. William Beach and James Sherk, "Growing the Labor Force," Letter to the Editor, *Washington Times*, May 3, 2006.
6. Pia Orrenius, "The Impact of Immigration," Commentary, *Wall Street Journal*, April 25, 2006.
7. Alexander T. Tabarrok and David J. Theroux, "Open Letter on Immigration," The Independent Institute, June 19, 2006.
8. Giovanni Peri, *Immigrants, Skills, and Wages: Measuring the Economic Gains from Immigration* (Washington, DC: Immigration Policy Center, 2006), 7.
9. Ibid., 6.
10. Gnanaraj Chellaraj, Keith E. Maskus, and Aaditya Mattoo, "The Contribution of Skilled Immigration and International Graduate Students to U.S. Innovation," March 17, 2005; Stuart Anderson, "America's Future is Stuck Overseas," *New York Times*, November 16, 2005.
11. Chellaraj, Maskus, and Mattoo, p. 5.
12. Ibid., 6–7.
13. Ibid., 9.

14. Marc Andreesen interviewed on *Lou Dobbs Tonight*, March 4, 2004.

15. AnnaLee Saxenian, "Brain Circulation, How High-Skilled Immigration Makes Everyone Better Off," *Brookings Review*, Winter 2002. In past years, the majority of H-1B visa holders have been from India and China.

16. Michael Cox and Richard Alm, "The Great American Job Machine," *New York Times*, November 7, 2003.

17. Daniel Griswold, *Mad About Trade* (Washington, DC: Cato Institute, 2009), 32.

18. Neil Irwin and Dana Hedgpeth, "Immigration's Bottom Line," *Washington Post*, April 30, 2006.

19. George J. Borjas and Lawrence F. Katz, "The Evolution of the Mexican-Born Workforce in the United States," Working Paper 11281, National Bureau of Economic Research, April 2005, 63.

20. Ibid., 37–39.

21. Ibid., 39–40.

22. David Card, "Is the New Immigration Really So Bad?" University of California–Berkeley, January 2005, 1.

23. Tyler Cowen and Daniel Rothschild, "Hey, Don't Bad-Mouth Unskilled Immigrants," *Los Angeles Times*, May 15, 2006.

24. David Card, "The Impact of the Mariel Boatlift on the Miami Labor Market," *Industrial and Labor Relations Review* 43, no. 2 (1990).

25. Card, "Is the New Immigration Really So Bad?"

26. Ibid. Emphasis in original. Card goes on to write, "The leading alternative to a local labor market approach is a time series analysis of aggregate relative wages. Surprisingly, such an analysis shows that the wages of native dropouts (people with less than a high school diploma) relative to native high school graduates have remained nearly constant since 1980, despite pressures from immigrant inflows that have increased the relative supply of dropout labor, and despite the rise in the wage gap between other education groups in the U.S. economy. While the counterfactual is unknown, it is hard to argue that the aggregate time series evidence point to a negative impact of immigration unless ones starts from that position *a priori*."

27. Ibid., 8. Card writes, "Again, the conclusion is that native mobility has virtually no offsetting effect on the relative supply shocks created by immigration. Indeed, once controls are introduced for city-specific trends in native population growth, the data suggest that native mobility responses may slightly reinforce the relative supply effects of immigration."

28. Ibid., 18. According to Card, "Although immigration presumably exerts downward pressure on the relative wages of dropouts, the wage gap between dropouts and high school graduates has been nearly constant since 1980, and has fallen by more than 50 percent relative to the gap between high school graduates and holders of bachelor's degrees."

29. Diana Furchtgott-Roth, "Immigrants Don't Depress Wages," *New York Sun*, April 12, 2006.

30. National Research Council, *The New Americans*, advance copy (Washington, DC: National Academy Press, 1997), S-5.

31. Adriana Kugler and Mutlu Yuksel, "Effects of Low-Skilled Immigration on U.S. Natives: Evidence from Hurricane Mitch," NBER, Working Paper 14293, August 2008, 3.

32. Gianmarco I. P. Ottaviano and Giovanni Peri, "Rethinking the Gains from Immigration: Theory and Evidence from the U.S.," August 2005, 28.

33. Ibid., 28.

34. Peri, *Immigrants, Skills, and Wages*, 1.

35. Ibid., 6.

36. Ibid., 6.

37. Giovanni Peri, "The Effect of Immigration on Productivity: Evidence from U.S. States," NBER Working Paper No. 15507 (November 2009), 1.

38. Peter B. Dixon and Maureen T. Rimmer, *Restriction or Legalization? Measuring the Economic Benefits of Immigration Reform* (Washington, DC: Cato Institute, 2009), 4.

39. Ibid., 4.

40. Interview with Peter B. Dixon.

41. Dixon and Rimmer, 4.

42. As cited in Jason L. Riley, *Let Them In* (New York: Gotham Books, 2008), 74.

43. Dixon and Rimmer, 11.

44. Testimony of James P. Smith, member, National Academy of Sciences Panel on the Demographic and Economic Impacts of Immigration, before Subcommittee on Immigration, Senate Committee on the Judiciary, on "Economic and Fiscal Impact of Immigration," September 9, 1997.

45. Ibid.

46. Ibid., "Responses of James P. Smith to Questions from Senator Abraham."

47. *The New Americans*, S-5.

48. "Responses of James P. Smith to Questions from Senator Abraham."

49. Testimony of Ronald D. Lee, member, National Academy of Sciences Panel on the Demographic and Economic Impacts of Immigration, before Subcommittee on Immigration, Senate Committee on the Judiciary, on "Economic and Fiscal Impact of Immigration," September 9, 1997.

50. Ibid.

51. Ibid., "Responses of Ronald D. Lee to Questions from Senator Abraham."

52. Ibid.

53. Ibid. For example, one assumption would be that immigrants and their descendants stay in the same state. It's possible that even if immigrants and their descendants moved, but exchanged states with other immigrants and their descendants in rough proportion, it would not affect the calculation.

54. Texas Comptroller of Public Accounts, *Undocumented Immigrants in Texas: A Financial Analysis of the Impact to the State Budget and Economy* (Austin: Texas Comptroller of Public Accounts, 2006), 20.

55. Stuart Anderson, *The Contribution of Legal Immigration to the Social Security System* (Arlington, VA: National Foundation for American Policy, updated March 2005), 1–2. Time has passed since the study was released, which means some of the numbers would have changed. However, the overall conclusion would

remain the same: increases in legal immigration would be beneficial to the Social Security system and decreases would be harmful.

56. According to the report, "A thirty-three percent reduction in legal immigration would increase the actuarial deficit by 10 percent over 50 years and result in lost revenues of $132 billion in present value over 50 years and $111 billion over 75 years, which would need to be made up for through higher taxes or other means. Such a tax increase would cost an American earning $60,000 in 2004 more than $720 in higher payroll taxes over the next 10 years, in the case of a 41% reduction in legal immigration, and $600 over the next 10 years for a 33% legal immigration reduction."

57. Opening Statement of Senator Spencer Abraham, before Subcommittee on Immigration, Senate Committee on the Judiciary, on "Economic and Fiscal Impact of Immigration," September 9, 1997.

SUGGESTED READINGS

Card, David. "Is the New Immigration Really So Bad?" University of California–Berkeley, January 2005.

Dixon, Peter B., and Maureen T. Rimmer. *Restriction or Legalization? Measuring the Economic Benefits of Immigration Reform.* Washington, DC: Cato Institute, 2009.

National Research Council. *The New Americans.* Washington, DC: National Academy Press, 1997.

Peri, Giovanni. "The Effect of Immigration on Productivity: Evidence from U.S. States." NBER Working Paper No. 15507, November 2009.

Peri, Giovanni. *Immigrants, Skills, and Wages: Measuring the Economic Gains from Immigration.* Washington, DC: Immigration Policy Center, 2006.

Texas Comptroller of Public Accounts. *Undocumented Immigrants in Texas: A Financial Analysis of the Impact to the State Budget and Economy.* Austin: Texas Comptroller of Public Accounts, 2006.

Eight

Assimilation

On the topic of immigrant assimilation, perceptions often take precedence over facts. Two perceptions are perhaps most important: (1) the belief previous immigrants were better than today's immigrants, and (2) the sense that the new immigrants will bring about unwanted change.

In her examination of more than a century's worth of newspaper coverage of immigration, American University professor Rita Simon discovered both overly optimistic evaluations of earlier waves of immigrants and excessively pessimistic views of current immigrants and their ability to adapt to life in the United States. According to Simon:

> In my study of public attitudes toward immigration, going back as far as one can, I have found that the American people, although they refer to the United States very proudly as a country of immigrants and they talk about the immigrant heritage and so forth, when you ask them specifically about immigration and about how many immigrants should be allowed to enter the country, they tend to put on rose-colored glasses and look backwards and suggest that those immigrants who came earlier, they were wonderful for this country. . . . But the immigrants who are coming now—and the now could be in the 1940s, the 1950s or any decade up until right now—they're no good for this country. They take more than they give. They're not really loyal. They're coming here only to make money. They will not make positive contributions. And we should really, as much as possible, not allow them in.[1]

Simon adds, "One of the reasons that we see the pattern that I described about liking immigrants who came in the past and being fearful of those who are coming now is there's genuinely a fear of change. And somehow I think there's a fear that these people are different, that they will not behave as all previous groups have behaved."[2]

Research by David Card (University of California–Berkeley) and his colleagues Ian Preston and Christian Dustmann of University College London supports Simon's evaluation. The research found people's attitudes toward immigration were much more likely to be shaped by their perception of "compositional amenities" than any impact, real or alleged, immigrants might have on jobs or wages.

Card defines "compositional amenities" as "The set of characteristics of an individual's environment that he or she values, and perceives as being potentially affected by a change in the presence of immigrants. It would include the racial/ethnic and income distribution of neighbors and co-workers, their religious affiliations, their language and culture."[3]

In Card's views, these perceptions go beyond what people may see around them. "That is extremely broad, because my feeling is that someone living in Tennessee, for example, may be concerned about the use of Spanish by immigrants in Miami. People often act like they have some feeling of 'ownership' over very wide domains. We don't have an easy way to make sense of this in economics other than as saying that it is something people obviously value."[4] He points out that he is often surprised at how someone from another state will comment forcefully on something that is going on (or believe is going on) at Berkeley.

By one measure, the research found "concerns over compositional amenities are roughly 4 times more important in explaining the variation in opinions on immigration policy within demographic subgroups than concerns over economic issues."[5] The study utilized data for 21 countries in the 2002 European Social Survey, but Card said, "I think the same ideas would apply in the U.S., perhaps to a slightly different extent."[6]

One reason for these results is that perceptions about immigrants in the minds of many people are different from the data. Many Americans may believe recent immigrants and their children are not interested in learning English, come here to get welfare benefits, are perhaps not that patriotic, and commit a disproportionate percentage of the crimes. The information in this chapter will help explain why these worries and perceptions are unnecessary.

DO IMMIGRANTS ASSIMILATE?

Do immigrants assimilate or stay forever apart from American society? This is a central question in the debate over immigration and has remained so for most of our nation's history. Discussing the restrictions on immigration imposed by Congress in the 1920s, historian Oscar Handlin wrote, "The objections to further immigration from Italy and Poland reflected the objectors' unfavorable observations of the Italians and the Poles they saw about them. The arguments that Greeks and Slovaks could not become good Americans rested on the premise that the Greeks and Slovaks in the United States had not become good Americans."[7]

When attempting to measure whether immigrants are assimilating, one should use longitudinal data, not averages or "snapshots," notes Jason Riley, author of *Let Them In.*[8] The reason is that new people added to a group tend to skew the data, which masks progress made over time by earlier members of a group.

Here is an example of a longitudinal approach (tracking individuals) vs. a group "snapshot" approach: Let's assume that the height of a typical 9th-grade boy entering a high school is 5′ 6″ but that the typical 12th-grade boy's height is 6′. If we tracked individual boys or even a cohort of 9th graders through to 12th grade, then we would find that typically the boys grow 6 inches taller over the course of their time at the high school. But if one measured only the average height of the boys in the school at a given time, it might be only 5′10″ tall. And if one measured the average height at the school three years later, it would likely still be 5′10″. However, one would not say, "None of the boys at this school ever grow."

Another element that can skew data on assimilation is the inclusion of illegal immigrants, particularly short-term migrants. An individual who expects only to be in the United States at most two to four years has less of an incentive to invest in the time, energy, or resources to acquire skills that would aid a long-term resident, such as learning English proficiently or going back to school to gain a higher level of education.

The issue is not academic, since sometimes data that include illegal immigrants have been cited to argue for changes to the legal immigration system. Generally speaking, critics of legal immigration want illegal immigrants to be deported, not to take civics classes, so including data on illegal immigrants when discussing potential changes to legal immigration makes little sense.

WAGE GROWTH

One way to tell whether immigrants assimilate or not is to answer the following question: Do immigrants enter the United States and never increase their earnings beyond their initial wages? If the answer is "yes," then immigrants are not able to assimilate economically in the United States. But the literature shows immigrants increase their earnings over time.

While much has been written about what American institutions may do that interferes with assimilation, few commentators note what America does right. Perhaps the most important assimilation policy the United States can maintain is flexible labor markets. Inflexible labor markets, such as in France, mean an employer may not wish to take a chance on hiring a new employee if it later will be difficult to dismiss that individual. The difficulty of young people or new immigrants entering the labor market because employers incur substantial risk of not being able to dismiss a new employee may be a contributing factor in the disaffection of Muslim immigrants in France and some other European countries. The world is complex, and one factor cannot explain everything. However, a government's economic policies are often a good place to start when looking for answers.

At least currently, the United States maintains a relatively flexible labor market when compared to most other countries. "Wages are less rigid in Canada and the United States than in Australia, with the general consensus that the U.S. labor market is the most flexible of the three," explain economists Heather Antecol (Claremont McKenna College), Peter Kuhn (University of California–Santa Barbara), and Stephen J. Trejo (University of Texas–Austin).[9]

Wage flexibility in America directly contributes to assimilation. "We find that wage assimilation is an important source of immigrants' earnings growth in both Canada and the United States, but the magnitude of wage assimilation is substantially larger in the United States," according to Antecol, Kuhn, and Trejo.[10] They found Australia offering unemployment compensation to newly arriving immigrants and rigidity in the labor market encouraged new immigrants to Australia to "invest less in skills that foster wage growth than immigrants to the United States."[11] Antecol, Kuhn, and Trejo conclude, "Our results are consistent with the hypothesis that national labor market institutions—in particular those that influence the dispersion of wage and the incomes of the unemployed—can play a key role in the immigrant assimilation process."[12]

Jeffrey S. Passel, senior research associate, Pew Hispanic Center, has developed techniques to differentiate between legal and illegal immigrants in census data and to track changes based on years in the country. Passel's research on immigrant wage growth and other issues demonstrates how important it can be to determine immigrant legal status when examining data on assimilation.

Census data show legal immigrants experience significant wage gains over time, even surpassing the average family income of natives, in the case of naturalized citizens. But illegal immigrants do not show that type of income gain based on years in the United States. "Average family income for both legal immigrants and refugees in the U.S. for more than 10 years is only 2 to 3 percent below that of natives," writes Passel. "For longer term naturalized citizen families, average family income is 23 percent higher than native income."[13] But the average income level of an illegal immigrant family remains well below the average native family (about 35 percent below) even among illegal immigrants in the country 10 years or longer.[14]

Research that did not distinguish between legal and illegal immigrants still found significant wage growth among immigrants. Economists Harriet Duleep and Mark Regets found that after a decade in the United States, the earnings gap between new immigrants and natives largely disappears, with immigrant wage growth faster than native (6.7 percent vs. 4.4 percent).[15]

EDUCATION

We can see a similar story on legal immigrants in the Pew Hispanic Center's analysis of census data on education and immigrants. Overall, 32 percent of legal immigrants have obtained a bachelor's degree or higher, compared to 30 percent of natives and 15 percent of illegal immigrants.[16]

What about those who did not finish high school (ages 18–24)? Among illegal immigrants, 49 percent did not graduate high school, compared to 21 percent of legal immigrants and 11 percent of natives. Even among illegal immigrants who completed high school, less than half went on to attend college.[17]

In contrast, among immigrants and natives who have completed high school, more legal immigrants have gone on to attend a college than natives—73 percent of legal immigrants vs. 70 percent of natives—according to Passel's research.[18] There may be legal impediments, such as denial of in-state tuition or lack of access to student loans, that can hinder illegal immigrants from pursuing college in the United States.

Education levels for legal immigrants improve across generations, just as they have historically for Americans. It is likely most people reading this chapter who have a college degree had parents or grandparents who did not attend college. "Turning to the data, educational assimilation appears alive and well," according to Pia Orrenius, senior economist, Federal Reserve Bank of Dallas. "High school dropout rates for immigrants improve across generations, dropping from 27 percent in the first generation to below the native average of 8.9 percent in the third generation."[19]

Orrenius finds "large differences among groups of immigrants," noting non-Hispanic immigrants, as a group, start below the dropout rates for natives and then improve further in the second generation. "Hispanic immigrants do much worse in general, but also improve the most," notes Orrenius. "In the first generation, about 44 percent lack a high school diploma, this rate improves to 15 and 16 percent, respectively, in the second and third generations."[20] She finds a similar pattern with wages, but points out an "education gap" explains most of the wage difference.

Some of this gap may be explained from Passel's data about the difference in education levels (and improvements) among illegal immigrants compared to legal immigrants, which Orrenius does not distinguish between, except in discussing possible solutions. "Legal status could open many doors, both lowering the costs of education and increasing avenues for financing education through access to student loans," she writes.[21] But Orrenius notes, "Surveys suggest that Hispanics have lower educational aspirations than other ethnic groups. This could reflect a discouraged youth to whom economic opportunity may not seem within reach. In addition, ethnicity does matter. Even when researchers account for all measurable factors that determine education levels, the fact that an individual is Hispanic or Black or Asian matters in and of itself."[22]

As with many immigration issues, the question turns back to Mexico. "Worrying about immigrant assimilation boils down to worrying about Mexican immigration," writes Orrenius. "Non-Hispanic immigrants consistently out perform natives, even after three generations."[23]

Two key points help place these concerns about Mexican immigrants in context. First, immigrants from Mexico represented only 17 percent of all legal immigrants to the United States in 2008, a smaller proportion than most people would imagine.[24] Second, according to the data, assimilation still works. Orrenius concludes the melting pot "continues to simmer successfully, much as it did 100 years ago." She makes a broader point, one that goes beyond immigration policy: "The problem we have uncovered is not one of immigrant assimilation, but rather what immigrants are assimilating to."[25]

ENGLISH LANGUAGE

Do immigrants and their children learn English? Do they want to learn English? Confronted with store signs in Spanish and service workers with sometimes limited English skills, many Americans believe the answer is "no." The data suggest otherwise.

In the report *The New Americans,* produced by the National Research Council, only 3 percent of immigrants in the country 30 years or more reported not speaking English well in the 1990 Census.[26] This illustrates that assimilation takes place, but also how important it is to make judgments on data that are longitudinal, since newly arriving immigrants can skew the totals.[27] The story is quite positive with the children of immigrants. According to a Pew survey, 88 percent of second-generation children from Latino immigrant families and 94 percent from the third generation said they spoke English very well.[28]

Contrary to concerns that Spanish-speaking immigrants will pass along to their children and grandchildren a proclivity to speak Spanish over English, research shows the opposite is true. A study by Frank Bean and Ruben Rumbaut (both University of California–Irvine) and Douglas Massey (Princeton University) found, "Although the generational life expectancy of

Spanish is greater among Mexicans in Southern California than other groups, its demise is all but assured by the third generation."[29]

Bean, Rumbaut, and Massey concluded, "Based on an analysis of language loss over the generations, the study concludes that English has never been seriously threatened as the dominant language in America, nor is it under threat today."[30]

IMMIGRANTS AND CRIME

Historically, no issue can incite a population against a minority or foreign-born group more than allegations of criminal activities. Pogroms against Jews in Russia, lynchings against black Americans in the antebellum South, and violence against Chinese immigrants in the West were at times triggered by accusations of criminal offences. Needless to say, public perception has often trumped reality.

In this case, the good news is that data show immigrants are less likely to commit crimes than the native born. In fact, data from California show immigrants are much less likely to do so "When we consider all institutionalization (not only prisons but also jails, halfway houses, and the like) and focus on the population that is most likely to be in institutions because of criminal activity (men 18–40), we find that, in California, U.S.-born men have an institutionalization rate that is 10 times higher than that of foreign-born men (4.2 percent vs. 0.42 percent). And when we compare foreign-born men to U.S.-born men with similar age and education levels, these differences become even greater," according to research by economists Kristin F. Butcher (Federal Reserve Bank of Chicago) and Anne Morrison Piehl (Rutgers University and the National Bureau of Economic Research). Looking only at prisons the researchers found, "U.S.-born adult men are incarcerated at a rate over two-and-a-half times greater than that of foreign-born men."[31]

National studies reach the same conclusion: foreign born (both legal and illegal immigrants) are less likely to commit crimes than the native born. "Among men age 18–39 (who comprise the vast majority of the prison population), the 3.5 percent incarceration rate of the native-born in 2000 was 5 times higher than the 0.7 percent incarceration rate of the foreign-born."[32] However, one of the ironies is that "assimilation" in the area of criminal behavior has actually meant a higher incarceration rate of native-born Hispanic males than their foreign-born counterparts, again raising the question into what societal problems are the children of immigrants assimilating.[33]

To those who have examined the issue, it is not surprising the crime rates of immigrants are low. "Currently U.S. immigration policy provides several mechanisms that are likely to reduce the criminal activity of immigrants," write Butcher and Piehl. "Legal immigrants are screened with regard to their criminal backgrounds. In addition, all non-citizens, even those in the United States legally, are subject to deportation if convicted of a criminal offense that is punishable by a prison sentence of a year or more, even if that is suspended. Furthermore, those in the country illegally have an additional incentive to avoid contact with law enforcement—even for minor offenses—since such contact is likely to increase the chances that their illegal status will be revealed."[34]

WELFARE USE

There is little evidence immigrants come to America to get on welfare, rather than to work, flee persecution, and/or join family members in the United States. Even if receiving services were a motive, it would make little sense because immigrants are generally ineligible for federal means-tested benefits programs unless they have been in the United States for five years or more in a lawful status. It should be noted that states have different eligibility rules and a child born in America is a U.S. citizen and can receive benefits if he or she meets a program's eligibility criteria, regardless of a parent's immigration status.

An analysis of census data released by the House Ways and Means Committee indicates the percentage of those who use AFDC/TANF (Aid to Families with Dependent Children/Temporary Assistance for Needy Children), Medicaid, and food stamps is generally about the same or lower for natives as it is for noncitizens and naturalized citizens. The data show the vast majority of immigrants are not receiving these types of public benefits. For example, less than one percent of naturalized citizens and noncitizens in 2006 received benefits under TANF (see Table 8.1).[35]

In 2006, 0.6 percent of natives used AFDC/TANF, compared to 0.3 percent of naturalized citizens and 0.7 percent for noncitizens. For Medicaid, 13.1 percent of natives used Medicaid, compared to 10.8 percent of naturalized citizens and 11.6 percent of noncitizens. And 7.7 percent of natives

TABLE 8.1
Use of Public Benefits by Nativity and Citizenship, 2006

Program	Percent of Natives Using Benefit	Percent of Naturalized Citizens Using Benefit	Percent of Non-Citizens Using Benefit
AFDC/TANF	0.6%	0.3%	0.7%
SSI	1.6%	3.0%	1.3%
Medicaid	13.1%	10.8%	11.6%
Food Stamps	7.7%	3.9%	6.2%

Source: House Ways and Means Committee, *2008 Green Book*, Appendix H, Table H-9—Estimated Benefit Usage by Citizenship Categories: 1995, 1999, 2001, 2006.

used the food stamp program, compared to 3.9 percent of naturalized citizens and 6.2 percent of noncitizens. For SSI (Supplemental Security Income), which most older natives would not use because they are eligible for Social Security benefits, 1.6 percent of natives used SSI in 2006, compared to 3.0 percent of naturalized citizens and 1.3 percent of noncitizens.

In 1996, Congress tightened the rules for immigrant benefit eligibility as part of a broader reform of the nation's welfare laws. The data illustrate this decrease in immigrant welfare use. "There were substantial declines between 1994 and 1999 in legal immigrants' use of all major benefit programs: TANF (−60 percent), food stamps (−48 percent), SSI (−32 percent), and Medicaid (−15 percent)," according to a report by the Urban Institute.[36]

Even before the changes in the law, there was little support for the view that individual immigrants were more likely to be on welfare than natives.[37] One of the difficulties in measuring welfare use is that eligibility for some benefits is geared toward individuals and for others is based on family, and families may live in households that go beyond two spouses and their children. If one labels a household as "using welfare" even when only one person in a house is receiving benefits, then it is likely to inflate the data on welfare use for immigrants, since the foreign born tend to maintain larger households. On the other hand, such a calculation could capture data on a U.S.-citizen child born to immigrant parents.

If immigrants are seeking out states with more lenient benefit eligibility, then they're not doing a good job. Many states with recent large increases in their immigrant populations are primarily states with low and below average social spending, such as Arkansas, North Carolina, South Carolina, Utah, and Georgia, notes Jason Riley.[38]

Prior to the 1996 reforms, there was concern that noncitizen parents were making excessive use of SSI. With the exception of refugees and other "humanitarian immigrants," veterans, active duty military and their families, and certain Native Americans born abroad, Congress enacted a complete ban on SSI for noncitizens who enter the United States after August 22, 1996.[39] Lawful permanent residents with credit for 40 quarters of work history in the United States can receive SSI once they have been in "qualified" status for five years or more (see Table 8.2).

In 1995, 3.2 percent of noncitizens used SSI, compared to 1.3 percent in 2006. Similarly, Congress barred most noncitizens arriving after August 22, 1996, from using food stamps, although this was modified in 2002 to allow noncitizen children and certain other lawfully residing immigrants to use food stamps. In general, a sponsor of an immigrant can be "required to reimburse the government for any means-tested public benefit the alien has received," notes attorney Susan Fortino-Brown.[40]

TABLE 8.2
Benefits Eligibility for Lawful Permanent Residents (LPRs)

Program	Eligibility for Immigrants Who Arrived after August 22, 1996
Temporary Assistance for Needy Families	Not eligible until after 5 years or more of lawful permanent residence status; deeming of sponsor's income and resources could affect eligibility
Food Stamps	Not eligible until after 5 years or more of lawful permanent residence status; lawful permanent residents who have worked for 40 quarters; deeming of sponsor's income and resources could affect eligibility; children under age 18 are eligible
Supplemental Security Income	Generally ineligible. Lawful permanent residents with credit for 40 quarters of work history eligible after 5 years in legal (resident) status; deeming of sponsor's income and resources could affect eligibility
Medicaid (Full-Scope)	Not eligible until after 5 years or more of lawful permanent residence status; deeming of sponsor's income and resources could affect eligibility; state options on children under 21 and pregnant women
Children's Health Insurance Program	Not eligible until after 5 years or more of lawful permanent residence status; deeming of sponsor's income and resources could affect eligibility; state options on children under 21 and pregnant women

Source: National Immigration Law Center. Rules as of January 2010. Note: Eligibility rules differ for immigrants who arrived in the United States prior to August 22, 1996, refugees, asylees, individuals granted withholding of deportation, Cuban/Haitian entrants, victims of trafficking, members of the Armed Forces on active duty and honorably discharged veterans and spouses/children of military/veterans. State eligibility rules can differ. Immigrants are eligible for Emergency Medicaid, including labor and delivery, if otherwise eligible for the program. In some circumstances under the law immigrants may become eligible for a benefit prior to 5 years of law permanent resident status if, for example, they were in "qualified" immigrant status for 5 years, such as a qualified battered immigrant or certain individuals paroled into the country who later became permanent residents.

OPINION SURVEYS OF IMMIGRANTS

One way to judge whether immigrants hold views that show they are good members of American society is to ask them their opinions on a variety of matters. A 2009 survey found that 76 percent of immigrants agreed with the statement, "The United States is a unique country that stands for something special in the world."[41] The survey, conducted by Public Agenda, a nonpartisan research group, involved more than 1,000 immigrants.

In the Public Agenda survey, 87 percent of the noncitizens who are legal residents say "they are either in the process or planned to become citizens in the future."[42] Eighty-four percent said a reason for becoming a U.S. citizen was to "show a commitment and pride in being an American." Eighty-eight percent cited "to have equal rights and protections in the United States" as reason for citizenship. And 90 percent cited attaining the right to vote.[43]

According to the survey, 88 percent of immigrants said it was extremely or somewhat important for immigrants "to work and stay off welfare." Eighty-four percent of immigrants believe it's somewhat or very hard for "new immigrants to get a good job or do well in the country without learning English."[44]

Overall, immigrants take a positive view of learning English. Seventy percent of those surveyed who spoke little or no English when arriving in America said they have taken classes to improve their English skills.[45]

On the issue of teaching English in public schools, 74 percent of immigrants said it was better to teach new immigrants English "as quickly as possible, even if this means they fall behind in other subjects." When parents were asked about how well their children (under 18) speak English, 67 percent said excellent, 21 percent good, 8 percent fair, and only 1 percent poor.

Eighty-eight percent of immigrants agreed with the statement, "A person has to work hard in this country to make it—nobody gives you anything for free."[46]

Although some have expressed the fear that Hispanics are less likely to share American values, public opinion surveys show this concern is unfounded. A 2004 American National Election Study found 91 percent of Hispanics said their love for America was "extremely" or "very" strong, the same percentage as whites.[47] In fact, a slightly higher percentage of Hispanics than whites—86 percent vs. 85 percent—said when they see "the American flag flying" it makes them feel "extremely good" or "very good."[48]

Supporting these survey results, Jason Riley of the *Wall Street Journal* points out those pushing what conservatives see as a "multicultural" agenda tend to be professors at elite universities, not "the women changing the linen at your hotel, or the men building homes in your neighborhood." His proposed solution: "Keep the immigrants. Deport the Columbia faculty."[49]

NOTES

1. Rita Simon interview, "The First Measured Century." Available at: http://www.pbs.org/fmc/interviews/simon.htm.
2. Ibid.
3. Interview with David Card.
4. Ibid.
5. David Card, Ian Preston, and Christian Dustmann, "Immigration, Wages, and Compositional Amenities," NBER Working Paper No. 15521 (November 2009): 2.
6. Interview with David Card.

7. As cited in "Should America Remain a Nation of Immigrants," hearing before the Subcommittee on Immigration, Committee on the Judiciary, U.S. Senate, August 11, 1997.

8. Interview with Jason Riley.

9. Heather Antecol, Peter Kuhn, and Stephen J. Trejo, "Assimilation via Prices or Quantities? Labor Market Institutions and Immigrant Earning Growth in Australia, Canada and the United States," IZA DP, no.802, June 2003, 1.

10. Ibid.

11. Ibid., 2, 31–32.

12. Ibid., 32.

13. Jeffrey S. Passel, *Unauthorized Migrants: Numbers and Characteristics* (Washington, DC: Pew Hispanic Center, 2005), 31.

14. Ibid., 31.

15. Harriet Orcutt Duleep and Mark C. Regets, "Immigrants and Human-Capital Investment," *American Economic Review* (May 1999).

16. Passel, 23.

17. Ibid., 22.

18. Ibid.

19. Pia Orrenius, "Immigrant Assimilation: Is the U.S. Still a Melting Pot?" Presentation, Federal Reserve Bank of Dallas, January 2004, 3.

20. Ibid.

21. Ibid., 4.

22. Ibid.

23. Ibid.

24. *2008 Yearbook of Immigration Statistics,* Office of Immigration Statistics, Department of Homeland Security, 2009. Table 3. Of 1,107,126 legal immigrants in 2008, 189,989 were born in Mexico.

25. Orrenius, 4.

26. National Research Council, *The New Americans*, advance copy (Washington, DC: National Academy Press, 1997), S-10.

27. Julia Preston, "Latino Immigrants' Children Found Grasping English," *New York Times*, November 30, 2007. For example, a Pew Hispanic Center survey found only 23 percent of first-generation Latino immigrants believed they spoke English well.

28. Ibid.

29. "Immigration No Threat to English Use in the U.S.: Study," Reuters, September 13, 2006.

30. Ibid.

31. Kristin F. Butcher and Anne Morrison Piehl, *Crime, Corrections, and California* (San Francisco: Public Policy Institute of California, 2008), 1–2.

32. Ruben G. Rumbaut and Walter Ewing, *The Myth of Immigrant Criminality and the Paradox of Assimilation: Incarceration Rates among Native and Foreign-Born Men* (Washington, DC: Immigration Policy Center, 2007), 1.

33. Ibid.

34. Butcher and Piehl, 3.

35. House Ways and Means Committee, *2008 Green Book*, Appendix H, Table H-9—Estimated Benefit Usage by Citizenship Categories: 1995, 1998, 2001, 2006.

36. Walter A. Ewing, *Not Getting What They Paid For* (Washington, DC: Immigration Policy Center, 2003), 1.

37. In research for the Urban Institute in 1994, Rebecca L. Clark wrote, "Among immigrants, high rates of welfare use are limited to one group of immigrants—those who entered as refugees—and one type of welfare—SSI. For other types of welfare, immigrants who did not enter as refugees are no more likely to use welfare than natives." From Rebecca L. Clark, "The Costs of Providing Public Assistance and Education to Immigrants" (Washington, DC: Urban Institute, 1994), 18, as cited in Julian L. Simon, *Immigration: The Demographic and Economic Facts* (Washington, DC: Cato Institute and the National Immigration Forum, 1995), 35–36.

38. Jason Riley, *Let Them In* (New York: Gotham Books, 2008), 108.

39. Thank you to Jonathan Blazer and Tanya Broder of the National Immigration Law Center for their assistance.

40. Susan Fortino-Brown, "Family-Sponsored Immigration, in *Navigating the Fundamentals of Immigration Law: Guidance and Tips for Successful Practice, 2007–2008 Edition*, ed. Grace E. Akers (Washington, DC: American Immigration Lawyers Association, 2007), 326.

41. *A Place to Call Home: What Immigrants Say Now About Life in America* (New York: Public Agenda and Carnegie Corporation, 2009), 15.

42. Ibid. 24.

43. Ibid., 26.

44. Ibid., 50–51.

45. Ibid., 52.

46. Ibid., 64.

47. As cited in Lack Citrin, Amy Lerman, Michael Murakami and Kathryn Pearson, "Testing Huntington: Is Hispanic Immigration a Threat to America Identity?" *Perspectives on Politics*, March 2007, 43.

48. Ibid.

49. Riley, 156.

SUGGESTED READINGS

Butcher, Kristin F., and Anne Morrison Piehl. *Crime, Corrections, and California.* San Francisco: Public Policy Institute of California, 2008.

Orrenius, Pia. "Immigrant Assimilation: Is the U.S. Still a Melting Pot?" Presentation, Federal Reserve Bank of Dallas, January 2004.

Passel, Jeffrey S. *Unauthorized Migrants: Numbers and Characteristics.* Washington, DC: Pew Hispanic Center, 2005.

A Place to Call Home: What Immigrants Say Now about Life in America. New York: Public Agenda and Carnegie Corporation, 2009.

Rumbaut, Ruben G., and Walter Ewing. *The Myth of Immigrant Criminality and the Paradox of Assimilation: Incarceration Rates among Native and Foreign-Born Men.* Washington, DC: Immigration Policy Center, 2007.

Nine

Conclusion

In any book that attempts to deliver a great deal of information on a complex subject in a relatively short space, it is easy to overlook some of the most basic questions that interest readers. To guard against that likelihood, this chapter is written in a question-and-answer format to focus attention on some of the key topics that interest people in the debate over immigration. Along with some concluding remarks, this chapter also presents an opportunity to provide some new information and summarize key findings in the book.

WHAT IS THE PERCENTAGE OF FOREIGN BORN IN THE UNITED STATES TODAY, AND IS THAT HIGH BY HISTORICAL STANDARDS?

Approximately 12.6 percent of the U.S. population was foreign born in 2007, according to the U.S. Census Bureau.[1] In historical terms, the current proportion of the foreign born is not high, or at least not higher than it was for a good part of our history. Between 1860 and 1920, the proportion of foreign born did not fall below 13.2 percent. In 1910, the percentage of foreign born in the U.S. population was 14.7 percent, according to the U.S. Census Bureau.[2]

Legal immigration today is also not historically high when measured by the annual flow based on the size of the U.S. population. In 2008, about three legal immigrants came in for every 1,000 people in the United States. In 1910, about 11 legal immigrants came to the United States for every 1,000 people in America.[3] An analogy demographer Ben Wattenberg has used to describe the current rate of immigration is to imagine a party in a ballroom with 1,000 people talking, eating, and enjoying themselves. Into that ballroom walk three people.

WHICH COUNTRIES SEND THE MOST IMMIGRANTS TO THE UNITED STATES?

For legal immigrants, in 2008 the biggest sending countries were Mexico, China, India, and the Philippines. For illegal immigrants, the biggest source countries in recent years have been Mexico, Guatemala, El Salvador, and Honduras, with Mexico by far the largest source country.[4]

WHAT DOES IT MEAN THAT IMMIGRANTS ARE SELF-SELECTED?

Immigrants who come to America are largely self-selected, meaning that it is often the most courageous and risk-taking members of a society who are willing to take a chance on immigrating to start over in a new land. This is particularly true of international students who later become employment-based immigrants. But even to come to America as a family-sponsored immigrant takes fortitude, given all the uncertainties of learning a new culture and perhaps a new language. It is common for family members eligible to immigrate to America to choose to stay in their home country rather than take such a risk.

Given this risk-taking mentality, it is not surprising immigrants in America are so likely to participate in family run startup businesses and start new businesses, 30 percent more likely than the rest of the population, according to the Small Business Administration.[5] In studying immigrant entrepreneurs, one finds that few could have started a company immediately upon arriving in the United States. Many were just children, international students, or H-1B professionals. But America helped shaped them into entrepreneurs as much as they helped shape America.[6]

British-born Ronnie Vasishta came to America to work at LSI Logic, a Silicon Valley company, and was later recruited to become CEO of eASIC, which designs and tests semiconductors. "It's a very daunting prospect to come to a different country and start from scratch," said Vasishta. "But one thing it really does for you—it's invigorating. Because you really feel like you have no safety net." Ronnie says at some point it was inevitable he would come to America. He asked himself: "Do I stagnate in another part of the world or do I come here? The United States does that. The ambitious people are drawn here."[7]

IS IT TRUE THAT FEW EUROPEANS IMMIGRATE TO THE UNITED STATES TODAY?

While the percentage of Europeans among new legal immigrants has fallen compared to the past, many Europeans still come to America. In 2008, 121,146 Europeans immigrated to the United States, with Russia, the

United Kingdom, Germany, and Poland as the largest source countries. The overall number of immigrants from Europe is similar to many decades ago, although such immigrants represent a lower percentage of the total. Between 1950 and 1959, 1.4 million immigrants from Europe came to America. Between 1990 and 1999, 1.35 million Europeans immigrated to the United States.[8]

It is natural that the proportion of immigrants from Europe has fallen in recent decades. Prior to 1965, U.S. immigration law was discriminatory, essentially barring people from Asia from coming to the United States to settle. It should be noted that Asian immigration to the United States after the 1965 Act is likely the most successful migration in the history of the world. In a relatively short period of time, Indian immigrants, for example, have surpassed the income and educational attainment of natives.[9]

Given the similar income levels in the United States and Europe, and the ability of many Europeans to move freely to other European Union nations, it is understandable the desire to come to America is not as strong in Europe as among people in other parts of the world.

DOES THE ANNUAL FLOW OF FOREIGN-BORN PROFESSIONALS ON H-1B TEMPORARY WORK VISAS DISCOURAGE U.S. STUDENTS FROM ENTERING SCIENCE-, MATH-, AND TECHNOLOGY-RELATED FIELDS?

There is no evidence that American college students, never mind high school students, are watching or making career decisions based on something as esoteric as the annual H-1B visa numbers. If they *were* paying attention to immigration policy, then the students would know H-1B visa fees have funded scholarships in technology-related fields for more than 50,000 American college students since 1999.[10] Moreover, H-1B visas represent a tiny proportion of the overall U.S. labor force—only about 0.07 percent of the U.S. labor force. In many recent years, the supply of new visas has run out for 12 months at a time, which means there would not even be any potential competition from new H-1B visa holders for anyone in the domestic labor market for up to a year at a time.

Given the innovations and productivity increases that can come from skilled professionals, foreign-born scientists and engineers are likely to complement the skills of Americans and increase employment opportunities. It is easy to forget that many of the jobs some argue should now be protected did not even exist 30 years ago.

Preventing high-skilled foreign nationals from working in the United States will not help U.S. students. It will harm them. Encouraging employers to hire foreign nationals overseas, rather than in America, will push capital from the United States to locations where the foreign talent is allowed to be hired. The entrepreneurship we have witnessed from skilled immigrants also would be lost. As America loses its leadership in technology fields, then there would likely be even less interest in U.S. students pursuing these fields. Finally, without international students, many graduate programs in science and engineering at U.S. universities would have insufficient numbers to sustain themselves.

American young people still aspire to careers in science and technology fields and pursue these dreams. They are not deterred from studying math, science, or engineering by the presence of foreigners in these fields. If U.S. students are so fearful of competition, then why have so many chosen such highly competitive fields as law and finance?

Foreign-born athletes such as the St. Louis Cardinals first baseman Albert Pujols and the Dallas Mavericks forward Dirk Nowitzki are visible on American television, yet that has not prevented American kids from playing baseball or basketball.

DO INTERNATIONAL STUDENTS CROWD OUT U.S. STUDENTS WHO WANT TO ATTEND COLLEGE?

There is no evidence that U.S. students are not able to enter engineering or other graduate-level programs in the United States due to the presence of international students.

Examining all U.S. graduate programs from 1982 through 1995, Mark Regets of the National Science Foundation found no sign that U.S. citizens were displaced in graduate programs by international students. Increases in the number of international students in a graduate department were associated with increases, not decreases, in the enrollment of U.S. citizens and permanent residents—about one extra U.S. student for every three extra international students. A rise in enrollment for one group that is associated with enrollment increases for all groups is "a result inconsistent with displacement," notes Regets.[11]

Examining degree granting in recent years, economists Keith Maskus, Aaditya Mattoo, and Granaraj Chellaraj found, "The number of PhDs granted to undergraduates of U.S. institutions, most of whom were U.S. citizens, did not change much during this period, while there was a substantial growth in the number of foreign bachelor's graduates obtaining U.S. doctorates. Thus the change in proportion is mostly due to the expansion of PhD programs, with a majority of the new slots being taken for foreign students rather than through substitution."[12] The economists concluded, "Foreign students, skilled immigrants, and doctorates in science and engineering play a major role in driving scientific innovation in the United

States." The bottom line: "reducing foreign students by tighter enforcement of visa restraints could reduce innovative activity significantly" in the United States.[13]

A joint study by the Association of American Universities and the Association of Graduate Schools found no evidence international students harm U.S. minority applicants, concluding, "[The] acceptance and enrollment rates of minority applicants are significantly higher in comparison to those of non-U.S. citizen applicants. . . . [T]his finding does suggest that institutions do show a preference for admitting U.S. minority applicants rather than non-U.S. citizen applicants."[14]

Data from the National Science Foundation show that between 1980 and 2000, the share of black Americans in science and engineering (S&E) occupations more than doubled from 2.6 percent to 6.9 percent, as did the share of women, from 11.6 percent to 24.7 percent. This happened at the same time that "the percentage of foreign-born college graduates (including both U.S. and foreign degreed) in S&E jobs increased from 11.2 percent in 1980 to 19.3 percent in 2000," according to the National Science Foundation.[15]

SHOULD THE UNITED STATES COMPEL INTERNATIONAL STUDENTS TO GO HOME SO AS TO PREVENT A "BRAIN DRAIN" FROM POORER COUNTRIES?

The United States should always err on the side of freedom, rather than attempting to choose for an individual whether or not he would be "better off" in his home country. Those who really desire to leave their home—the most ambitious—will go to other countries if they are not allowed to stay in the United States.

Some might argue that if an individual stays in America after completing his or her studies that is a loss to the student's home country. That is not true. If the individual stays in America and becomes successful, he or she will likely maintain ties to his or her home nation, perhaps returning to invest in a business, establish export ties, or conduct charity work, as has been done by many successful Indian Americans, such as Vinod Khosla, a cofounder of Sun Microsystems. In contrast, if the individual returns to that nation right after graduation, he or she may possess limited skills to make a major impact. This is particularly the case if the country the student returns to is run by corrupt or inept leaders who limit economic opportunities for entrepreneurs or those with creative talent. In the case of nurses in the Philippines, women (primarily) train with the intention to earn money abroad, meaning if that option was closed off, they likely would not have trained as nurses in the first place.

WHY IS IT A BAD IDEA TO ESTABLISH A COMMISSION TO REGULATE LOW- AND HIGH-SKILL TEMPORARY VISAS AND GREEN CARDS?

U.S. employers would be wise to oppose any immigration legislation that includes a commission to regulate the future flow of high- and low-skilled foreign workers. Such a commission is likely to harm U.S. competitiveness, push more work outside the United States, fail to reduce illegal immigration, and increase the number of immigrants who die each year at the border due to a lack of legal avenues to work in America.

As described in a short book in 2009 by former Carter labor secretary Ray Marshall—and endorsed by the AFL-CIO and Change to Win in a press release—the commission would include nine members, appointed by the president and members of Congress for nine-year terms, and would possess the authority to set the conditions and annual limits for both high- and low-skilled temporary visas and green cards, including the power to eliminate entire visa categories. And, perhaps most importantly, its findings and recommendations would become law unless blocked by Congress.[16]

In an analysis of the commission proposal, the American Council on International Personnel notes, "To date, no one has made the case that a commission would not become a new set of obstacles employers must overcome to hire foreign nationals. Even worse, a commission could be an irreversible policy change that threatens to end American companies' access to highly educated professionals."[17]

In addition to all current requirements, the commission model endorsed by the AFL-CIO and Change to Win would set a new and formidable threshold for admitting foreign workers—a finding of a "certified labor shortage" in an occupation—that its own architect (Ray Marshall) says has not existed in America at any time in recent memory. Therefore, one could conclude that if the commission had been functioning over the past two decades, few, if any, skilled immigrants who have come to America in the past 25 years would have been allowed into the country.

The labor market is global, not only domestic, a fact ignored in any commission proposal. A key reason a "labor shortage" may not show up in any government data is that employers find "work arounds" and take creative action, such as "offshoring," to address an inability to hire people they need. In the technology field, if companies cannot find the individuals they need in the United States, they can send the work to be done elsewhere, such as China, or hire people in other countries and expand their labor force abroad. In agriculture, one reason it is difficult to document a labor shortage in agricultural workers is that analyses do not distinguish between legal and illegal workers. Most farm workers are here illegally, according to the Department of Labor. Therefore, a commission would ratify and encourage what many see as undesirable outcomes.

Under the notion that foreign nationals would not be admitted for employment purposes unless "certified labor shortages" are identified by a commission, there appears no room for an employer to hire someone because that individual would make an important and measurable impact on the company. The data do not exist to determine fine gradations in specific fields or the demand among all U.S. employers for specific specialties. There may exist government data on recent biology majors but not on who can perform research (or at what level) in gene manipulation for agriculture or in treatments for genetic diseases and how many U.S. employers need such skills this year. The commission would prevent talented people from being hired *in the United States*.[18]

One argument offered for a commission is it would keep politics out of immigration policy. A nonpolitical commission in Washington, DC, is an oxymoron. Elected officeholders would choose all of the members. Lobbying from all sides of the issue would move to these commission members. Employers would be forced to go "hat in hand" to ask if the commission could certify certain types of employees, while others will lobby the commission to oppose the entry of any workers. A commission will not end lobbying, but simply shift its focus to this new, unelected body of bureaucratic officials.

The Migration Policy Institute (MPI), a Washington, DC, think tank, has presented an alternative vision of a commission that suffers from a number of the same problems, although comes from a less-restrictive perspective. In truth, no supporter of a commission can be confident how it would work in practice. The mandates given to the commission by all advocates of the idea are general enough that commission members would be able to recommend anything they wish based upon personal preference, citing whatever data they desire to conform to their opinions. At best, everything would rest upon who is appointed, a dangerous "roll of the dice" for employers, immigrants, and their families. It is possible critics of family immigration will seek to include family-sponsored immigrants within the authority of the commission.

An earlier commission on immigration, chaired by congresswoman Barbara Jordan, produced a series of proposals—later rejected by Congress—that many family, business, and religious groups viewed as ill conceived and highly political. The commission proposed more recently is far more powerful and represents a far greater threat, since its powers are contemplated to be both operational and permanent. The authority to have immigration recommendations become law unless overruled by a vote of Congress is significant. "If Congress establishes a commission with essentially legislative powers, then members of Congress would have created a new power center in Washington, DC, whose authority, in many respects, will rival their own on immigration policy," concludes the American Council on International Personnel.[19]

WHAT IS THE PROCESS OF BECOMING A CITIZEN?

Becoming an American citizen is often the proudest day of an immigrant's life. A lawful permanent resident (green card holder) can apply for naturalization after five years in that status, or three years if married to a U.S. citizen. The questions asked on the civics portion of the exam have been revised in recent years. Whether this has made the test more difficult or just more uniform is still being evaluated. In addition to passing the civics exam, immigrants must show proficiency in English and not have committed crimes that would disqualify them from becoming citizens.

DO IMMIGRANTS COME HERE TO GO ON WELFARE?

It is illogical to argue both that immigrants are taking jobs from Americans and are also coming here to go on welfare. The good news is immigrant welfare use is low, and there is little evidence immigrants as a group come here because of the benefits.

U.S. policies on immigrants using public benefits are stricter than in European countries. If a foreigner wanted to immigrate based on the opportunity for welfare, they would be better off trying a country different than the United States. Immigrants are generally ineligible for federal means-tested benefits programs unless they have been in the United States for five years or more in a lawful status. It should be noted that states have different eligibility rules, and a child born in America is a U.S. citizen and can receive benefits if he or she meets a program's eligibility criteria, whether or not a parent is an immigrant. Congress tightened immigrant benefit eligibility as part of a broader reform of the nation's welfare laws in 1996.

Census data analyzed by the House Ways and Means Committee show the percentage of those who use AFDC/TANF (Aid to Families with Dependent Children/Temporary Assistance for Needy Children), Medicaid, and food stamps is generally about the same for natives as it is for noncitizens and naturalized citizens. In 2006, 0.6 percent of natives used AFDC/TANF, compared to 0.3 percent of naturalized citizens and 0.7 percent for noncitizens, while 7.7 percent of natives used the food stamp program, compared to 3.9 percent of naturalized citizens and 6.2 percent of noncitizens.[20]

ARE IMMIGRANTS MORE LIKELY THAN NATIVES TO COMMIT CRIMES?

The data show immigrants are less likely to commit crimes than the native born. "When we consider all institutionalization (not only prisons but also jails, halfway houses, and the like) and focus on the population that is most likely to be in institutions because of criminal activity (men 18–40), we find that, in California, U.S.-born men have an institutionalization rate that is 10 times higher than that of foreign-born men (4.2 percent vs. 0.42 percent). And when we compare foreign-born men to U.S.-born men with similar age and education levels, these differences become even greater," according to research by economists Kristin F. Butcher (Federal Reserve Bank of Chicago) and Anne Morrison Piehl (Rutgers University and the National Bureau of Economic Research). Looking only at prisons, the researchers found that "U.S.-born adult men are incarcerated at a rate over two-and-a-half times greater than that of foreign-born men."[21] National studies reach the same conclusion: foreign born (both legal and illegal immigrants) are less likely to commit crimes than the native born. "Among men age 18–39 (who comprise the vast majority of the prison population), the 3.5 percent incarceration rate of the native-born in 2000 was 5 times higher than the 0.7 percent incarceration rate of foreign-born."[22]

WHY DON'T MORE IMMIGRANTS AND THEIR CHILDREN WANT TO LEARN ENGLISH?

Because someone is more comfortable speaking in a native tongue when out with a friend or relative, that does not mean he or she does not speak English or is not interested in learning English. Work schedules, raising children, and a limited availability of night classes could make it difficult for immigrants to become proficient in a new language. Considering how valuable English language skills can be in the quest for a better job and higher income, immigrants already possess a great incentive to learn English.

Time in the country is the most important factor in immigrants learning English. Only 3 percent of immigrants in the country 30 years or more reported not speaking English well in the 1990 Census.[23] The children and grandchildren of immigrants are likely to lose the ability to even speak Spanish. "Although the generational life expectancy of Spanish is greater among Mexicans in Southern California than other groups, its demise is all but assured by the third generation," according to research by Frank Bean and Ruben Rumbaut (both of the University of California–Irvine) and Douglas Massey (Princeton University).[24] "English has never been seriously threatened as the dominant language in America, nor is it under threat today."[25]

WOULD A "TIME-OUT," MORATORIUM, OR SIGNIFICANT REDUCTION IN LEGAL IMMIGRATION LEVELS HELP THOSE IMMIGRANTS ALREADY HERE TO ASSIMILATE?

Those who suggest America needs a "time-out" to help current immigrants assimilate generally have not wanted immigrants allowed into

America in the first place. That makes it hard to accept their argument as efforts to assist immigrants. To put it another way: How much time and effort have anti-immigration organizations devoted to teaching immigrants English?

The last two "time-outs" were not proud moments in American history.

The 1882 Chinese Exclusion Act suspended the immigration of Chinese for 10 years and was part of a broader racial animus against Chinese immigrants that included lynchings, boycotts, and mass expulsions.

The national origins quota laws of 1921 and 1924, which largely determined the admission of immigrants to the United States for four decades, were based on bizarre eugenics theories about races and skull sizes. A popular book at the time by Madison Grant explained, "In dealing with the European populations the best method of determining race has been found to lie in a comparison of proportions of the skull."[26] In formulating restrictive immigration legislation, the House Judiciary Committee relied on a eugenics expert, Harry Laughlin, who had drafted the "model eugenics law" that served as the basis for forced sterilization in Virginia.[27]

Advocates of the 1924 bill played up anti-Jewish sentiment in gaining legislative support, with Congressional supporters using documents quoting U.S. consuls abroad as saying legislative action was needed to prevent the mass entry of Jews who were "abnormally twisted," "inassimilable," "filthy, un-American, and often dangerous in their habits."[28]

There is no evidence keeping Americans from sponsoring close family members or preventing businesses from hiring needed workers will help immigrants learn English better or understand more about American history and culture. "Some argue for another timeout to immigration, yet when we look back at the theories and sentiments that drove Congress to close the door to immigrants, we should realize that those were sad chapters in America's past, not guideposts to its future," noted Senator Spencer Abraham in a hearing at Ellis Island.[29]

DO MORE PEOPLE ENTERING THE LABOR FORCE MEAN DEPRESSED WAGES AND INCREASED UNEMPLOYMENT?

If simply having a large labor force meant living standards are bad for workers, then people in Haiti, Cuba, and other small countries would be much better off than Americans, which is certainly not the case. Donald Boudreaux, chair of the Department of Economics at George Mason University, said it is a common mistake to assume more workers means trouble. "Unsophisticated economic theory sees a larger pool of workers as a drag on wages," said Boudreaux. "Correct theory, in contrast—dating back to Adam Smith—understands that productivity, wages, and prosperity are enhanced by a deeper division of labor made possible by a larger supply of the ultimate resource: human effort and creativity."[30]

Concerns about unemployment and immigrants derive from the false notion that a fixed number of jobs exists, so a newcomer must "take away" a job from a current job holder to become employed. "There is no fixed pie or fixed number of jobs, so there is no way for immigrants to take away jobs from Americans. Immigrants expand the economic pie," said economist Mark J. Perry.[31] As consumers, immigrants increase the demand for goods and services, and thereby expand the demand for labor. Savings, investments, creating jobs through starting businesses, allowing for economies of scale, and filling niches in the labor market are all ways immigrants and other newcomers to an economy can create additional jobs.

If new entrants to the labor market increased unemployment, then the U.S. unemployment rate would rise every summer when college and high school graduates enter the labor market after completing their degrees, which does not happen. Economists Richard Vedder, Lowell Gallaway, and Stephen Moore found no evidence that immigration increases state unemployment levels.[32]

Economists generally view more people in an economy as beneficial. "The most important benefit of population size and growth is the increase it brings to the stock of useful knowledge," wrote Julian Simon. "Minds matter economically as much as, or more than, hands or mouths. Progress is limited largely by the availability of trained workers."[33]

A NUMBER OF GROUPS OPPOSED TO IMMIGRATION ARE ALSO IN FAVOR OF POPULATION CONTROL BECAUSE THEY BELIEVE FEWER PEOPLE IN THE UNITED STATES WOULD HELP THE ENVIRONMENT. DOES IMMIGRATION HARM THE ENVIRONMENT?

By many measures the standard of living and environment in the United States have improved dramatically at the same time that America's population has increased. One of the best measures of health in a country is life expectancy. In 1930, life expectancy in the United States was 60; by 2000 life expectancy had increased to 77.[34]

A 2008 report by the Environmental Protection Agency related how key indicators of pollution had improved in recent years: "Nationwide, emissions of criteria pollutants (or the pollutants that form them) due to human activities have decreased. Between 1990 and 2002, emissions of carbon monoxide, volatile organic compounds (which lead to the formation of ozone), particulate matter, sulfur dioxide, and nitrogen oxides (which lead to the formation of ozone and particulate matter) decreased by differing amounts, ranging from 17 to 44 percent. For lead, emissions have decreased by 99 percent, but this reduction is based on data that span a longer timeframe (1970 to 2002)."[35] And the "total acreage of forest land nationwide declined between the 1930s and the 1970s, but increased over the last three decades."[36]

Gregg Easterbrook, author of *The Progress Paradox*, points to many environmental indicators that have improved while the U.S. population has risen. He notes: "Twenty-five years ago, only one-third of America's lakes and rivers were safe for fishing and swimming; today two-thirds are, and the proportion continues to rise."[37] He also writes, "Since 1970 smog has declined by one-third, even as the number of cars has nearly doubled and vehicle-miles traveled have increased by 143 percent" and "Toxic emissions by industry declined 51 percent from 1988 to 2002."[38] Easterbrook concludes, "The steady environmental improvement in the United States should be a subject of national pride."[39]

WHY DON'T WE LIMIT THE ADMISSION OF HIGH-SKILL PEOPLE TO THOSE WHO CAN GET AN "EINSTEIN VISA"?

One problem with trying to limit the admission of high-skill people to only certified, accomplished geniuses is that it would unduly restrict America's access to talented people and thereby harm growth and innovation.

Even America's immigrant Nobel Prize winners were often just promising students when they first began the process of immigrating to the United States. For example, Elizabeth Blackburn came to America originally in 1975, more than 30 years before earning the Nobel Prize in Medicine and a decade before she published her research that led to the prize.

It is a red herring to argue, as some do, that American employers could satisfy their labor needs by hiring foreign nationals using O-1 visas, which are restricted to those with "extraordinary ability . . . which has been demonstrated by sustained national or international acclaim," according to the law.[40] Only 9,014 O-1 visas were issued in FY 2008, and many were granted to individuals other than scientists and engineers.[41] If America only admitted those who had already made significant breakthroughs that garnered "national or international acclaim," then outstanding foreign nationals would, by definition, be producing those innovations outside the United States. At that point in their careers, such people would have much less interest in coming to a new country, particularly one whose immigration laws had for so long barred their entry.

WHAT IS ONE OF THE MOST UNKNOWN CONTRIBUTIONS OF IMMIGRANTS?

The foreign born make up more than 27 percent of the physicians and surgeons practicing in the United States, and 18.7 percent of the dentists.[42]

Foreign-born physicians play an important role in many rural areas. "International medical graduates fill various safety-net needs at a rate disproportionately higher than that for U.S. medical school graduates, including in areas with high infant mortality rates, low socioeconomic status, high non-white population and states with high rural population percentages," according to Keith Mueller of the Rural Policy Research Institute.[43]

WHY DO OPPONENTS OF IMMIGRATION AND SOME LEGISLATORS TARGET FAMILY IMMIGRATION CATEGORIES FOR REDUCTION?

The animosity toward family immigration among some critics of immigration is difficult to explain. In describing the efforts of Paul Ehrlich to encourage the birth of as few people as possible in the world to limit the size of the population, the late Julian Simon wrote, "The Ehrlich argument boils down to the inverted (or perverted) Golden Rule: Do unto others—prevent their existence—what you are glad no one did to you."[44]

In a similar fashion, critics of immigration, who likely are only in the United States due to an earlier family member being allowed to immigrate, are also largely guilty of a reverse or inverted Golden Rule. Much of the push to eliminate family immigration categories comes from a desire to reduce overall immigration as much as possible. While the public makes a distinction between legal and illegal immigration, many critics view both as equally problematic. That is because the critics generally view the world through the viewpoint that each new person adds to the population and incorrectly assume that means harm to the economy, culture, and environment. Suspecting that efforts to reduce illegal immigration will fall short, critics seek to restrict what can be most easily controlled, namely the quotas on legal immigration categories.

Another intangible factor is it appears a greater value is placed on certain family relationships in other countries. Some U.S. lawmakers have questioned whether an adult brother or sister should be considered a close family member, at least in the context of immigration policy. That seems strange to most people from Latin American and Asian countries, where sibling relationships can be very close. It is particularly odd that some U.S. lawmakers and immigration critics call sons or daughters who reach the age of 21 "extended" family members.

WHAT IS THE BEST WAY TO REDUCE ILLEGAL IMMIGRATION?

"Illegal immigration occurs because foreign workers can earn much more in the United States than they can at home and U.S. immigration restrictions prevent them from entering the country through legal means," writes economist Gordon H. Hanson. "Simply by moving to the United States, the [Mexican] worker's annual income would rise by 2.5 times, even after controlling for cost-of-living differences between the two countries."[45]

The only proven way to reduce illegal immigration is to increase the use of temporary visas. That would allow Mexicans, Salvadorans, and others to work legally in the United States and free up law enforcement resources that can be focused on genuine criminal or security threats. This can be accomplished, as recommended in this book, by combining a sufficient number of fully portable work permits—not tied to a specific employer—with bilateral administrative agreements between the United States and countries that send illegal immigrants to America. This approach would provide labor market freedom and, therefore, protection for new workers; at the same time, it would elicit cooperation on immigration enforcement from Mexico and (eventually) other key countries. Reducing illegal immigration can also be accomplished by establishing a new temporary visa category, if the category is relatively free of bureaucracy (easy to use by employers and employees) and of a sufficient annual number to replace the illegal flow of workers.

The actions of Mexican farm workers between 1953 and 1959 demonstrate that allowing legal paths for work can reduce illegal immigration and save lives. After enforcement actions in 1954 were combined with an increase in the use of legal visas via the Bracero program, illegal entry, as measured by INS apprehensions at the border, fell by 95 percent between 1953 and 1959 (see Chapter 4). This demonstrated how access to legal means of entry can affect the decision-making of migrant workers. "Without question, the Bracero program was . . . instrumental in ending the illegal alien problem of the mid-1940s and 1950s," wrote the Congressional Research Service.[46]

Neither legalizing those in the United States illegally nor increasing immigration enforcement will reduce illegal immigration or limit immigrant deaths at the border. The 1986 IRCA legislation adopted a policy of legalization and increased enforcement, while failing to allow the means for individuals to work legally in the United States at lesser-skilled jobs. As a result, illegal immigration increased dramatically in the years following passage. One can expect a similar outcome should Congress repeat the mistakes of 1986 and leave out a significant temporary visa component in any new immigration reform legislation.

WHAT IS THE BIGGEST LONG-TERM THREAT TO LEGAL IMMIGRATION?

The biggest threat to legal immigration and a rational policy toward illegal immigration is not organized labor, anti-immigration groups, or cultural anxiety about immigrants. The most serious long-term threat to a generous immigration policy is the United States establishing economic policies that result in high rates of structural unemployment as we have seen in Western Europe. High unemployment rates limit public support for legal immigration, notwithstanding that both economic theory and research demonstrate increased immigration should not increase the unemployment rate for natives.

For decades, with a few exceptions, the labor policies of European countries have resulted in far higher unemployment rates than those experienced in the United States. Policies that make it more difficult for employers to fire or lay off workers can it make it less likely for companies to hire people in the first place. High levels of mandated benefits, wages, or leave time generally increase the cost of employing people and can inhibit hiring. As a rule, employers will hire as many people as is profitable, but to hire those unprofitable to employ, for example, because they earn more than can be recovered through sales, can put a business at risk.

The Economist magazine recently explained the dilemma:

> Falling unemployment made it easier for some countries to loosen the regulations that gummed up their labor markets, helping to push the jobless numbers down further as well as making economies more competitive. . . . Rising unemployment will make it far harder to push through labor-market reforms. It will make it politically impossible to scrap or blur the divide that exists in many countries between protected "insiders" on permanent contracts and unprotected "outsiders" stuck with temporary ones. This means that the first and biggest sufferers from rising joblessness will be outsiders, a group disproportionately made up of the young, women and people from ethnic minorities. . . . The risk is that many governments will instead react much as they did in the 1980s, when they encouraged schemes to promote early retirement, to shorten working hours and to reduce part-time working. These policies betrayed an atavistic belief in the "lump-of-labor" fallacy, which holds that as there is a fixed amount of work to be spread around, easing some people out of jobs generates additional jobs for others. Both experience and economic theory have shown this to be false.[47]

The "lump of labor" fallacy still dominates discussions of immigration policy, which means persistently high unemployment rates in the United States will make it difficult to enact needed reforms and could lead to immigration policies that are worse than the status quo.

America is a nation of immigrants. The dream of a better life for themselves and their children has led immigrants for the past 400 years to take a chance on a new land. The journeys have enriched both the immigrants and America. President Ronald Reagan once commented on the uniqueness of the American experience. He told a class of young people, "I got a letter from a man the other day, and I'll share it with you. The man said you can go to live in Japan, but you cannot become Japanese—or Germany, or France—and he named all the others. But he said anyone from any corner of the world can come to America and become an American."[48]

If we can adopt the right policies, then America can continue to be that beacon of freedom and opportunity that has summoned so many to its shores.

NOTES

1. "Census Bureau Data Show Characteristics of the U.S. Foreign-Born Population," U.S. Census Bureau, Press Release, February 19, 2009. See main table. Foreign born is anyone who is not a U.S. citizen at birth, which includes temporary visa holders and illegal immigrants, as well as lawful permanent residents and naturalized citizens (38,059,694 foreign born out of a U.S. population of 301,621,159).

2. Campbell Gibson and Kay Jung, "Historical Census Statistics on the Foreign-Born Population of the United States, 1850–2000," Working Paper No. 81 (Washington, DC: Population Division, U.S. Census Bureau, 2006).

3. U.S. Census Bureau; *2008 Yearbook of Immigration Statistics.*

4. Michael Hoefer, Nancy Rytina, and Bryan C. Baker, *Estimates of the Unauthorized Immigrant Population Residing in the United States: January 2009* (Washington, DC: Office of Immigration Statistics, Department of Homeland Security, 2010); *2008 Yearbook of Immigration Statistics* (Washington, DC: Office of Immigration Statistics, Department of Homeland Security, 2009).

5. Robert W. Fairlie, *Estimating the Contribution of Immigrant Business Owners to the U.S. Economy,* Small Business Administration, Office of Advocacy, November 2008, Executive Summary.

6. Stuart Anderson and Michaela Platzer, *American Made: The Impact of Immigrant Entrepreneurs and Professionals on U.S. Competitiveness* (Arlington, VA: National Venture Capital Association, 2006).

7. Ibid., 12.

8. *2008 Yearbook of Immigration Statistics*, Table 2.

9. "Nearly 75 percent of Asian Indians older than 24 years of age hold a four-year college degree, which dwarfs the national average of 28 percent," write Richard T. Herman and Robert L. Smith. "In 2007, the median household income for Americans born in India was $91,195, the highest of any identifiable group, according to the U.S. Census Bureau." Richard T. Herman and Robert L. Smith, *Immigrant, Inc.* (Hoboken, NJ: John Wiley & Sons, 2010), 31.

10. FY 2010 National Science Foundation Budget Request to Congress, EHR-20-21.

11. Mark Regets, "Research Issues in the International Migration of Highly Skilled Workers: A Perspective with Data from the United States," Working Paper, SRS 07-203, June 2007, 11.

12. Gnanaraj Chellaraj, Keith E. Maskus, and Aaditya Mattoo, "The Contribution of Skilled Immigration and International Graduate Students to U.S. Innovation," March 17, 2005, 9.

13. Ibid.

14. Association of Graduate Schools, "Participation in Doctoral Education at Major Research Universities by U.S. Citizens, Women, and Underrepresented Minorities," vol. 1, no. 1 (April 1993): 2–3.

15. National Science Board, *2006 Science and Engineering Indicators* (Arlington, VA: National Science Foundation, 2006), 3–19.

16. Ray Marshall, *Immigration for Shared Prosperity*, Economic Policy Institute, Washington, DC, 2009, 22–23, 25; "Change to Win and AFL-CIO Unveil Unified Immigration Reform Framework," Press Release, Change to Win and AFL-CIO, April 14, 2009.

17. *Examining Proposals to Create a New Commission on Employment-Based Immigration* (Washington, DC: American Council on International Personnel, 2009), 2.

18. Even if an individual cleared a hurdle established by the commission, he or she would still have to contend with existing requirements in current law (and potentially new and more restrictive ones) before being admitted to the country.

19. *Examining Proposals to Create a New Commission on Employment-Based Immigration*, 2.

20. House Ways and Means Committee, *2008 Green Book*, Appendix H, Table H-9—Estimated Benefit Usage by Citizenship Categories: 1995, 1999, 2001, 2006.

21. Kristin F. Butcher and Anne Morrison Piehl, *Crime, Corrections, and California*, Public Policy Institute of California, February 2008, 1–2.

22. Ruben G. Rumbaut and Walter Ewing, *The Myth of Immigrant Criminality and the Paradox of Assimilation: Incarceration Rates among Native and Foreign-Born Men* (Washington, DC: Immigration Policy Center, 2007), 1.

23. National Research Council, *The New Americans*, advance copy (Washington, DC: National Academy Press, 1997), S-10.

24. "Immigration No Threat to English Use in the U.S.: Study," Reuters, September 13, 2006.

25. Ibid.

26. Madison Grant, *The Passing of the Great Race*, 4th ed. (New York: Charles Scribner's Sons, 1922), 19.

27. Elof Axel Carlson, *The Unfit: A History of a Bad Idea* (Cold Spring Harbor, NY: Cold Spring Harbor Laboratory Press, 2001), 255–256.

28. John Higham, *Strangers in the Land, Patterns of American Nativism, 1860–1925* (New York: Antheum, 1973), 309–310.

29. "Should America Remain a Nation of Immigrants," hearing before the Subcommittee on Immigration, Committee on the Judiciary, U.S. Senate, August 11, 1997, 3.

30. As cited in Stuart Anderson and L. Brian Andrew, *Coming to America* (Arlington, VA: National Foundation for American Policy, 2006), 4.

31. Interview with Mark J. Perry.

32. Richard Vedder, Lowell Gallaway, and Stephen Moore, *Immigration and Unemployment: New Evidence* (Arlington, VA: Alexis de Tocqueville Institution, 1994), 2, as cited in Stuart Anderson, *Employment-Based Immigration and High Technology* (Washington, DC: Empower America, 1996), 66.

33. Julian Simon, *The Ultimate Resource 2* (Princeton, NJ: Princeton University Press, 1996), 12.

34. Table 12, "Estimated Life Expectancy at Birth in Years, by Race and Sex: Death-Registration States, 1900–1928, and United States, 1929–2001," *National Vital Statistics Reports* 52, no. 14 (February 18, 2004): 33.

35. Environmental Protection Agency, *EPA's 2008 Report on the Environment: Highlights of National Trends*, June 2008, 5.

36. Ibid., 29.

37. Gregg Easterbrook, *The Progress Paradox* (New York: Random House), 41.

38. Ibid., 42–43.

39. Ibid., 100.

40. Section 101(a)(15)(O)(i) of the Immigration and Nationality Act.

41. U.S. Department of State. *Classes of Nonimmigrants Issued Visas, Fiscal Years 1989–2008.*

42. *Critical Care: The Role of Immigrant Workers in U.S. Healthcare* (Washington, DC: Immigration Policy Center, 2009), 2.

43. Kristi L. Nelson, "Foreign-Born Doctors Fill Gaps in Health Care System," *Knoxnews.com*, September 28, 2008.

44. Simon, 562.

45. Gordon H. Hanson, *The Economics and Policy of Illegal Immigration in the United States* (Washington, DC: Migration Policy Institute, 2009), 7.

46. Congressional Research Service, *Temporary Worker Programs: Background and Issues.* A report prepared at the request of Senator Edward M. Kennedy, Chairman of the Judiciary Committee, United States Senate, for the use of the Select Commission on Immigration and Refugee Policy, February 1980, 41.

47. John Peet, "Europe Isn't Working," *The Economist, The World in 2010*, November 13, 2009, 84.

48. Ronald Reagan, remarks to students at Suitland High School in Suitland, MD, January 20, 1988.

SUGGESTED READINGS

Examining Proposals to Create a New Commission on Employment-Based Immigration. Washington, DC: American Council on International Personnel, 2009.

Gibson, Campbell, and Kay Jung. "Historical Census Statistics on the Foreign-Born Population of the United States, 1850–2000." Working Paper No. 81. Washington, DC: Population Division, U.S. Census Bureau, 2006.

National Science Board. *2010 Science and Engineering Indicators.* Arlington, VA: National Science Foundation, 2010.

Simon, Julian. *The Ultimate Resource 2.* Princeton, NJ: Princeton University Press, 1996.

Selected Bibliography

Anderson, Stuart. *The Impact of Agricultural Guest Worker Programs on Illegal Immigration*. Arlington, VA: National Foundation for American Policy, 2003.

Anderson, Stuart. "The Multiplier Effect." *International Educator*, Summer 2004. Available at: www.nfap.com.

Anderson, Stuart, and L. Brian Andrew. *Coming to America*. Arlington, VA: National Foundation for American Policy, 2006. Available at: www.nfap.com.

Anderson, Stuart, and Michaela Platzer. *American Made: The Impact of Immigrant Entrepreneurs and Professionals on U.S. Competitiveness*. Arlington, VA: National Venture Capital Association, 2006. Available at: www.nfap.com.

"Annual Report of Immigrant Visa Applicants in the Family-Sponsored and Employment-Based Preferences Registered at the National Visa Center as of November 1, 2009." Washington, DC: Bureau of Consular Affairs, U.S. Department of State, 2009.

Butcher, Kristin F., and Anne Morrison Piehl. *Crime, Corrections, and California*. San Francisco: Public Policy Institute of California, 2008.

Card, David. "Is the New Immigration Really So Bad?" University of California–Berkeley, January 2005.

Castañeda, Jorge. *Ex Mex: From Migrants to Immigrants*. New York: New Press, 2007.

Characteristics of Specialty Occupational Workers (H-1B): Fiscal Year 2008. Washington, DC: Department of Homeland Security, 2009.

Chellaraj, Gnanaraj, Keith E. Maskus, and Aaditya Mattoo. "The Contribution of Skilled Immigration and International Graduate Students to U.S. Innovation." Policy Research Working Paper Series. Washington, DC: World Bank, 2005.

A Commission to Regulate Immigration? A Bad Idea Whose Time Should Not Come. Arlington, VA: National Foundation for American Policy, 2009. Available at: www.nfap.com.

Cornelius, Wayne. *Controlling Unauthorized Immigration from Mexico: The Failure of Prevention through Deterrence and the Need for Comprehensive Reform.* San Diego: Center for Comparative Immigration Studies, University of California–San Diego, 2008.

Dixon, Peter B., and Maureen T. Rimmer. *Restriction or Legalization? Measuring the Economic Benefits of Immigration Reform.* Washington, DC: Cato Institute, 2009.

Examining Proposals to Create a New Commission on Employment-Based Immigration. Washington, DC: American Council on International Personnel, 2009.

Fairlie, Robert W. *Estimating the Contribution of Immigrant Business Owners to the U.S. Economy.* Washington, DC: Office of Advocacy, Small Business Administration, 2008.

Fairlie, Robert W. *Kauffman Index of Entrepreneurial Activity, 1996–2008.* Kansas City, MO: Ewing Marion Kauffman Foundation, 2009.

Fermi, Laura. *Illustrious Immigrants.* Chicago: University of Chicago Press, 1968.

Gibson, Campbell, and Kay Jung. "Historical Census Statistics on the Foreign-Born Population of the United States, 1850–2000." Working Paper No. 81. Washington, DC: Population Division, U.S. Census Bureau, 2006.

Haines, David W., ed. *Refugees in America in the 1990s.* Westport, CT: Greenwood Press, 1996.

Handlin, Oscar. *The Uprooted: The Epic Story of the Migrations That Made the American People*, 2nd ed. New York: Little, Brown, 1979.

Herman, Richard T., and Robert L. Smith. *Immigrant, Inc.* Hoboken, NJ: John Wiley & Sons, 2010.

Higham, John. *Strangers in the Land, Patterns of American Nativism, 1860–1925.* New York: Atheneum, 1973.

Hoefer, Michael, Nancy Rytina, and Bryan C. Baker. *Estimates of the Unauthorized Immigrant Population Residing in the United States: January 2009.* Washington, DC: Office of Immigration Statistics, Department of Homeland Security, 2010.

Hutchinson, E. P. *Legislative History of American Immigration Policy, 1798–1965.* Philadelphia: University of Pennsylvania Press, 1981.

Jones, Maldwyn Allen. *American Immigration*, 2nd ed. Chicago: University of Chicago Press, 1992.

Kenney, David Ngaruri, and Philip G. Schrag. *Asylum Denied.* Berkeley: University of California Press, 2008.

Massey, Douglas. *Backfire at the Border: Why Enforcement without Legalization Cannot Stop Illegal Immigration.* Trade Briefing Paper No. 29. Washington, DC: Center for Trade Policy Studies, Cato Institute, 2005.

Mithas, S., and H. C. Lucas. "Are Foreign IT Workers Cheaper? United States' Visa Policies and Compensation of Information Technology Professionals." Working Paper. College Park: Smith School of Business, University of Maryland, 2009.

National Research Council. *The New Americans.* Washington, DC: National Academy Press, 1997.

National Science Board. *2010 Science and Engineering Indicators.* Arlington, VA: National Science Foundation, 2010.

Navigating the Fundamentals of Immigration Law: Guidance and Tips for Successful Practice. Washington, DC: American Immigration Lawyers Association. (Updated annually.)

Orrenius, Pia. "Immigrant Assimilation: Is the U.S. Still a Melting Pot?" Presentation, Federal Reserve Bank of Dallas, January 2004.

Passel, Jeffrey S. *Unauthorized Migrants: Numbers and Characteristics.* Washington, DC: Pew Hispanic Center, 2005.

Peri, Giovanni. "The Effect of Immigration on Productivity: Evidence from U.S. States." NBER Working Paper No. 15507, November 2009.

Peri, Giovanni. *Immigrants, Skills, and Wages: Measuring the Economic Gains from Immigration.* Washington, DC: Immigration Policy Center, 2006.

A Place to Call Home: What Immigrants Say Now about Life in America. New York: Public Agenda and Carnegie Corporation, 2009.

Ramos, Jorge. *Dying to Cross.* New York: HarperCollins, 2005.

Riley, Jason L. *Let Them In.* New York: Gotham Books, 2008.

Rumbaut, Ruben G., and Walter Ewing. *The Myth of Immigrant Criminality and the Paradox of Assimilation: Incarceration Rates among Native and Foreign-Born Men.* Washington, DC: Immigration Policy Center, 2007.

Simon, Julian. *The Ultimate Resource 2.* Princeton, NJ: Princeton University Press, 1996.

Texas Comptroller of Public Accounts. *Undocumented Immigrants in Texas: A Financial Analysis of the Impact to the State Budget and Economy.* Austin: Texas Comptroller of Public Accounts, 2006.

2008 Yearbook of Immigration Statistics. Washington, DC: Office of Immigration Statistics, Department of Homeland Security, 2009.

Urrea, Luis Alberto. *The Devil's Highway.* New York: Little, Brown, 2005.

U.S. Department of State Visa Bulletin. (Updated monthly.)

The U.S. Refugee Admissions and Resettlement Program at a Crossroads: Recommendations by Refugee Council USA. Washington, DC: Refugee Council USA, 2009. Available at: www.rcusa.org.

Wadhwa, Vivek, AnnaLee Saxenian, Richard Freeman, and Alex Salkever. *Losing the World's Best and Brightest: America's New Immigrant Entrepreneurs, Part Five.* Kansas City, MO: Duke University, University of California–Berkeley, and Ewing Marion Kauffman Foundation, 2009.

Wadhwa, Vivek, AnnaLee Saxenian, Ben Rissing, and Gary Gereffi. "Skilled Immigration and Economic Growth." *Applied Research in Economic Development 5*, no. 1 (May 2008).

Wyman, David S. *Paper Walls: America and the Refugee Crisis, 1938–1941.* New York: Pantheon Books, 1985.

Index

ABOUT THE AUTHOR

STUART ANDERSON is executive director of the National Foundation for American Policy, a research group in Arlington, Virginia, and formerly head of policy at the Immigration and Naturalization Service and staff director of the Senate Immigration Subcommittee. Stuart's work on immigration has been published in the *Wall Street Journal, New York Times*, and other publications.

Recent Titles in the
Greenwood Guides to Business and Economics

The National Economy
Bradley A. Hansen

The Corporation
Wesley B. Truitt

Income and Wealth
Alan Reynolds

Money
Mark F. Dobeck and Euel Elliott

The Stock Market
Rik W. Hafer and Scott E. Hein

Entrepreneurship
Alan L. Carsrud and Malin E. Brännback

Globalization
Donald J. Boudreaux

Energy
Joseph M. Dukert

Demography, Education, and the Workforce
Robert I. Lerman and Stephanie Riegg Cellini